Octopus Economics

Taxless States and Commercial Government Theory

Written by
Jordan Weisinger

INFINITY
PUBLISHING.COM

ISBN 0-7414-5434-3

Head shot and Octopus cover art supplied by Candice Gill.

Published by:

INFINITY
PUBLISHING.COM

1094 New DeHaven Street, Suite 100
West Conshohocken, PA 19428-2713
Info@buybooksontheweb.com
www.buybooksontheweb.com
Toll-free (877) BUY BOOK
Local Phone (610) 941-9999
Fax (610) 941-9959

Printed in the United States of America

Published October 2010

Table of contents:

THE PORTENT

Chapter 1

Commercial Government Theory

For most people taxes are the bane of their existence. Every week your paycheck is considerably less than it could be because somewhere some person decided that your money would be better spent on some obscure government program. Nobody likes to pay taxes but we recognize they are necessary for national security and public welfare. Public schools, roads, airports, farm and energy subsidies, courts, law enforcement agencies, and the military must be publicly subsidized. Each service and piece of equipment must be bought or bartered for. Since we aren't communists one must conclude that taxes are therefore unavoidable. Not necessarily, a government which is able to invest a small proportion of its tax receipts in private equities over an extended period of time will earn for itself a renewable and sustainable resource that compensates for most, if not all, of the costs of its constituent government agencies and welfare programs.

Rather than continuing to apply conventional techniques of public finance, which only results in immense deficits and dangerous underfunding of necessary government services, a nation can implement a Mandatory Contribution Permanent Fund System to slowly make itself independent of taxation. The MCPFS will be coordinated across every municipal, county, state, and national jurisdiction so that each government will have the means to eventually subsidize all of their government expenditures with investments rather than taxes. Make no mistakes, this is a slow process. There is no way a government can substitute some meager investments for the sum total of all its tax receipts. It takes decades for any such program to mature but it is almost inevitable once begun. Most governments are already free to invest in and earn profit from private equities and the precedent for governments comingling public moneys with private moneys are found in the histories of public pensions and Sovereign Wealth Funds.

Public employee pensions are the most widespread example of government's being vested in private equities. Every state in the U.S. offers its employees a pension plan for retirement, and every department of the treasury manages the investment accounts supporting the plan. Many of the Sovereign Wealth Funds in Europe are in fact public employee pension funds and were created to offset the rising costs of national government employee benefits. All of the pension's profits are redirected into former employee's retirement benefits. This includes a cash income stipend and health benefits. The only beneficiaries are retired employees so the government insulates itself from many of the conflicts of interests inherent in investing in private equities but the fact remains that the government is still involved in earning profits for its residents. Public pensions are an incredible concentration of wealth with some managing several hundreds of billions of dollars.

Take for example the California Public Employees' Retirement System (CalPERS). It is the largest pension fund in the United States. It provides pension funding, healthcare, and other retirement services for approximately 1.5 million California public employees. In October 2007, it owned $260.6 billion worth of stock, bonds, funds, private equity, and real estate. Another example is the California State Teacher Retirement System (CalSTRS). It had funds in excess of 179.6 billion. After the economic down turn and collapse in securities markets both were re-evaluated. CalPERS is now holding 179.2 billion while CalSTRS has 113.7 billion. Although their assets have recently depreciated they will eventually regain value and exceed their previous asset tallies. Both CalPERS and CalSTRS are an example of governments investing in private equities for the benefit of its employees. They are just two examples of Public Employee Retirement Systems. There are similar systems in New York and New Jersey and most other states. Most counties and large cities also maintain their own pension systems.

An enormous amount of money is captured in our public employee retirement systems. If one summed up the entire municipal, county, city, and state government pension plans there would be trillions of dollars of assets located in government managed funds throughout the world. It is estimated that nearly half of all the securities offered in the U.S. economy are owned by public and private pensions. Governments frequently participate in corporate board elections and shareholder votes within the companies they have vested interests in. We never doubt the integrity of the management now even when they employ extracurricular agendas with the representation. CalPERS is also an example of socially or politically motivated investment. They have excluded companies doing business in Sudan and have pressured many companies for reforms of executive compensation; they promote cooperation with Unions, and exclude business employing unfair labor practices. These retirement funds have extraordinary influence in the markets; hundreds of billions of dollars are at their disposal. Despite this trend in pension management there isn't a foreboding threat of communism looming in our future as a result of this public wealth.

An MCPFS will dramatically increase the volume of state capital involved in domestic and foreign economies and certainly accelerate the interface between government and businesses but the integrity of the commercial system will be protected by the fiduciary duty fund managers have with beneficiaries. In fact, most business owners welcome government investment and are quite comfortable with the intermingling of interest. The concentrated equity of public pension plans provides capitalization to the private sector which would not ordinarily be present in the securities markets. Hedge funds and mutual funds do not invest for long terms in public companies. Pensions generally do. Long term commitments provide stability to the equity markets and this is needed for sustained growth. Public Employee Retirement Systems are ordinarily accepted as being within the normal confines of government responsibility and more direct efforts to commercialize government should be similarly received. The risk of conflict is the same for State or local employee pensions as a in an MCPFS.

Many nations have recently created Sovereign Wealth Funds to defray their national tax rates, to offset bond and retirement liabilities for government employees, to provide capital for stimulus and economic development, to stabilize their currencies, and even to forward their own foreign policy agendas. They are becoming more and more common as their versatility becomes more recognized. The first Sovereign Wealth Fund was the Kuwait Investment Authority, a commodity SWF created in 1953 from oil revenues before Kuwait even gained independence from Great Britain. Kuwait's fund is estimated to now be worth approximately $250 billion. Twenty one countries have sovereign wealth funds of significant size. Seven have what are considered super funds and have amassed sums in excess of 100 billion. These funds are: ADIA (Abu Dhabi Investment Authority, $627 billion); The Government Pension Fund of Norway ($326 billion); Government of Singapore Investment Corporation ($247.5 billion); Kuwait Investment Authority; China Investment Corporation ($190 billion); Singapore's Temasek Holdings ($85 billion); and the National Welfare Fund of Russia (total of $219.9 billion).

As a proportion of GDP the five largest funds are Abu Dhabi Investment Authority, Brunei ($30 billion), Kuwait, the Qatar Investment Authority ($60 billion) and Singapore's GIC. Singapore actually manages two sovereign wealth funds (GIC and Temasek for combined assets of 350 billion) so the proportion of public wealth to GDP is much higher. Many countries operate multiple funds; Russian owns its Stabilization Fund and National Wealth Fund. China has its SAFE fund, Africa Fund, a Social Insurance Fund, and its foreign currency assets (estimated to be nearly 2 trillion dollars worth of equity).

The Western democracies are under-represented in terms of the volume of state capital which they have access to. France manages 28 billion in their Strategic Investment Fund, Canada has 14.9 billion in their Alberta Heritage Fund, and Ireland has 22.8 billion in their National Pension Reserve Fund. Australia makes a good effort with 42.2 billion in their Future Fund while the U.S. states of Alaska, Alabama, New Mexico, and Wyoming have an approximate total of 60 billion combined in their Permanent Funds. Norway is the most progressive western democracy with nearly 330 billion locked away in their Government Pension Fund. This tally pales in comparison to the trillions held by oil producing states of the Middle East, Africa, and Asia.

Even developing countries such as Azerbaijan, Trinidad & Tobago, Ecuador and Nigeria have small funds. The GDP for the entire world is only 15 trillion dollars. The amount of money captured in Sovereign Wealth Funds is already 3.3 trillion and that amount is expected to increase dramatically. Japan, India, and several other countries intend on creating funds to manage private equities, currencies, or public debt so the list is expected to change dramatically over the next decade or two. Within a matter of decades public wealth may represent the greatest concentrations of wealth in the world's economies.

There are roughly 240 nations or groups of associated people claiming sovereignty and already forty have established funds. If the remaining 200 also create their own then there will be an astounding amount of state capital flowing into and out of local economies. The U. States' permanent funds and the Albertan Heritage Fund create precedent for provincial, county, or state governments to contribute resources to the overall amount of state capital employed in the global economy. If towns, cities, and boroughs capitalize themselves with private equity in a like manner as states or nations soon there may be tremendously more state capital involved in the economy than private capital. The proliferation of Sovereign Wealth Funds, Permanent Funds, and Government Pension Funds may usher in a new era of Competitive State Capitalism with a dominant proportion of assets under the direct control of various democratic or authoritarian governments. Commercial Government Theory is a direct response to this trend in global economics.

Commercial Government Theory is the belief that a government's investment into securities, commodities, and private equities will make it more efficient, more versatile, and more viable. It is the belief that when governments compete in jurisdictions they do not administer law to they will naturally seek profits like any other ordinary commercial party. Commercial Government Theory provides organization and structure when government ownership grows to proportions that rival personal ownership. Maintaining limits on government entitlements to invest in securities, commodities, and private equities ensures that residents are not exploited, businesses are not co-opted for other than financial gains, it preserves free markets, and it protects the political integrity of participating governments. Fears of government monopoly and exploitation must not stunt an opportunity to create, through further inquiry, debate, and refinement, a nation completely independent from taxes. A properly administered MCPFS will prove that although government services are necessary, taxes are not.

Central to commerce is the exchange of trust and only those nations with popular election systems have the political integrity necessary to compete as commercial governments. Dictatorial governments competing or investing heavily in its own economy resembles more of a communist system than a capitalist system no matter how the profit is managed or disguised.

Authoritarian governments can bully and cajole domestic businesses into unsatisfying arrangements, resident's property and legal rights can be marginalized without recourse, and foreign companies may face unfair competition. Trust is pivotal and a people must have the necessary political mechanisms to accommodate legitimate argument against government ownership or competition. The system of law hearing argument against commercial government must be administered by people and be accountable to the people. Thus only democratic political systems have the adaptability and integrity to employ commercial governments.

The general organization of democratic governments lends itself to preservation of the divide between industry and state. There is the separation of powers through a tripartite government structure. The executive branch will remain at odds with the legislative and judicial branches. The judicial will reign in overreaching legislatures and executives. The legislatures will protect the interests of their residents and create fair and equitable markets. Combining the tripartite government with the bi-cameral party system (at least two antagonistic parties) should mitigate conflicts within the same tier of government and create conflicts in opposing governments. Each regional government (state, county, or province) will be in competition with the other regions. Within the regional government each municipality and city will guard against unfair political advantage of competing municipalities regardless of their affiliation. The cornerstone of sound political economy is conflict and more fuel is thrown on the fire when governments are allowed to compete with each other and private industry.

Commercial Government Theory asserts that the nation can be dissected into competitor jurisdictions and administrative jurisdictions in order to mitigate the possible conflicts and compromise normally associated with government investment and competition. Isolating jurisdictions into competitive units complements the adversarial multi-party political system and dividing government powers among different branches. Competitor jurisdictions are those jurisdictions where the asset owning governments can become fully involved in every aspect of commerce because they have little influence on legislation and enforcement governing commerce in that region. Administrative jurisdictions are those jurisdictions where the government administers law and any commercial involvement will be strictly regulated. Administrative jurisdictions are based on the pre-existing political boundaries established through municipal charters and state constitutions.

When conflicts arise between governments and residents, or commercial parties and competitor jurisdictions, the normal regulatory apparatus of the states, provinces, counties, towns, cities, and nation, with their respective courts, will mitigate and diffuse any improprieties or abuses. Competitive interests of one jurisdiction will be held in check by the administrative interests of another jurisdiction. Most host jurisdictions will favor consumers with protective regulations and judicial decrees rather than alien government corporations. Employees of government owned businesses will almost exclusively have residency in the host jurisdiction and are less prone to take advantage or abusing their neighbors at the behest of another government's appointed executive. It is expected that most competitive government corporations will be more responsible in their business practices or product lines simply because their managers are ultimately accountable to the voters of the owning jurisdiction. The fear of scandal will keep most government business managers and executives honest and forthright in their dealings with other jurisdictions or companies.

In most configurations of commercial government the national tier of government will be prohibited from owning positions in companies operating within the country. Its agencies and departments will be free of those conflicts lower governments inherit when first beginning to invest and become business owners. It will be the final means to negotiate difference between the competing states, cities, small businesses and Mega-corporations. The national government will continue to police against graft, fraud, corruption, and coercion regardless whether the perpetrator is private or government. All these checks and balances are in excess of the natural tendency of a people to guard against the improprieties of their elected agents. The press will remain privately owned and residents can continue to rely on their judgment and curiosity as the primary means to check corruption and to remedy abuses.

Governments always reserve the right to organize and operate business but they seldom do so for profit. The principle argument for nationalization or municipalization of services or products is public welfare. Government is the only business entity entitle to uncompetitive business practices. It can hold monopoly, conduct price fixing, and dumping in order to protect the general welfare of its residents. Conventional government incorporations don't earn profits because they generally operate within the administrative jurisdictions of the owning governments. Often providing a service for residents is more important than producing profits. Commercial governments will have no incentive for funding failing businesses in competitor jurisdictions and as a result the larger market economy will be protected. The only reason one government operates a business in another jurisdiction is to earn profits and reduce its own resident's tax liabilities.

The right to employ uncompetitive business practices will naturally be forfeited when operating within a competitor jurisdiction. A government competing in another government's jurisdiction for market share will not be entitled to forward the general welfare of the opposing government's residents as a reason to act in that jurisdiction. Alien governments are unable to operate nonprofit businesses within any jurisdiction other than its own. It must seek as much profit as the market permits and it will have to adhere to the municipalities' ordinances and regional governments' laws while doing so. No government will be eligible to earn profit from business transactions occurring within their administrative jurisdictions. Neither will they be able to deliver products to residents or businesses whose addresses are within their jurisdictions.

If the commercial government is eligible to own and operate a business it may make one contribution to its initial assets and must rely on standard modes of recapitalization from that point forward. Government corporations will have to price their product or service competitively to ensure they earn enough revenue to keep operations fully funded. Unprofitable businesses will be liquidated unless they find other investors or contract for a commercial loan. This will make it near impossible for government businesses to undercut privately owned vendors because they all face bankruptcy if revenue doesn't exceed overhead. The most important reason for a single contribution system is so that government companies don't have access to unlimited financing. Government businesses must be accountable to the market economy and limiting their funding to conventional methods will create parity between private and government owned businesses.

This experiment would be disastrous if government businesses had an overwhelming advantage over private businesses and it is likely the whole market economy would collapse.

Competitive government owned businesses will be treated exactly like ordinary privately owned companies whenever they participate in commerce within a competitor jurisdiction. Government businesses will be subject to the same administrative regulations, the same city ordinances, and all applicable state, national, or international laws that private businesses are. Government will owe a fiduciary duty to their residents and they will be expected to earn the greatest amount of profits with the least exposure of risk. Representatives are expected to vote in corporate board elections and shareholder referendums with the sole intent on producing profits and marinating dividends. This should put other shareholders at ease with an influx of government investment. A huge proportion of securities are already owned by pension funds and sovereign wealth funds and most business welcome the government money as openly as they do private investors.

Collusion between governments will be strictly forbid so that representatives can't negotiate for uncompetitive exchanges of services or products, so that laws do not favor one party over another, and enforcement is applied evenly and without prejudice. Commercial governments cannot leverage their own political integrity for the compromise of another region or nation's integrity. Government businesses won't ever be able to lobby government employees or representatives from competitor jurisdictions. They can't make campaign contributions, nor donate PAC moneys, nor offer bribes or gifts. This is especially true for the elected representatives and appointed officials of the owning jurisdiction. It is imperative that private companies are not disadvantaged by government owned business's natural proximity to representation. Government investment and competition will reform the traditional relationship between commercial parties and the state, where most instances of commercial influence on political campaigns will be eliminated by exclusions created by investment by the government, or as a result of business transactions with that jurisdiction's companies.

The combination of exclusions should produce a system of politics insulated from commercial influence be it prompted by private parties or government parties. Simultaneously governments will realign their interests with those of the business community so that the most efficient regulations and most productive incentives are in place. Private small businesses and large public businesses can all be assured that they will not be exploited, nor marginalized, or discouraged, and that all markets will be accessible to them as they are for government owned businesses. Reinforcing the separation of State and Industry through restrictions on lobbying and campaign contributions is the greatest secondary benefit of a fully funded MCPFS. Public welfare will be intertwined with profit as a government's ability to provide for its citizens is intimately tied to its success in business in competitor jurisdictions and as a result governments will reciprocate competitive markets and reasonable regulations. When governments no longer rely on businesses as the primary source of tax revenue they will be better able to apply scrutiny and an unbiased eye to industry regulation.

The many commercialized aspects of traditional government authority will not be compromised. The U.S. governments FDIC could still seize management of banks that become insolvent. The Federal Reserve could still rescue an ailing mortgage company, like Fannie Mae or Freddie Mac, or insurance companies like AIG by assuming substantial amounts of their stock. Likewise, a nation desiring to make a transition to a nationalized healthcare system (i.e. the United Kingdom) would retain the authority to do so. A government always has authority to act in otherwise uncompetitive ways to ensure public welfare or economic stability. Its ability to offer subsidized services to residents will never be compromised but all of their funding must come from the General Fund and not their Permanent Funds. This will preserve the integrity of moneys set aside for public welfare and moneys set aside for investment.

Governments will be able to provide a managed market economy without directly interfering with private wealth. It has all the advantages of a managed market without any of the adverse effects of overregulation and misappropriation. Disposable incomes for individuals or corporations can be adjusted by changes in tax rates or dividends, and credit markets can be adjusted by mandating cash reserves held in government Permanent Funds, artificial demand for securities or commodities can be created by changing risk allocation requirements, and higher governments can dictate the volume of money invested in domestic or foreign securities or bond markets. These measures of control will be in addition to manipulating interest rates, legislating tax breaks, or regulation of industry and all of the other conventional methods of implementing economic and fiscal policies.

The nation will have more influence in the global political arena when its constituent governments intertwine themselves within the corporate boards of banks and other financial institutions, technology and manufacturing companies, defense contractors and emergency equipment suppliers. With control of corporate boards contracts can be funneled towards other resident owned businesses operating abroad. Business contacts and transaction are an incredible source of intelligence that agencies can gain access to and embargos will be much more effective at causing banks runs, high unemployment, and higher inflation, losses in securities markets, real estate, markets, and economic crisis in general. Accumulating public debt from a foreign nation can aid in negotiating United Nations and World Bank Votes. Investment dollars can supplement humanitarian aid to help develop undercapitalized regions. A fully vested MCPFS provides countless tools for a nation to manipulate and forward its interests.

The MCPFS is modeled after the State of Alaska and its Alaskan Permanent Fund. The Alaskan Permanent Fund is a constitutionally established fund, managed by semi-independent corporations established by Alaska in 1976. The Alaskans set aside a share of certain oil revenues to continue benefiting current and future generations of Alaskans. The result is that Alaskans do not pay state income or sales taxes. Residents only pay local and federal taxes. The Fund continues to receive revenue from mining, oil, and gas operations in the state and reinvests the proceeds in stock, bonds, and other instruments. It is free to invest in local, national, and multinational corporations. This is the only instance where a democratic government takes tax dollars and invests in private equities with the goal to eliminate or depreciate all taxes normally associated with government operation.

The Alaskan Permanent Fund grew from an initial investment of $734,000 in 1977 to the current sum of approximately 40 billion dollars in 2007. There are obviously risks of economic or political compromise considering the large amount of state capital is involved but Alaska mitigates any potential for conflict by outsourcing management of its fund to a 3rd party. The Alaska

Permanent Fund Authority manages the Fund's assets and is required to earn the maximum prudent return. The Fund is not employed to apply a social or political agenda with the invested moneys. In addition to subsidizing the majority of the Alaskan State budget it produces a dividend for its residents. There is debate regarding the original intention of the Fund; some say that it was to ensure complete subsidy or the state budget when oil supplies ran dry but popular sentiment is overwhelmingly in favor of dividend production (started in 1982). As a result the State General Fund runs at a deficit despite the fact that when both the General Fund and the permanent Fund are balanced a surplus remains.

Alaska has a small population and high revenue source. It receives billions of dollars annually from the use of the Alaskan pipeline and from the rental of mining rights of vast mineral, oil, and gas resources. The rest of the states don't resemble Alaska in this manner, but the other states have vastly greater access to tax revenue from commercial and private incomes, property taxes, and sales taxes. Rather than natural gas or oil, the other States can exploit their economies as consumption and productivity are readily available and renewable resources. In a short period of time, States can create stores of capital from almost negligible tax that equals the capital reserves of Alaskan Permanent Fund in proportion to their own populations.

Take NJ's 2006 State budget for example. The total amount of all indirect and direct taxes collected was 28 billion dollars and if there is a legislated maximum contribution of 3% of the budget, then the New Jersey Permanent Fund will receive around 840 million every year in contributions. After 25 years nearly $ 61 billion would be held in escrow for the subsidy fund if 7% was earned on the principal. Approximately $4.2 billion would be available for subsidy every year going forward after maturity (without depreciating the principal). This equals nearly 18% of the original total government expenditures of 28 billion. If income taxes were 11% then they would be reduced to 9.0%. Sales taxes can be reduced from 7% to 6%.

This reduction in taxes results from only a single 25 year cycle. Subsequent cycles will accelerate the reduction in taxes. After 2 cycles totaling 50 years, state income taxes will be down to 6.8% and sales tax down to 5%. A national corporate profits tax will fall from 40% to 24%. Fifty years may seem like a long time to an individual but it is merely a moment in the life span of a nation. A third MCPFS cycle ending in the 75 year after inception will erode taxes to near minimal levels. Rather than an 11% income tax there will be a rate closer to 4.4%. Sales taxes will be depressed to 4% as well and corporate profits taxes will be only 16%. There is no reason a government subsidy program needs to end when taxes are completely suppressed. They can begin fully funding dividend programs and simply redistribute their earnings amongst their residents.

The 25 year cycle is not written in stone. A more applicable maturity date would be 40 or 50 years. This is similar to the length of time an average American works and saves towards retirement. Working with the same 28 billion dollar budget and using the same 3% contribution and 7% earnings estimate the projected principal grows to nearly $192 billion with a yearly subsidy of approximately $13.4 billion after 40 years. This would account for nearly 48% of the budget. Rather than 11% income tax it would be 5.7%. Sales taxes would depreciate to 3.5%. Corporate profits taxes would be 20.8% rather than 40%. The economy would boom the year after the first 40 year cycle completed. If the program were continued into subsequent 40 year cycles then there would be virtually no taxes after the second completed cycle and positive earnings after the third.

Subsequent Permanent Funds would have to have a contribution rate equivalent to the current budget plus subsidy. Otherwise the amount contributed would diminish with the smaller tax revenue and future subsidy will be proportionally less. A subsidy rate of 20% for the second cycle would be equivalent to only 15% of the whole budget (budget + subsidy). The third cycle's subsidy of 20% would really equal only 10% of the whole budget. In each case it would still enable a subsidy rate of 20% but that would be applied to the already diminished tax rate. A 3% contribution rate based on the original tax rate is not overly burdensome even if it has doubled relative to the adjusted tax rate. True, it would be a larger proportion of the new 5.7% tax rate but it would still be the same low rate paid in the decades before.

If the Permanent Funds were not staggered waiting for complete subsidy could take upwards of 80 or 90 years without any immediate benefits. Many generations would pay into the system and get very little out of it with a waiting period that long. People react to immediate success and a long wait could diffuse support for the MCPFS. A staggered budget subsidy program is fairer to more people and can be more easily measured for success. It is also more compatible with dividend production or other MCPFS goals. Regardless of whether a 15, 25, or 40 year cycle was selected it could alternate uses so one year budget subsidy is produced, the next year proceeds can be translated directly into dividends, and the year after that the government could revert to budget subsidy or simply expand its spending by the amount earned in interest off the principal.

These are slightly unfair comparisons. The projections don't account for budgetary or monetary inflation. The truth is if budgets continued to increase at the rate most current do then the gains from even a 40 year maturity date would be profoundly eroded. Fortunately states like NJ can't sustain growth of 6.1% year after year. Taxes would simply choke off commerce and making living in the region unbearable. In only a decade or two of such gross overspending taxes would double or treble. No resident would stand for income taxes of 22%, sales taxes of 14%, or property taxes of 2% or more. It is imperative for any government's sustainability that government spending be reigned in from current levels. Contributions to permanent funds are correlated to increases in government spending so a proportion of the inflation is captured. Smaller more reasonable adjustments in government spending won't erase all of the benefits of an MCPFS but fiscal responsibility is still needed to make this public finance system work. Hopefully managing income generating assets will rub off on our politicians and they will learn that balancing revenues with spending is necessary for survival.

A more modest yearly return on investment will produce far less subsidy. If contributions of 3% of the budget are made every year, and investments earned only 5%, then after a wait of 40 years a principal of 92 billion would produce only 5 billion in subsidy. This would still account for nearly a quarter of the taxes needed to sustain the state but much less than if more aggressive investment strategies are used. Most money managers and business owners expect to earn much higher than 5% on their investments. Historically securities markets in the U.S. have produced an average of 10% returns (not taking into account the recent market collapse). If managers earned 9% during a 40 year cycle, with arbitrary 1.4% combined budgetary and monetary inflation, then approximately 275 billion in principal will have been saved, with 25 billion in subsidy accounting for nearly 63% of the costs of a budget. Taxes will be 37% of what they would normally be without the MCPFS. Year to year the return rates will change depending upon the changing composition of the Permanent Funds but the average should remain between 6 and 8% producing a fairly predictable return on the investment.

The efficacy of a MCPFS can be manipulated through changing contribution rates as well. If the contribution rate was higher significantly more money would be available at the end of a cycle. With a contribution rate of 5%, a base budget of 28 billion, and a profit rate of 7%, then at the end of a 40 year cycle approximately 320 billion would be available for budget subsidy producing nearly 22 billion in interest and accounting for 45% of the tax receipts after adjusted for 1.4% inflation (78% non-inflated). Needless to say, if contribution rates were smaller then much less subsidy would occur unless offset by extraordinarily high rates of return. Contribution rates can be determined by previous performance so that the Permanent Fund produces the expected amount of subsidy in the prescribed time frame. More mature MCPFS can use contribution rates to influence the volume of money involved in local economies. Reducing rates expands the volume and increasing contribution rate contracts the volume of money disposable incomes consumers have.

There may even come certain times when continued contributions to a MCPFS becomes untenable. A ruined economy can make the extra tax too hurtful to the economy. Reckless investments can give the appearance of excessive losses and causes a public to lose trust in its ability to succeed. Whatever the reason a MCPFS can be suspended for a short time while its purpose or value is re-evaluated. The assets already locked within the Permanent Fund will continue to produce dividends and increase in value. If a onetime contribution of 3% was made on a 28 billion dollar budget, and if it were left alone for one hundred years while it earned an average of 7% interest, it would produce a subsidy large enough to account for 45% even after an inflation rate of 1.4%. Waiting 100 years may not be the best scenario but 45% subsidy after a single contribution is extraordinary on its own. Suspending contributions to a MCPFS for only a few years merely delays the inevitable product of budget subsidy.

There isn't a tremendous amount of variety between tax rates of different countries especially when considering the cohort of western democracies. German industry pays and average of 29.8% on profits. Its residents pay between 15 and 45% in income taxes and 19% for sales tax (only 7% on necessities). French businesses are charged a 33.33% tax on their profits and French workers pay between 10 and 40% in income taxes. Like Germans, the French pay around 19.6% on products and service with 5.5% for food and other select items. The English pay a corporate profit tax between 21 and 28%, income taxes of 0%, 20%, or 40%, a national insurance rate between 0 and 11%, and a Vat/Gat/Sales tax of 17.5%. Unlike the U. States most European countries offer significant government benefits such as national health insurance and free universities, but businesses in the U.S. still pay between 15 and 39% in federal corporate profits tax, between 0 and 12% in State corporate profits tax, and between 0 and 7.65% in payroll taxes. Wage earning residents pay between 0 and 35% in federal income tax, between 0 and 10.3% in state income taxes, and between 0 and 7.65% in FICA and OASDI taxes. Consumers pay between 0 and 10.25% in sales taxes.

Without taxes crime, corruption, and abuse would reign. Populations would not be educated, industry would not be regulated, and we would lack protection from foreign invaders and domestic usurpers. Taxes allow our governments to perform their expected roles. An MCPFS makes it possible to continue funding necessary government programs while suppressing the taxes imposed on residents and their businesses. Those nations that hesitated and did not convert to a commercial government format years earlier will find themselves at a grave disadvantage. How could a country like France or the U.S. compete when their corporate profits tax remains at 39% while England and Germany offers a 10% corporate profits tax? Their security markets will boom when corporate profits skyrocket with a reduction in income and sales taxes equal to a 25% increase in domestic consumption. Imagine the appreciation in real estate values when property taxes are zeroed out. All of these tax reductions will occur without depreciating government spending and programs like national health insurance, subsidized universities, unemployment insurance, and other government sponsored benefits.

Low taxes will enable companies to retain more of their revenues for profit and be able to produce services and goods at lower costs. Residents will have more disposable income and their standards of living will improve. The country will produce more competitive exports erasing any unfavorable imbalance in trade. Credit markets will be more liquid allowing for businesses to expand faster. More capital will be available for start up businesses and mergers. Even the most conservative commercial governments will see unprecedented growth in their GDP's and historic lows in unemployment rates. In addition to the obvious advantages low taxes bestow on a State and its economy, all commercial governments will have tremendously more economic and political influence than traditional capitalist democracies. Their assets can be used in the myriad of extracurricular ways already mentioned. Assets provide leverage, intelligence, access, and support even when used innocuously in allied economies. Eventually commercial governments will eclipse and replace most traditional capitalist democracies.

Paramount to understanding the feasibility of budget subsidy through a MCPFS is the ability to justify creating such a program and then waiting 25 or 50 years for it to mature. Fifty years seems considerable when compared to the entire 200 year history of the U. States but 50 years is a rather unsubstantial amount of time when weighed against the histories of other countries. Most European countries have histories spanning many hundreds of years. A wait of 50 years is negligible compared to a 1000 year old country. It is hardly worth mentioning if the history of the country goes back 2 or 3 thousand years. In a matter of 100 years, or a span of 1/10 its total age, England could fundamentally change its system of public finance so that the entirety of its government expenditures is offset by investment into securities, commodities, and private equities. At some point the government will cease needing more money to subsidize its budgets and be free to produce wealth for its residents. Once government successfully reorganizes its priorities to include wealth creation for its residents the Capital State will be born.

Unfortunately, in order to fund a MCPFS taxes would have to be increased a small amount. It does seem a little counterproductive to insist on a tax increase to fund a program purposefully created with the sole intention of eliminating all taxes. Make no mistake the long term benefits are absolutely worth the temporary inconvenience. Fortunately the magnitude of the increase is relatively small. If a government is regulated to a maximum contribution of 3% of the budget (or tax revenue), the inception of the program would not cause a gross increase of 3 points in taxes; it merely causes a 3% increase in taxes. For example; if property tax was 1% and a government investment plan was initiated with a maximum 3% contribution, then property taxes would only raise to 1.03% not to 4% (0.0103 versus 0.04). The 0.03% increase is minimal compared to the promise of a reduction of taxes after the accounts mature. Trading a slight increase in taxes for an inevitable large decrease is in everybody's best interests.

The extra tax will simply be absorbed by residents and their businesses without any horrible economic impact. The overall negative impact of higher taxes should remain nearly inconsequential to the incomes and living standards of the majority of residents in the jurisdiction especially when the corporations within the state see a torrent of extra investment capital enter into the credit and securities markets. All of the contributions will be applied to purchasing real estate, securities, and commodities so the money isn't effectively removed from the economy. It is simply redirected. The competitive disadvantages between governments offering a 39.3% corporate tax rate and one requiring a 40.2% tax rate is negligible. Residents paying an income tax of 7% will not be disenfranchised if that rate rose to 7.21%. The cost of a MCPFS is minimal when compared with the inevitable gains. Any depreciation of competitiveness will likely made up by the government's focused reinvestment into their own security, commodity, and real estate markets and the higher rate of capitalization will almost definitely compensate for the marginal increase in taxes.

A MCPFS does require a small sacrifice from those that will be unlikely to benefit: They will take an average of 25 years to mature and older segments of the population are at risk of paying into the system without seeing a reduction in their tax liabilities. The tax dollars are conserved in the economy but confined to a relatively small sector of the domestic economy. Companies will find it far easier to raise capital through security and bond sales. Investments made through private equity arrangements and commercial loans will make it much easier for small business to grow and developers to begin construction. Government investment will provide most businesses with a consistent and reliable source of capitalization. Still a significant portion of the population will not immediately benefit.

The burden of a slight increase in taxes for the first few generations is infinitesimal in importance when comparing it with the humongous benefit minimized taxes has for all the remaining generations after the Subsidy program has matured. The wealth lost during the first 25 years by residents contributing to the fund is more than compensated by the gain or retention of wealth in the decades or centuries subsequent to a successful program. The people will be able to generate their own wealth more quickly and preserve it more efficiently. The end result is a bulwark of public wealth located in local towns, cities, and states. Governments will be stronger, more efficient, their solvency will be ensured, and sovereignty secured.

There is already precedent for the appropriation of money from individuals and businesses not relevant to benefiting those people or industries. A large portion of social programs designed and implemented by the government (state or federal) already do not benefit many individuals paying the cost. A substantial portion of current budgets go toward sheltering and feeding the poor, subsidizing poorer school districts, protecting small farmers in the west, and aid to foreign governments. One can argue that all are necessary services but it is undeniable that a majority of the nation's population is not in direct receipt of such services. Government investment will benefit all the residents of a particular jurisdiction albeit at a future date. So it is unfortunate that a few generations will see an increase in their taxes, but a much larger number of people will see a much greater reduction in their taxes.

Most governments don't stay on budget. They tax 28 billion but spend 30 billion. They employ municipal bonds and treasury bills to compensate for the difference. This mechanism for public funding will not change. In some ways this is unfortunate because Most of the traditional capitalist democracies are suffering under the threat of insolvency. National and municipal government public debts are at an all time high in most countries. Their dangerous addiction to wild spending and excessive borrowing will cause their bankruptcy. Insolvency, although often not a fatal disposition, will severely hamstring a government's ability to provide emergency or necessary services. Their militaries will be crippled from underfunding, farming will be unsustainable without subsidies, and its infrastructure will crumble and decay. When the needs of a people go unsatisfied for long enough a government's sovereignty can be challenged and then prove fatal to the political system. Commercial governments produce a second revenue source reducing the amount of money they need to borrow thus insulating them from the threat of coercion by other competitive nations. Better yet, the extra revenue can defray the cost of bond liabilities already accrued.

The good news is that a Mandatory Contribution Permanent Fund System will not impair the integrity of bond markets. Not only will commercial bond markets boom from the flood of government capital but governments will still have incentive to issue bonds or sell treasury bills. The bond market is one of the most important facets of free market economy. It sets precedent for interest rates and offers some of the least risky investments for money managers. Pension funds rely on low yield but stable government bonds to offset high yield and high risk securities. One fair criticism of commercial government theory is that its success may erode the quantity of high quality bonds offered by governments when the majority of their expenditures are covered by investment revenue. They could maintain low taxes without offering bonds thus impairing the bond market. This is blatantly untrue. Many of the same pressures that cause a government to borrow money now will cause it to borrow money in the future.

In fact the act of budget subsidy actually creates new circumstances where a government will be inclined to issue bonds or borrow from commercial institutions. Whenever there is a deficit of funding, meaning when the fixed amount of budget subsidy produced by the Permanent Fund misses projections, a government will offer bonds to make up the difference. This can occur when the stock markets or real estate markets are depressed, it can occur from mismanagement, or it can occur when government spending outpaces government subsidy. The likelihood of shortfalls in budget subsidy from year to year actually makes commercial governments more dependent on consumer demand for bonds. Bond markets are safe for another reason. When a government is able to offset 15% of its budget cost with investment the public won't stand for the same government then increasing spending by 15%. The public will expect to see the reduction in taxes and will resist governments increasing their spending and eroding the gains. Governments will borrow the difference between their spending and the adjusted tax rate.

Maintaining low taxes is the exact mechanism at work when current governments issue bonds.

There is even incentive for a government to issue bonds at one rate and invest in private equities for a higher rate of return. Yes, they can leverage their tax revenues for larger permanent fund contributions. This is the very same mechanism that corporation use to attain faster rates of growth and higher returns. No, this is not the safest strategy to employ but it can guarantee continued funding of the MCPFS without raising taxes on residents. The single biggest inconvenience of a government subsidy program is an increase in taxes and issuing bonds can eliminate or marginalize that aspect. If a government is wary of creating bond liabilities within the general fund for permanent fund uses than the permanent fund can issue its own bonds. Permanent Fund bonds will still lower resident's tax liabilities by substituting bond revenues for tax contributions. Permanent fund bonds should be comparable with general fund bonds because both are supported by taxes.

The safest way to ensure future strength in the bond market is to place restrictions on budget subsidy so that only on budget expenses are considered. In reality this is also the most convenient method to calculate contribution rates. On budget expenses more closely represents the total amount of tax receipts collected. A government could adjust its savings for both on and off budget expenses but that would require a much, much larger contribution rate. Three percent of a budget actually equates to 5 or 6% of the tax rate when both on and off budget expenses are included. There will be a prerogative to keep current tax rates low even when budgeting for a MCPFS so governments will be more inclined to peg contributions to on budget expenses only. Thus governments will still be forced to secure at least part of its total revenue from bond sales from year to year.

For older more mature commercial governments certain restrictions can be put in place to ensure a high functioning bond market. It is almost inevitable that if a government begins saving a small proportion of its tax revenue every year that it will eventually have such a massive amount of principal that it becomes conceivable that budget subsidy will be able to accommodate both on budget and off budget expenses. Using this system it will take more than 100 years but given the average age of most nations this is hypothetically relevant. If this be the case then Governments can simply be prohibited from including off budget expenses into budget subsidy. By rerouting the surplus subsidy money into the dividend fund the bond markets can be preserved. Dividends are the perfect outlet for surplus revenue because it helps deflate the regressive nature of tax depreciation and it creates immediate controls on government spending.

Public wealth would no longer refer to park spaces or government administration buildings. Instead it will be partial or complete ownership of profit seeking businesses in competitor jurisdictions. They will own retailers, equipment suppliers, contractors, and manufacturing or distribution companies. Public wealth will be seen in terms of gross ownership and market share. In every instance it is private property held in common for all the residents of that region or locality. The public wealth of one community would not be wealth for another community. It is exclusively owned just like individual private wealth or corporate wealth is. It will be a source of pride and identity for the residents. It will be a source of income and collateral. Public wealth will not only be concentrated in the 50 state governments, it will be distributed among thousands of municipal, county, or city governments. There are 87 thousand independent towns, cities, counties, and states in the United States (or other nations). Each one will develop its own fund and will be natural competitors to one another with commercial interests set at odds with each other.

Money already captured in public pensions or Sovereign Wealth Funds is extremely durable. Most funds can survive even the harshest of economic climates. In fact, despite the fact they may have earned terrific losses in short term values, the fact that new contributions will be vested in a depreciated market means that when the markets recover they should be in a better position than before the collapse. Pension funds, Permanent Funds, and Sovereign Wealth Funds can usually hold their assets long enough to recover any value lost during an economic downturn. The scope of a government fund is in decades or centuries and they should be able to weather almost any type of negative scenario. Even if the fund accrues losses in a critical payout phase responsible governments can create an insurance system to provide assistance until the fund can right itself. An MCPFS creates permanent wealth for a government and its residents which can be used across generations for any purpose that forwards the people's interests.

Despite the obvious implications of public wealth commercial government systems are most definitely not a form of communism. Individual property rights continue to be protected. There is no government monopoly on production and distribution of goods and services. Banking services are not centralized. Agriculture and manufacturing are not consolidated and managed according to a planned economy. Political parties are not usurped by the proletariat, the family structure remains intact, and the economy is still monetized. Yes public wealth has socialist underpinnings, especially when governments begin to be represented on corporate boards or gain influence on private businesses, but there is no usurpation of property and no coercion from profit. Government entitlements to invest in private equities can be reasonably structured to eliminate most conflicts in interest, to reduce the incidence of graft and corruption, and to preserve private ownership as the dominant theme in its economy.

Every reasonable financial planner espouses the need for individuals to dedicate a small percentage of their earnings to retirement savings. The idea is that after 30 or 40 years of consistently saving between 3 and 5% of their yearly income they will have enough principle to produce an investment income to replace their labor income. This formula must be applied to public finance as well. No the government won't retire from its working task of administering law and providing necessary services for residents but it can become self sufficient. It can free its citizens and residents from burdensome property, sales, income, and profits taxes. Using alternative forms of public finance will make the nation stronger, more versatile, and safer. It is just as reckless for an individual to neglect retirement savings as it is for a nation to squander its opportunity to initiate a Mandatory Contribution Permanent Fund System.

Most commercial government systems preserve free markets and promote entrepreneurship. When governments are actors in a competitor jurisdiction where they have no responsibilities for public welfare and the administration of law, they will be an ordinary commercial party in every capacity. Municipalities, counties, and states become engrossed in the economies of rival municipalities, counties, and states. They will be investors, partners, and competitors with private businesses. Lower taxes will spur growth, innovation, and enfranchisement within both the private and government sectors. Public wealth will provide nation's security and better guarantee their sovereignty. The era of Competitive State Capitalism has begun. It has already started transforming the economic and political landscape of the world and will continue to gain momentum until it is the single most dominant theme in the global economy.

CODEX MECHANICUS

Chapter 2

Account attributes and entitlements:

Once the argument for commercial governments is forwarded and supported the next logical step is discuss their form and structure. This section is to serve as an in-depth list of the most important properties of commercial governments. The three primary categories of commercial government characteristics are account attributes, entitlements, and market impact. The category of account attributes and it is split into five major subclasses. They are tier of government, operations, purpose, method, and domain. The category of entitlements is divided into instrument, jurisdiction, and degree. The category of market impact is split into gross ownership and market share. Each category and its options are listed in an outline form so that a key for each sample system can be produced. Utilizing a key makes quick comparisons possible and lends itself for manipulating options into a not yet specified system. All of the listed characteristics will be explained as to their function or importance within the sample systems.

I. Account Attributes;

   A. Tier of government owning fund:
      1. Federal (Central)
      2. Regional (State)
      3. Local (county, city, village, or town)

   B. Operation (management of fund):
      1. Government must manage own money.
         a. Social Agenda
         b. Profit seeking only
      2. Private company (3rd party) must manage government money
      3. Government can choose to outsource management
         a. May apply social agenda when self managing
         b. Profit seeking only when self managing

C. Purpose (use):
   1. Subsidy of budget (reduce tax liabilities)
   2. Production of dividend checks for residents
   3. Improving government benefits (increase government spending)
   4. Combination of uses
      a. Subsidy/dividend production
      b. Dividend/improve benefits
      c. Subsidy/improve benefits
      d. Unstructured;

D. Method:
   1. Rollover contributions and interest (Savings)
      a. 15 year cycle
      b. 25 year cycle
      c. 40 year cycle
   2. Immediately apply interest earned (Defrayment)
   3. Hybrid: (split contribution between savings and defrayment)
      a. savings with 15 year cycle/defrayment
      b. savings with 25 year cycle/defrayment
      c. savings with 25 year cycle/defrayment

E. Domain:
   1. Centralized
      a. One permanent fund for all taxes
         x. separates off budget from on budget expenses
      b. Multiple subsidy funds, one for each tax
   2. Departmentalized (divided into department/ agency/or program)

Each tier of government can have values or entitlements that are different from the other tiers of government within the same nation. Generally the lower tier governments will have greater allowances to invest due to the larger number of competing governments, the more limited supply of investment capital, and less potential for conflict. Confining Permanent Fund attributes to a single category of government entitles higher governments to more easily legislate or regulate that specific class of lower government. For ease of classification only three types of government are listed. They are the federal (or national) tiers, the regional (state or provincial) tiers, and the local (municipal and county) tiers of government.

A. Tier of government:
   1. Federal (National)
      And/or
   2. Regional (State)
      And/or
   3. Local (county, city, village, or town)

It is possible to dissect the local tier into three distinct parts; the county, the city, and the town but this is generally unnecessary as all three already have limited potential for conflict when the majority of their investments and ownership occurs outside of its administrative jurisdiction. Cities pose a specific problem considering some incorporate multiple counties (or boroughs) and can be as large in area and population as certain opposing regional (or state) governments. If necessary, cities exceeding a predetermined threshold of population can be treated as regional governments in terms of depreciated entitlements and checks on potential conflicts.

Most of the models offered concern one principle nation but the process can be updated to incorporate Unions (i.e. the European Union). The Union will have an extra delineation within the tier of government attribute and the jurisdiction attribute. Different degrees of ownership can coincide with whether or not competitive jurisdictions are located within the union or whether it lies outside of the union. The Unionized countries will have to determine amongst themselves the appropriate entitlements for each of their own tiers of government and which classes of commercial government are acceptable for members. If the Union government levies taxes than it can have its own permanent fund but this isn't always necessary.

Who actually manages the permanent funds determines the classification of commercial government. Some governments will manage their funds themselves while others will outsource management to 3rd party money managers. Different tiers of government within a single nation can decide to manage their funds differently. Allowing individual municipalities or counties to manage their Permanent Funds directly causes little concern for abuse. However, regional (or state) governments and certainly federal (or national) governments may need to outsource management of assets to offset the considerable potential for conflict.

B. Operation (management):
   1. Government must manage own money.
      with
      a. Social or political Agenda
         or
      b. Profit seeking only
         or
   2. 3rd party must manage government money.
      or
   3. Government can self manage or outsource
      and
      a. may apply social agenda when self managing
         or
      b. Profit seeking only when self managing

There is a fundamental difference in whether or not a government can manage its own allocation of investments in a general subsidy portfolio or whether it must outsource the management of such funds to a 3rd party firm. First, conflicts can be minimized or eliminated by outsourcing the management of contributions. Second, governments which reciprocate capital influence on commerce represent a deviation from the traditional role of democratic government. Both are appropriate limits on commercial government and more conservative nations can opt to enforce both by forcing lower governments to outsource management of the funds.

Mandating governments to outsource management eliminates the concerns that a government will apply a social agenda with invested capital. The fiduciary must earn the highest yield with the least risk; tax dollars cannot be co-opted for reasons of economic development or political favor. Forcing governments to use 3rd party money managers protects commercial interests from extracurricular uses of government money. When outsourcing management politicians or public administrators will not decide which companies are invested in, there will be no opportunity for a politician to offer favors or a company to solicit for favors, how business is conducted at the firm, and which whom the businesses enter into transactions with. Commerce will be insulated from interloping governments.

Most governments impact industry strictly through regulation, enforcement, and tax policy. Commercial governments that manage their own portfolios have an opportunity to influence industry through capital investment and regulation. These governments can represent their constituencies through shareholder votes and corporate elections or through direct interface with commercial parties through contracts, sales, exchanges, or mergers. When legislation causing some change in law fails to pass a governor or mayor can still attempt to force compliance through representation on certain companies' boards. Although one government may only have negligible representation due to diversification, several governments with complementing agendas and working in unpremeditated concert will have significant enough representation to enforce their constituencies' prerogatives. These governments can weigh social gains against financial gains, and although profits will be their primary concern, they can consider sacrificing some profitability for extracurricular noncapital returns.

Certain governments may choose to manage their own portfolios but be prohibited from forwarding a social agenda. In this case the managing government has a fiduciary responsibility to cause the greatest gain in new wealth. These governments forfeit their representation on corporate boards to the companies' active management or allowing their brokers to apply their own prerogatives to the vote. These governments can't participate in elections and votes while 3rd party money managers can. This configuration is the least effective because it combines a high potential for conflicts and excessive losses due to self inflicted mismanagement with a disabled ability to influence industry. Despite the fact it would be much more profitable for these governments to outsource management the option remains available so that government need not relinquish control of their assets if they also feel that government interloping in the economy would be harmful.

The third attribute relates to the general purpose of the MCPFS. Most commercial governments should be organized around a purpose of budget subsidy. Budget subsidy adequately rewards those contributing the most in terms of taxes. It is also the easiest goal to understand. Most people are viscerally affected by taxes and substantially reducing them will produce a tangible and immediate reward. The MCPFS will then be justified. Lower taxes can make businesses more competitive and profitable, it can translate to more disposable income for residents which will raise their living standards and bolster consumerism. Lower taxes can substantially inhibit inflation when companies are empowered to charge less for products and services but make more money from their sales.

C. Purpose (use):

1. budget subsidy

   or

2. production of dividend

   or

3. improving government benefits

   or

4. Any combination of uses (unstructured)

Although most MCPFS should be concerned primarily with budget subsidy there may be occasions where representatives feel that a reduction in taxes is less productive than an increase in production of dividends. A people's perception of realized benefits will be greatly increased due to the tangible effects of receiving a yearly or quarterly dividend check. A people are much more likely to think a single dividend check provides them with more money than an equivalent amount of tax savings if they are spread out from paycheck to paycheck. This will add legitimacy to the continued funding of an MCPFS.

In addition to the psychological reasons for implementing a dividend production system there are incredible economic advantages. Dividends can be immediately applied to consumption. The lower and middle classes are much more likely to spend the cash dividend on rent, food, and clothing. Whatever is left will probably be spent on entertainment. This increased consumption will inflate company revenues; it will drive up stock prices, and strengthen the real estate markets. The results are nearly equivalent to budget subsidy but not reducing taxes will preserve a people's motivation to keep government spending low and government benefits at a minimum.

Those governments that trend to socialism can select improving government benefits. Communism isn't necessarily the final product for a commercial government selecting this option but it certainly is one product. A segment of the population will rather see an increase in spending rather than dividends or tax breaks. This can take the form of more defense spending, more grants for research, and more public assistance. Government spending accounts for a larger percentage of the economic activity of most nations and using public wealth to accelerate the exchange will produce tangible benefits in regards to better programs and a healthier economy.

When only lower governments are authorized to make improvements to government benefits (by increasing spending or creating I-A Corporations- see **Neo-Populism**) it complements market competition for real estate and residency. Municipalities and counties could start offering health and life insurance benefits, wealth management services and retirement benefits, and of course leisure and recreation outlets. Local governments generally won't have the capital reserves to severely handicap competition by usurping market share by government benefits. As long as this is checked by oversight from a national or regional government there should be very little concern that a people will be overcome with communist motivations.

It is always acceptable for a government to select an unstructured purpose for their own permanent fund. An unstructured purpose gives government's authority to devote proceeds to what they deem most important for that quarter or year and that can be of great benefit but the money will be diffused among the multiple goals. Taxes can change from quarter to quarter or year to year to combat inflation. Dividends can be speedily sent out when an economy needs acceleration. Governments could even sponsor smaller more recreational and entertainment events with the proceeds. With an unstructured purpose a government could devote part of their profits to taxes or dividends and still have enough left over to implement so form of government benefit. There is a downside to the unstructured purpose characteristic. Without focus the proceeds generated by government investment will only yield negligible or mediocre results. Rather than a 15% reduction in taxes, it may only produce 3%. Rather than many thousands of dollars in dividends, only a mere hundred may be offered. No doubt the government could not offer substantial benefits with a permanent fund divided among many purposes. Architects will have to trade efficacy for versatility at least until they set themselves on a path of singular function.

Generally the intent of governments within one nation will be uniform but different combinations have different consequences and advantages in different tiers. Some states will make the reduction of taxes a priority and some will promote production of dividends. National government should focus on budget subsidy but other governments, especially municipalities, could offer amenities or improved benefits. This variety will make more sense when in the next section cycles are described in more depth because different purposes can be paired with different duration cycles. The more variety there is in one nation the more successful it will be. It will be able to conserve wealth much more efficiently when tax rates can fluctuate wildly from one county to the next, where dividends are not the status quo but an extra advantage, and where towns and cities can specialize in benefits targeting businesses or residents.

Each government can apply a different strategy to public wealth accumulation and use. There are three principle methods and each one has certain advantages. A government can save and horde its assets until a substantial income is derived from the public wealth. All the profits made from investment are kept distinct from the government's general fund and reinvested with payout scheduled every 10, 25, or 40 years. This method will achieve the stated goal of budget subsidy fastest when all profits from successful investment are rolled over and preserved within the fund. A predictable amount of payout will occur in predictable periods allowing governments to plan better.

D. Method:
  1. Savings
     a. 10 year cycle
     b. 25 year cycle
     c. 40 year cycle
        or
  2. Defrayment
        or
  3. Hybrid (split savings and defrayment)
     a. savings with 10 year cycle/defrayment
     b. savings with 25 year cycle/defrayment
     c. savings with 40 year cycle/defrayment

A defrayment method relies primarily on the accumulation of yearly contributions as the means to achieve budget subsidy, produce dividends, or improve government benefits. The contributions are invested but the profits are not rolled over. Instead the government utilizes the profits in the way specified in the purpose section. The trade off is steadily lower taxes throughout the duration of the MCPFS. Having immediate and tangible results may legitimize government investment and competition. The defrayment method is the least effective in creating public wealth but it can certainly appease an inpatient public. Many residents will object paying into a MCPFS if the rewards are not expressed for 25 or 40 years.

A defrayment policy can be utilized much more effectively than a savings method when managing the economy with public wealth. Coincidentally those economies that need the most government management, i.e. Neo-Populist models, generally incorporate defrayment methods and unstructured purposes which make this more possible. Planned markets are usually rife with supply problems, demand problems, pricing problems, and labor problems. Managing an economy with public wealth can alleviate some of these inefficiencies but not eliminate them. When an economy is compromised by uncompetitive entitlements more comprehensive management of public wealth can infuse some fluidity into the capital and credit markets. In fact a Neo-Populist economy may not function properly without such management.

Hybrid methods provide the most flexibility for wealth accumulation. Hybrid models are generally split between savings and defrayment so that the benefits of both are gained. The contributions made into the savings portion of the hybrid permanent fund follow the same schedule as savings permanent funds. Half of the contributions will be saved and half will be immediately available. If 4% of a budget was collected, 2% would be applied to a savings program and 2% to a defrayment program. The hybrid method of wealth accumulation allows a government to offer budget subsidy and dividend production simultaneously. Most other states will have to operate multiple permanent funds to gain the advantage of both products or alternate between goals after complete permanent fund cycles. More involved MCPFS may in fact operate multiple hybrid permanent funds so that they can simultaneously combine multiple wealth accumulation methods with multiple goals. Normally a savings method is applied to budget subsidy and defrayment to dividend production but if one fund is already organized around this structure a second simultaneous fund could offer the savings method for dividend production and defrayment for budget subsidy.

Although defrayment account attributes aren't associated with a fixed duration, or cycle, once their contributions produce income equivalent to the percent raise in taxes another program can be initiated and assume the previous percent raise in taxes for contributions. This is only true if the first program is intended to produce budget subsidy because the interest generated will immediately cancel its cost in tax dollars. The second program would be funded without raising taxes a second time and the first program could continue funding itself. The second permanent fund could then be used to produce dividends or increase government spending. Obviously if the purpose didn't change in subsequent programs the effect would be redundant. However, one defrayment program need not necessarily be followed by another defrayment program. In this respect the same advantages of a hybrid method can be achieved but there would be two distinct permanent funds to manage.

The last section in account attributes is labeled domain because it sets the most intimate structure of Permanent Funds. Typically, each whole government will have one permanent fund to manage. It will be authorized by the legislature and operated by the executive branch. This is the easiest format to digest. It also makes the most sense but for practical reasons there are a variety of configurations. Most governments have both on budget and off budget expenses and one fund would confuse moneys meant for different programs. If this is true then specific taxes can contribute to otherwise independent permanent funds. Still others will see an advantage in maintaining many different permanent funds with each one under the control of a different government department or agency.

E. Domain:
  1. Centralized
     a. One subsidy fund for all taxes
        with
        x. separates off budget from on budget expenses
        or

b. Multiple subsidy funds, one for each tax

or

2. Departmentalized (divided into department or agency)

Each variation has its advantages. Having only one permanent fund enables a government to own larger positions in industries. All of the capital wealth of a region or locality is focused into one fund and can be managed by the same official or organization. Having multiple funds causes greater diversification and risk can be better mitigated. It may be harder to coordinate majority ownership but that is also a benefit. When public wealth is dispersed across government departments are agencies a people can be protected against political coercion, graft, or corruption. Public wealth will not be concentrated in just a few political organizations and private industry won't be compromised.

Different domains will translate into different entitlements because of the variety in responsibilities and culpabilities of tiers in government and competing departments. Although a certain government may be prohibited from using a specific instrument its constituent agency may pose less a threat and be authorize to own the company or product. Domain can change between cycles in a MCPFS which adds to the variety of the initiative; not only can the purpose or wealth accumulation be adapted to circumstances, but different facets of government can be entitled to different concentrations of wealth. Central capitalization can even be used simultaneously as departmental capitalization in the same respects contributions are split within a hybrid permanent fund. Complicated tangles of different operational methods, different wealth management methods, and different modes of capitalization can create very versatile models of commercial government.

The second section limits those instruments a government may invest in. It determines whether the degree of ownership may be a majority managing portion or whether it is relegated to minority or marginal positions, and it designates which jurisdictions the instrument may originate from or operate in. Some instruments can be dissected into subgroups, or specific products, and this complements the different tiers of vested government, the different domains in government structure, and management styles used for public wealth because each variation can be constrained to a specific jurisdiction and degree.

II. Entitlements:

A. Secondary market Instruments- (modified by degree and jurisdiction):

1. The government may not invest in secondary market instruments
2. The government can invest in broad spectrum instruments only (mutual, hedge, index, REIT, derivatives).
3. The government can invest in any investment instrument (stocks, options, derivatives, and commodities).

B. Debt markers (Instrument modified by jurisdiction, *always marginal degree*):

1. The government is prohibited from investing in any debt markers.
2. The government can invest in government's debt markers.
3. The government can invest in corporate debt markers (bank products, junk bonds, rated corporate bonds).
4. The government can invest in personal debt (mortgages, credit, past due amounts).

C. Real estate (modified by jurisdiction):

1. The government is prohibited from any investment in any real estate.
2. The government can invest in real estate.
   a. commercial
   b. residential

D. Currency (unmodified):

1. The government is prohibited from trading any currencies.
2. The government can invest in currency excluding the national currency.
3. The government can invest in currency including their national currency.

E. Venture Capital (primary markets, modified by jurisdiction and degree):
  1. The government is forbidden from owning private equities
  2. The government may initiate and manage new businesses.
  3. The government may purchase portions of private companies

Jurisdiction (modifies instrument and degree):
  x. The government can invest in foreign jurisdictions
  xx. The government can invest in domestic territories but not operating within the same jurisdiction.
    (c). jurisdiction is defines as same regional government
    (cc). the jurisdiction is defined in terms of opposing municipal governments.
  xxx. The government can invest in domestic instruments operating in the same jurisdiction (administrative jurisdiction).

Degree (Modifies instrument and jurisdiction):
  i. The government is relegated to a marginal share
  ii. The government can invest in minority shares.
  iii. The government can invest in majority shares.

III. Market Accumulation (<48% rules):
  A. Intra-company
    1. <48% of collective government ownership
    2. >48% of collective government ownership
  B. Inter-company
    1. <48% of market share
    2. >48% of market share

The principle support for commercial government is that conflicts can be limited by limiting the degree of ownership and the jurisdiction within competitor jurisdictions. Without this mechanism government involvement in the local economy would be too dangerous even to consider. There are two principle jurisdictions; foreign jurisdictions in competing nations and domestic jurisdictions within the same nation. Domestic jurisdictions are then divided into competing regional jurisdictions, competing municipal jurisdictions, and administrative jurisdictions.

Jurisdiction (modifies instrument and degree):

x. The government can invest in foreign jurisdictions.

or

xx. The government can invest in domestic markets but not operating within the same jurisdiction.

and

(c). the jurisdiction is defined as same regional government (state or province).

or

(cc). the jurisdiction is defined in terms of opposing municipal governments.

or

xxx. The government can invest in domestic instruments operating in the same jurisdiction (administrative jurisdiction).

The administrative jurisdiction is the economy which is local to the vested government; there it has regulative powers, legislative powers, and enforcement powers. Investment or competition in administrative jurisdictions causes the greatest incidence of conflicting interests and for that reason most governments are forced to be restricted to only the most menial rate of involvement. This is complicated when larger companies operate within several nations or states. Whenever revenues from a particular state (or city) exceed 5% of the company's total revenue then governments from that same state (or city) is generally limited to marginal positions at most. This limitation includes revenue generated through assets held by the company (and funds, i.e. mutual funds, hedge funds, and index funds) in addition to its ordinary commercial role. Thus any revenue derived from the jurisdiction in question is tallied and used as criteria for exclusion or limitation. This also applies to jurisdictions where private or public industry is incorporated. Political and judicial integrity can be compromised if the authoritative government has significant positions in companies dependent on its courts or laws.

Many instruments originate from multi-regional or multinational companies and eligibility will be based on such location. A company can be incorporated in Delaware but receive 20% of its revenue from New York City. In this instance all Delaware and New York governments will be excluded from investing in the company. If the company receives 33% of its revenue from New York markets, 33% of its revenue from New Jersey markets, 33% of its revenue from Pennsylvania markets, and was incorporated in Delaware, it would be excluded from all four of those states because they would all have overwhelming incentive to protect the company's profitability. Most commercial governments are strictly forbid from profiting off of their own residents. This will help ensure that coercive legislation is forwarded to discriminate against their own consumers. This will protect the integrity of regulatory agencies and courts.

This also applies to the origins of other financial instruments. For example derivatives are products offered by one company and are based on the successes of another company. This will provide three exclusionary criteria. The first is that the product is offered by a company residing in a specific jurisdiction. The second is that the derivative insurance against losses accrued by a company also located within a jurisdiction. The third is where the company is incorporated. If any of the locations happen to be within the administrative jurisdiction of the vested government consumption of the product will be guided by the entitlements afforded to the jurisdiction in question. This exclusion principle can be extended to commodities or any other instrument where it is appropriate. Florida would be prohibited in trading futures on Oranges or Tomatoes and New Jersey could not traffic in Eggplant futures.

The initial reaction of most readers should be to immediately restrict all government involvement in opposing foreign or competitive domestic jurisdictions only. This is not necessary and unfairly discriminates against small and medium businesses within the same jurisdiction of the vesting government. Marginal positions eliminate most concerns of usury or political coercion. Any impropriety will hardly be worth public condemnation or criminal prosecution when revenue created by the manipulation is only a tiny fraction of their overall profits. If a marginal position is defined as a maximum of 3% equity stake then why would a manager open themselves up to prosecution for a profit of 0.21%

on the original capital investment? The risks far outweigh the gains in these cases. In most instances a marginal degree of ownership also sets the maximum proportion of overall exposure within the permanent fund. With only 3% of the fund being able to be legitimately devoted to the single source of revenue the government will certainly focus on other more pressing and lucrative positions.

An important distinction is made in the jurisdiction selection. Although all commercial governments must operate primarily within opposing jurisdictions the definition of opposing jurisdiction is subject to variation. In conservative examples opposing jurisdictions will relate to opposing regional governments so that municipalities and counties can only compete in those jurisdiction located in another regions political domain. This is not an arbitrary division; conflicts will occur far less frequently if intra-state profiting is prohibited. It is assumed that regional governments have significantly more momentum in asserting their interests and more leverage for lobbying for their concerns. Simply put, dissecting the nation along competitive jurisdictions based on regional boundaries greatly reduces the danger of corruption and political coercion and most classes and models will reiterate this fact.

A competitor jurisdiction is any territory where the vesting government does not have control over regulatory agencies, legislation, and taxes. Foreign jurisdictions represent an opportunity for domestic governments to invest with the least potential for conflict of interests. There is no intersection of administrative jurisdictions; a competing nation controls all legislation, regulation, and enforcement. Therefore investments into foreign jurisdictions do not necessarily have to be limited to marginal or non majority positions; since virtually no conflicts arise from intersecting administrative jurisdictions governments can be permitted to own majority or owning positions. Nearly all commercial governments will allow for any government to manage controlling interests in industry that originates and operates within a completely foreign economy. The freedoms allowed in foreign jurisdictions may eventually translate into greater domestic allowances when regulation and enforcement are more practiced and can be guaranteed.

The jurisdiction must be in agreement with the degree of ownership allowed. Greater potential for conflicts due to intersecting administrative jurisdictions corresponds with lesser degrees of ownership. Less potential for conflict will usually result in greater degrees of ownership. There are three principle degrees of ownership; marginal, minority, majority. Most commercial governments will relegate themselves to marginal positions when the instruments originate from or operate within their administrative jurisdictions. More liberal systems will allow minority and majority degrees of ownership but they will only manifest in opposing regional jurisdictions and foreign jurisdictions (both competitor jurisdictions).

Degree (Modifies instrument and jurisdiction):

i. The government is relegated to a marginal share

or

ii. The government can invest in minority shares.

or

iii. The government can invest in majority shares.

The marginal rate is the most important rate because it is applied to most intra-administrative investment and is used as the default rate in minority entitlements. Most marginal rates should be set at 3% because that allows significant involvement without predisposing a company to too much interference while still generating statistically significant revenues. They can be adjusted to 1%, 2%, or even 4 or 5% but should be lower considering their use within administrative jurisdictions but more confidence or greater expectations can be complement by higher rates. It will inevitably be whatever the public deems acceptable in terms of risk and reward. If the public absolutely forbids intra-administrative investment then the marginal rate must still be set for use in minority entitlements.

Minority positions encompass any position which is subordinated to a larger controlling share. In order to subordinate the position the government is restricted to an aggregate position of no more than ½ the total position of the largest shareholder. A minority position will always be less than 33% of the total outstanding shares or equity. This does not mean a government cannot acquire a substantial share but it can never have the principle share. This entitlement will help preserve competitive free markets because private interests will generally have leadership positions. Included within the minority entitlement is the authority to invest at the marginal default rate. This means that when a minority position would result in an amount less than the default rate it may instead apply the marginal rate (either ½ of the largest private position, or 3%, whichever is greater).

Majority or ownership positions allow governments to acquire management of the company. They may have the largest share of outstanding stock or they can own all of the stock (private ownership). Consensus may still be needed to execute prerogatives but the government will have the principle position. In most instances assets held within the administrative jurisdiction must be liquidated and auctioned off and the acquired company may not compete at all in the same region as the owning government.

Only those governments able to invest to a majority share degree in primary market instruments are able to initiate new businesses. Creating new businesses is the most overt commercial action a government can undertake. Creating a new business can be much less expensive than acquiring an already established business through primary or secondary security instruments. It is of course much riskier, and requires much more work, but the gamble can pay off with immense returns. Only the most liberal commercial governments will allow majority ownership and it must be stressed that all of the normal goals of commercial government can be met by either marginal or minority degrees of ownership.

The degree of ownership determines what proportion of the governments fund may be comprised by that specific instrument. If relegated to a marginal position then the instrument must be equal to 3% (or less) of the total value of the fund. If a minority position is allowed than the total value of that position must be equal to or less than 6% of the total value of the fund. No limitations apply when majority entitlements are allowed but most legislatures will demand adequate diversification. Weighing a fund too heavily with one class of instrument predisposes the government to catastrophe if markets become compromised. The object of commercial government theory is to imbue fiscal responsibility and security within participating governments. Those that don't diversify won't be able to sustain incomes to offset their budget liabilities. Government investment and competition will then be an exercise in futility.

Higher governments can exert control over lower governments by creating Permanent Fund Guarantee companies. These insure the revenue stream of mature permanent funds when they are in the payout phase (i.e. completed cycles). During the life of the permanent fund it pays insurance premiums to the guarantee company. If there is an excessive loss in revenue the Permanent Fund Guarantee Company starts paying into the government's general fund so that taxes don't have to be raised to compensate for the loss in value of assets. A PFGC can set diversification standards so that the risk of PF insolvency is minimized. It can work exactly like the U.S. Pension Benefit Guarantee Company, collecting premiums, insuring benefits, and instilling diversification rules. Every regional government can operate their own in addition to a national guarantor.

There is a huge variety of instruments a government can invest with to earn an income. There are so many in fact that the simplest method to apply limitation on entitlements based on jurisdiction and degree of ownership is to lump a great many types of investments into a single class and regulate all of them the same way. In this respect, entitlements are dissected in secondary instruments, currencies, real estate, debt, and primary security instruments. Each class entails different measures of responsibility and may be limited to different jurisdictions or degrees of ownership. When and if more scrutiny is applied to commercial government theory more qualities may become more important and more types of securities or bonds available they can quickly be incorporated into the structure of the program by naming and qualifying such additions into the bill authorizing the investment program.

Most instruments are categorized into the class of secondary market instruments. This section includes common stock, preferred stock, options, mutual funds, hedge funds, index funds, REITS, commodities, derivatives, and most other securitized instruments (or funds). It is the catchall for the various products which must be offered. This list is not definitive, if a government would rather lump REIT with the real estate section, or derivatives and securitized mortgages within the bond section, they can do so by simply installing directions through legislation. Neither is the list comprehensive. If a specific product was left off then a government can enact specific legislation to regulate its use. Instruments are almost always modified by degree and jurisdiction. Following each category of instrument will be a designation describing the appropriate limits in degree or jurisdiction.

A. Secondary market Instruments- (modified by degree and jurisdiction):
   1. The government may not invest in secondary market Instruments.

      or

   2. The government can invest in broad spectrum instruments only (mutual funds, hedge funds, index funds, REIT, etc).

      or

   3. The government can invest in any investment instrument (stocks, options, derivatives, commodities, most securitized instruments).

It should be obvious that investment into the stock of specific companies represents a bigger concern for conflict. So do contracts for specific commodities or derivatives. For this reason governments can be restricted to broad spectrum instruments. The use of broad spectrum instruments limits the potential for specific companies to be favored by legislation or enforcement and preserves the natural divide between commerce and government. In the most conservative commercial governments all investment into secondary instruments can be prohibited. Their configurations can be based solely on currency, real estate, or government bonds. Whatever a people's reservations are regarding government investment they can find a configuration that satisfies their requirements.

Debt is often a primary instrument used by investors to offset higher risk in specific instruments. The bond markets are the second most popular instrument with more money only being applied to derivatives. It would be impossible for a government to achieve a proper allocation of risk without making such investments legal. Government bonds are tax backed and therefore produce the most reliable incomes. The purchase of treasury bills produces the least inherent conflict and should remain unregulated for the most part. But this can lead to future problems. Certain municipalities or regional government may be able to leverage the purchase of other government's municipal bonds for political favors; it is important to mitigate the potential of conflict by restricting the purchase of municipal bonds from other governments outside of the regional jurisdiction of the investing government.

B. Debt markers (Instrument modified by jurisdiction):
   1. The government is prohibited from investing in any debt markers.
      or
   2. The government can invest in government's debt markers.
      and/or
   3. The government can invest in corporate debt markers (commercial paper, bank products, junk bonds, regular corporate bonds).
      and/or
   4. The government can invest in citizen debt (mortgages, credit, past due, etc).

Corporate debt should be regulated similar to how secondary market instruments are. Lower level governments should have greater freedoms and more entitlements than higher governments. Corporate debt includes commercial paper, junk bonds, regular corporate bonds, and commercial bank loans. Companies use bond sales to fund day to day operations, mergers, expansion, and reorganizations. They enjoy high yields but don't allow for consumers to vote on their corporate boards. This may make corporate bonds a more attractive instrument than common stock because governments will be able to interfere with commerce less. Since less influence can be exerted on companies by governments through bond consumption there is no need to apply maximum degrees of ownership but because degree also impacts portfolio distribution the standard amount must be the marginal rate. If more regulation is needed for the different variety of corporate debt it can be applied individually so that governments are still able to capitalize by their involvement.

Debt is also the most controversial instrument for a government to invest in. This is true when it concerns citizen debt like mortgages, credit, or past due amounts. Government can acquire an inordinate amount of influence on those citizens that owe the debt. Such a privilege must be accompanied with procedures for exercising legal remedies and forgiving such debt. Under no circumstance should a government be able to traffic in debt instruments of its residents and citizens (yet it occurs in some Traditional Competitive Socialist States, see subsequent chapter). Personal debt is included because it is an ordinary function of a great many different industries and in order for there to be authority for a government to initiate new businesses it must be given entitlement to traffic in the instruments.

Profit seeking governments will naturally view real estate as one instrument that offers a high yield and relatively low risk. It may depreciate in value, and it does carry a tax liability, but it is tangible and is well preserved over time. Real estate can be improved with new construction, renovated, rented, or resold. The same concerns regarding resident debt holds true for investment into real estate. Under no circumstances should a government be enabled to own and operate real estate for profit in their own administrative jurisdiction (unless through nonprofit cooperatives in Neo-Populist systems). Otherwise imminent domain laws could be abused, zoning laws could be exploited, and tax policies could discriminate against non government owners.

C. Real estate (modified by jurisdiction):
   1. The government is prohibited from any investment in any real estate.
      or
   2. The government can invest in real estate.
      a. commercial
         and/or
      b. residential

A distinction is made between commercial and residential properties so that a government can profit from managing real estate while distancing itself from interacting with the majority of the population. In most instances whenever a government can exploit residential properties it will always be able to manipulate commercial properties but being able to traffic in commercial properties is not always precedent to employ residential properties for profit. Commercial interests can better protect themselves from aggressive governments considering they generally have more access to capital for use in defense and have more established political lobby. Residential property owners do have voting rights so they can protect themselves but their lack of organization can expose smaller numbers of owners to abuses. Real estate offers tremendous opportunity for profit and most governments should be given authority to implement capital strategies that incorporate land and property ownership.

Under no circumstances will aggressive governments be able to purchase territories and then usurp government functions in those areas. They will never be able to collect taxes or vote in elections for the properties they acquire through their permanent funds. Other governments must be assured that vesting governments have no ulterior motives of expansion. Profit is the only legitimate purpose from one government to purchase real estate within another government's jurisdiction unless both jurisdictions agree to the conditions of exchange under a **Mutable Boundaries system** (see annex). In order for a property to change jurisdictions consideration must be paid to the former jurisdiction at a value based solely on tax receipts. Government services must be guaranteed for residents until the transition is complete. The two functions must be clearly separated so that one is not confused with another and no exploitation occurs.

Most banks traffic in currency trades. Many countries hold reserves of foreign currencies to add value to their own national currency. Some businesses actually earn more revenue from currency trades than they do from all the sales of their products or services. The FOREX (foreign currency exchange) trades at a higher volume than the secondary stock market. Trades are liquid and occur at a high frequency. Money traded one day can be removed the next day. Alternative investments (i.e. stocks, real estate, and debt) require long periods of maturation and make large amounts of capital unavailable. Currency represents an opportunity for governments to make high profits while preserving the availability of the capital.

D. Currency (instrument, unmodified):
   1. The government is prohibited from trading any currencies.

      or
   2. The government can invest in currency excluding the national currency.

      or
   3. The government can invest in currency including their national currency.

National governments should be excluded from making any currency transaction concerning their own money. The national government can exert too much influence on the price of its currency through manipulation of the national interest rate or printing more money. Lower governments (municipalities and states) should not be restricted in any measure considering the layers of insulation between them and the national government. Leaked information poses the greatest risk but the concern exists now and will not be exaggerated by transition to a commercial government system. Fixing the national currency requires too much coordination to be possible from the stand point of states and is nearly impossible for cities and towns to accomplish. The three options for currency trades provide enough flexibility to accommodate most concerns and can even allow the national government to earn income with this instrument.

Governments may elect to invest in primary stock markets through venture capital. This will enable a government to purchase partial ownership of non stock (public) companies. Most small and medium businesses do not offer public stock and would normally be excluded from government investment. One pretense of commercial government is stable recapitalization of resident businesses. Governments would otherwise be limited to commercial bank loans (corporate debt) to capitalize smaller businesses if venture capital was not a legitimate entitlement. It opens the flood gates and governments can completely immerse themselves in commerce. This provides the most visceral interaction between vested governments and ordinary citizenry because small business is the largest component of the economy.

Only those governments which can invest to a majority degree of ownership will be able to initiate new business but this adds an important dynamic to government competition. It no longer has to rely on previously created businesses. Initiating a new company may be risky but it takes a lot less capital than buying an already thriving company. All new businesses must operate outside the administrative jurisdiction; the sale and performance of the product/service must be initiated and conclude in another location. Government owned business will not be allowed to deliver products to address located within their administrative jurisdictions and can't offer rebates to residents traveling abroad to acquire the product or service.

Government businesses must also be incorporated in a competitive jurisdiction so that no intersection of interests occurs in the courts or legislation of the owning government. Profits will continue to be funneled to the owning jurisdiction but there should never be an instance where its laws or courts determine fault or liability Competitive Government Corporations (C-G Corporations) will be treated in every respect like an ordinary commercial party and receive no special rights. Only the most liberal of commercial governments will exercise this option. Competition in opposing regional jurisdictions may elicit volatile sentiment from some of the residents and business owners of the jurisdiction when their profitability suffers.

E. Venture Capital (primary markets, modified by jurisdiction and degree):
   1. The government is forbidden from initiating a new business
      or
   2. The government may initiate and manage new businesses.
      and/ or
   3. The government may purchase portions of private companies

The last section deals primarily with market saturation of government investment. In order to preserve free markets governments can be limited to less than 48% of outstanding shares in a company. This limit pertains to all government ownership so that no group of governments can acquire a collective majority in any one company. This helps ensure that private commercial interests make the majority of executive decisions. When singular or collective government ownership exceeds this 48 percent rule then it should be considered a C-G Corporation.

III. "Market Accumulation" (<48% rules):
   A. Intra-company
      1. <48% of collective government ownership
         or
      2. >48% of collective government ownership
   B. Inter-company
      3. <48% of market share

or

4. >48% of market share

If majority ownership is permitted and limitations on gross ownership are relaxed a new limitation can protect an otherwise free market economy. Limiting all government owned companies (C-G Corporations) to less than 48% industry market share will ensure that an economy is still primarily governed by private interests. Thus governments will not be able to form a monopoly of industry regulation and market share. It is common for lower jurisdictions to be allowed to transgress either limit when higher governments are still restricted. Gross ownership and market share laws need not be uniform throughout the nation.

When government investment is completely unrestricted in terms of gross ownership and market share the nation is much more likely to become Competitive State Capitalist. Relaxing all limitations does not immediately make a nation or jurisdiction socialist because a majority of businesses may still be privately owned but in all likelihood the nation will eventually have a higher concentration of C-G Corporations than private industry and at that point it will be considered Competitive Socialist. In order to prevent this evolution a nation could simply revert to previous limitations and require constituent governments to sell those shares that contradict maximum gross ownership or market share restrictions. All of the Competitive State Capitalist and Neo-Populist systems require their C-G Corporations to be securitized. Thus market share and equity can more easily be returned to the public if the market becomes overly burdened by public wealth.

Complete List of available traits for Commercial Governments:

I. Account Attributes;
   A. Tier of government owning fund
      1. Federal (Central)
      2. Regional (State)
      3. Local (county, city, village, or town)
   B. Operation (management of fund)
      1. Government must manage own money.
         a. Social Agenda
         b. Profit seeking only

2. Private company (3rd party) must manage government money.
3. Government can choose to outsource management
    a. May apply social agenda when self managing
    b. Profit seeking only when self managing

C. Purpose (use)
    1. Subsidy of budget (reduce tax liabilities)
    2. Production of dividend checks for residents
    3. Improving government benefits (increase government spending)
    4. Combination of uses
        a. Subsidy/dividend production
        b. Dividend/improve benefits
        c. Subsidy/improve benefits
        d. Unstructured

D. Method:
    1. Rollover contributions and interest (Savings)
        a. 15 year cycle
        b. 25 year cycle
        c. 40 year cycle
    2. Immediately apply interest earned (Defrayment)
    3. Hybrid: (Split)
        a. savings with 15 year cycle/defrayment
        b. savings with 25 year cycle/defrayment
        c. savings with 25 year cycle/defrayment

E. Domain:
    1. Centralized
        a. One permanent fund for all taxes
            x. separates off budget from on budget expenses
        b. Multiple subsidy funds, one for each tax
    2. Departmentalized (agency/department/program)

II. Entitlements:

A. Secondary market Instruments- (modified by degree and jurisdiction):
    1. The government may not invest in secondary market instruments
    2. The government can invest in broad spectrum instruments only (mutual, hedge, index, REIT, derivatives).

3. The government can invest in any investment instrument (stocks, options, derivatives, and commodities).

B. Debt markers (Instrument modified by jurisdiction, *always marginal degree*):
   1. The government is prohibited from investing in any debt markers.
   2. The government can invest in other government's debt markers.
   3. The government can invest in corporate debt markers (bank products, junk bonds, rated corporate bonds).
   4. The government can invest in citizen debt (mortgages, credit, past due amounts).

C. Real estate (modified by jurisdiction):
   1. The government is prohibited from any investment in any real estate.
   2. The government can invest in real estate.
      a. commercial
      b. residential

D. Currency (unmodified):
   1. The government is prohibited from trading any currencies.
   2. The government can invest in currency excluding the national currency.
   3. The government can invest in currency including their national currency.

E. Venture Capital (primary markets, modified by jurisdiction and degree):
   1. The government is forbidden from initiating a new business
   2. The government may initiate and manage new businesses.
   3. The government may purchase portions of private companies

Jurisdiction (modifies instrument and degree):
   x. The government can invest in foreign jurisdictions
   xx. The government can invest in domestic territories but not operating within the same jurisdiction.

(c). jurisdiction is defines as same regional government

(cc). the jurisdiction is defined in terms of opposing municipal governments.

xxx. The government can invest in domestic instruments operating in the same jurisdiction (administrative jurisdiction).

Degree (Modifies instrument and jurisdiction):

i. The government is relegated to a marginal share

ii. The government can invest in minority shares.

iii. The government can invest in majority shares.

III. Market Accumulation (<48% rules):

A. Intra-company

1. <48% of collective government ownership
2. >48% of collective government ownership

B. Inter-company

1. <48% of market share
2. >48% of market share

Examples (code and key):

Explication of Account Attributes;

1.) **I.A.1** denotes the account attributes of a national government.

2.) **I.A.1, B.2**, denotes that the account attributes of the national government include the operational mandate for the government to outsource management of its Permanent funds.

3.) **I.A.1, B.2, C.1, D.1.b**: National government (I...A.1), requiring outsourced management of the Permanent fund (I...B.2), with budget subsidy (I...C.1) as its primary goal, and using a rollover method with a cycle of 25 years before payout (I...D.1.b).

Explication of Entitlements;

4.) **II.A.3** denotes the ability of the government to invest in secondary market instruments (i.e. stock, commodities, funds, and derivatives).

5.) **II.A.3.xx** denotes a government entitlement to invest in secondary stock instruments of companies operating in (or products produced in) an opposing regional political jurisdiction.
6.) **II.A.3.xx(c).ii** translates to a government which can invest in secondary market securities to a minority degree in companies that primarily in competing regional jurisdiction.
7.) **II.A.3.xx(c).ii, B.2.3.x.xx.** translates to a government which can invest in secondary market securities to a minority degree in companies that primarily in competing regional jurisdiction, and it can invest in public and corporate bonds in competitor jurisdictions as well as foreign jurisdictions.

Full explication (Account attributes + Entitlements);

7.) **I.A.1, B.2, C.1, D.1.b; II.A.3.xx(c).ii, B.2.3.x.xx.** translates into: National government (I...A.1), requiring outsourced management of the Permanent fund (I...B.2), with budget subsidy (I...C.1) as its primary goal, and using a rollover with a cycle of 25 years before payout (I...D.1.b), and where it can legitimately use secondary market instruments (II...A.3) originating from opposing regional jurisdictions { xx(c)}, and investing to a maximum of minority degree (.ii), and public and corporate bonds (II...B.2.3.x.xx) from competitor jurisdictions as well as foreign jurisdictions.

Generally each tier of government will be defined to the exclusion of another tier but those templates with attributes and entitlements universal to multiple tiers of government will combine them within a single line. After the expression of options in code form, a detailed explanation of those options will follow in outline form, with an even more detailed explication occurring in paragraph form. Certain models of commercial government will be based on earlier explanations with only substitutions to the previous code listed. One must reference the template cited in order to understand the adjusted form.

Considering the many variables involved in determining substance and entitlement of a government investment fund and the possibility for variety among the many tiers of government, there is no reasonable method to reproduce all useful combinations of attributes for commercial governments. These are sample constructions and one class may be constituted by any combination of the listed attributes and be named in any manner the creator sees fit. There are almost an innumerable amount of combinations each with competing advantages. Instead of making an exhaustive list and describing all the advantages of possible combinations only the most important or divergent combinations are offered. They are reduced into themes with the combination of attributes and entitlements only depicting the most obvious traits.

In order to form a perspective in regards to conventional government entitlements one should compare the models offered to a translation of Alaska and its Permanent Fund into comparable values.

Alaskan Permanent Fund;

I.A.2, B.2, C.3, D.2, E.1.a.x; II.A.3.x.xx.xxx.iii, B.2.3.4.x.xx.xxx, C.2.a.b.x.xx.xxx, D.3, E.2.3.x.xx.xxx.iii; III.A.2.x.xx.xxx, B.2.x.xx.xx

The state of Alaska **(I.A.2)** outsources management of the fund **(II...B.2)** to a special committee in charge of allocating funds within the Permanent fund. The Alaskan Permanent Fun's main charge is to compensate for the state budget but Alaskan dividends have recently become nearly as important **(I.C.3).** They primarily use a hybrid savings-defrayment method for wealth accumulation **(II...D.3)** but they are juggling budget subsidy, dividend production, and growth all at the same time. Most other Permanent or Subsidy funds will have to wait several years before beginning to make payments into their General funds or paying out dividends. The Alaskan Permanent Fund is also organized around the central government **(II...E.1.a.x)** with the legislature authorizing its creation for offsetting state general fund expenditures.

The Permanent Fund resembles a fairly average configuration of account attributes for commercial governments but it has wild entitlements for investments. There is virtually no limit to the degree of ownership it can acquire **(II.A.3.x.xx.xxx.iii, E.2.3.x.xx.xxx.iii).** There is no evidence that the permanent fund ever initiated their own businesses but they can purchase shares of companies in the primary securities markets (venture capital). It can own real estate in any jurisdiction **(II...C.2.a.b.x.xx.xxx),** traffic in any bonds, bills, or instruments it wishes to **{II...B.2.3.4.x.xx.xxx),** and trade currencies **(II...D.3).**The mitigating factors are the size of the fund, only 40 billion, and strict mandates for diversification have thus prevented gross concentrations of ownership by Alaska's use of state capital. Nobody has ever thought of enacting gross ownership or market share limits because Alaska acts alone in capitalizing its budgetary process **(A.2.x.xx.xxx, B.2.x.xx.xxx).** Most Sovereign Wealth Funds have comparable entitlements. The sovereign wealth fund of Norway, the Future Fund of Australia, and the Temasek Fund in Singapore all have virtually no limits placed on their involvement with commercial institutions within their own economies or foreign economies.

Alaska's investment does not jeopardize the domestic economy with oversaturation of government investment but Alaska is a relatively small state. It has a population of only 600,000 despite being the largest state in the Union. It is only one of 50 states and when the other states and their constituent county and municipal governments, including California, New York, and Texas, capitalize their budgetary processes and form their own Permanent Funds, an overwhelming amount of state capital will invade the market. A death knell would certainly sound when national capital began to flow in and out of public and private companies competing within the national economy. With the onset of a MCPFS state capital will become a prevalent force in domestic and foreign economic theatres. Without structure state capitalism could overwhelm traditionally capitalist and typically free market economies..

Singapore is one example where the government employs capital from their sovereign wealth fund to manage domestic private companies. Singapore's Funds hold large stakes in their largest private companies. Fund managers have the ability to influence the corporate governance of those telecommunications, entertainment, utilities, and financial services companies where they own either a quarter or third of all outstanding stock in those companies. They have intimate access to financial records, proprietary information, corporate policies, and actively participate in shareholder votes and corporate board representative elections. The Singapore Fund may have recently reduced its positions in their national companies but the previous interaction with corporate boards did not produce horrendous results. Most governments will make the same decisions regarding management as other institutional investors would and seek profits at the exclusion of social and political agendas. Singapore's formerly significant positions prove that government can interface with private industry and not destroy profitability or disrupt services.

The innate responsibilities of a government determine the scope of its entitlements. Local governments have the most options available concerning investment and competition in the national economy because there is an abbreviated potential for conflict. As long as it does not involve itself in companies profiting within their own municipalities then there is very little cause for alarm. They should be perceived as ordinary commercial parties in every respect. The same goes for regional governments seeking profit in competitor jurisdictions. Regional governments will always be excluded from competing in their own administrative jurisdictions which will dispel many of the arguments against commercialization and profit seeking. Still, they will be heavily regulated and will often have less dramatic entitlements. The national government should be the most restricted in its involvement in the national economy because it has the greatest potential for abuse or conflict. Often they will be relegated to compete in foreign jurisdictions only but occasionally they can take marginal positions or employ hedge funds, mutual funds, index funds, or other broad spectrum investment vehicles.

Within the same national framework of one political system constituent lower governments can have different account attributes and entitlements from higher governments. Lower governments must always abide by higher governments rules pertaining to the maximum degree of investment but may limit themselves and those governments subordinate to their order to lesser degrees of investment. In a country as large as the U.S. it is imaginable that some states would elect to remain uncompetitive and simply deposit their contributions in savings accounts at local banks, while other leverage their contribution to gain significant positions in domestic and foreign public companies; some states would limit themselves to minority positions, while others will wholeheartedly embrace majority positions, and some may elect to satisfy their fiscal needs with broad spectrum instruments only. Commercial Government Theory has enough variety in it to accommodate most any reservation or enable any ambition.

There are three main classes of commercial government. They are the Neo-Capitalist, the Competitive State Capitalist, and the Neo-Populist systems. The Neo-Capitalist class is comprised of two varieties of Capitalocracy and two varieties of Corporatocracy. They attempt to protect private industry while fostering investment revenue for governments. The Competitive State Capitalist class is divided into three variations of Solocorporatocracy. They apply the least restraint to government involvement in competitor jurisdictions but preserve many of the market dynamics afforded by well regulated competition. Competitive State Capitalist systems conserve wealth the most efficiently of all commercial governments when most corporate profits are applied to reduce tax liabilities or produce dividends for residents. The Neo-Populist class is dissected into two variations of Monocorporatocracy and one Commucorporatic model. They compromise competition in their administrative jurisdictions by authorizing nonprofit government cooperatives (I-A Corporations) to offer low cost products and services. Each of the major classes addresses a different prerogative or trend in Commercial Government Theory. They utilize different account attributes, are empowered with different entitlements, and they permit vastly different concentrations of government ownership.

THE LUCERNE

Chapter 3

Neo- Capitalist Systems:

The primary purpose of the Neo-Capitalist states is to make their resident businesses more profitable and as a result most will not deviate from budget subsidy as the intended goal of government investment. In the long term, after a few cycles, these governments will offer tax rates far below par when compared to other uncapitalized capitalist nations. This will depress resource costs, manufacturing costs, labor costs, and transportation costs making resident business far more competitive. The volume of exports should rapidly expand as resident businesses will be able to market products and services of equal value but lower costs than competitor companies located in conventional capitalist countries. This will also promote consumerism in the country bolstering profits and the more competitive industries will keep a greater percentage of their revenue due to lower taxes. The Neo-Capitalist systems empower governments to significant incomes from investment but protect the free market by reigning in entitlements and by ensuring private individuals and institutions remain as the dominant business owners in the domestic economy.

There are two principle classes of Neo-Capitalist commercial governments. The first is the Capitalocracy which tends to limit the degree of ownership constituent governments can acquire to minority positions. The second is the Corporatocracy which allows majority ownership of private and public companies. There is only one model of Capitalocracy which permits gross ownership of public companies to exceed the 47% threshold but all of the Corporatic systems exploit excesses in gross ownership. These two classes and all of their subclasses attempt to restrict government ownership to preserve a free market system. In every instance government involvement is restricted to less than majority positions of market share to preserve private industries' dominance. Throughout all of the sample systems conservative entitlements progress to more liberal configurations but it must be stressed that the primary goal of budget subsidy can be accomplished with even the most conservative combinations of account attributes and entitlements.

Capitalocracies and Corporatocracies will distribute wealth more evenly within the country. The richest one percent of the population owns nearly 40% of the wealth. Concentrating wealth in competing municipalities, counties, states, and national governments will help defray this inequality. The lower classes will become co-owners in the commercial infrastructure of the country. Neo-Capitalism, simply put, is profit sharing between the classes after public wealth is applied to capitalize private and public industry. The same process that makes resident businesses more profitable will expand the disposable incomes of the general public. The 90% of the population owning only 3% of the total equity in the country will see their disposable incomes increase with property and income tax reductions and possibly dividends. All roads lead to Rome. With consumption driving 75% of the real economy any reductions in tax liabilities for the lower classes should cause an incredible amount of wealth for the owner's class.

Neo-Capitalism doesn't rely on a gross usurpation of wealth; it persists from an equitable redistribution through an almost negligible tax. Most often resident businesses are the recipients of government investment and private equity loans. Those that pay more into the MCPFS see the most gain when their businesses receive the capitalization they need for expansion or reorganization. Government investment will invigorate the financial industries as more money will be in savings accounts, more money will be vested in annuities, and more money will be applied to mutual funds, hedge funds, index funds, and private equity. Higher governments can also manage the public wealth of lower governments to the benefit of private industry. Investing and competing in foreign economies will draw important capital from those systems and input into our own. This can defray the negative effects of ordinary trade imbalances.

Government involvement eliminates the coercive interference from corporations on politics but it realigns government prerogatives to incorporate profit as facet of public welfare. Yes, a great many private and public companies will be excluded from making campaign contributions or effectively lobbying government for favorable legislation but the very same government will become interested in the performance of the market and more specifically seek profit. Right now profit is seen as an adversary to public welfare. A Neo-Capitalist nation's profitability is a facet of public welfare. Not only do successful industries translate to tax revenue from corporate profits and individual incomes but the governments will entitled to their fair share of dividends. Governments will balance public welfare with competitive markets by creating a regulatory apparatus that protects residents and fosters business.

Capitalocracies (*aka Capital Democracies*) are the most conservative Neo-Capitalist models of commercial government. There are more conservative versions of commercial government but they don't fit the criteria of Neo-Capitalist because they don't allow government to directly interact with commerce through corporate board elections and shareholder votes. The Capitalocracy limits government involvement and ownership to responsible proportions without limiting potential revenues. It sets the precedent for government investment and involvement but does not commandeer commerce for unprofitable purposes. It can easily evolve into more liberal incarnations of commercial government when an adequate regulatory apparatus is created. Experimentation is expected and entitlements can be expanded or rescinded based upon their impact on the economy. The Capitalocratic class is divided into three subclasses, or models. There is a minor variety, a major variety and a general variety.

Capitalocracy, minor:

Code:
I; A.1, B.3.a, C.1, D.1.b, E.1.a.x, II; A.3.x.ii, B.2.3.x, C.2.a.b.x, D.1, E.3.x.ii, III; A.2.x, B.2.x

I; A.2.3, B.3.a, C.1, D.1.b, E.1.a.x, II; A.3.xx(c).xxx.i, A.3.x.ii, B.2.3.x.xx(c).xxx, C.2.a.b.x.xx(c), D.3, E.3.xx(c).xxx.i, E.3.x.ii, III; A.2.x, A.1. xx.xxx, B.2.x

Key:

I. (Account attributes) **A.1** (national government), **B.3.a** (option to manage itself with social agenda), **C.1** (budget subsidy only), **D.1.b** (savings method with 25 year cycle), **E.1.a.x** (permanent funds for both on and off budget expenses), **II.** (Entitlements) **A.3.x.ii** (may invest in any secondary instrument to minority degree in foreign jurisdictions), **B.2.3.x** (may invest in any public or corporate debt in foreign jurisdictions), **C.2.a.b.x** (may utilize any residential or commercial real estate in foreign jurisdictions), **D.1** (currency trades prohibited), **E.3.x.ii** (may invest with venture capital or primary security instruments to a minority degree in foreign jurisdictions only), **III.A.2.x** (gross ownership is unrestricted in foreign jurisdictions), **B.2.x** (market share is unrestricted in foreign jurisdictions)

I. (Account attributes) **A.2.3** (regional and local governments), **B.3.a** (option to self manage permanent funds with social agenda), **C.1** (budget subsidy only), **D.1.b** (savings method with 25 year cycle), **E.1.a.x** (multiple funds for on and off budget expenses), **II.** (Entitlements) **A.3.xx(c).xxx.i** (may invest in any secondary instrument to a marginal degree in competitor regional jurisdictions and its administrative jurisdiction), **A.3.x.ii** (may invest in any secondary instrument to a minority degree in foreign countries), **B.2.3.x.xx(c).xxx** (may use any form of public or corporate debt, regardless of where it originates), **C.2.a.b.x.xx(c)** (may purchase any residential or commercial real estate in foreign or opposing regional jurisdictions), **D.3** (may trade any currency), **E.3.x.ii** (may invest in primary security instruments, up to a minority degree, in foreign jurisdictions), **E.3.xx.xxx.i** (may invest in primary instruments, up to a marginal degree in competitor regional jurisdictions and their administrative jurisdictions); **III. A.2.x** (gross ownership is unrestricted in foreign theatres), **A.1.xx.xxx** (gross ownership is constrained to less than 48% in administrative and opposing regional jurisdictions), **B.2.x** (these governments are allowed unrestricted market share in foreign economies).

By nature of its role, the national governments of Capitalocracy-minor will be the most restricted in terms its entitlements to investment but they can take full advantage of foreign markets and instruments. There is no doubt that national taxes are usually the highest within the country and that a properly managed MCPFS should be employed to subsidize a portion of national government expenditures. A portion of the country's national taxes will contribute to the nation's national permanent fund. All nations reserve the right to create their own sovereign wealth funds with unlimited entitlements and they can elect to fund one through their General fund but this form of commercial government seeks to eliminate any potential abuses or political interference in its institutionalized mandatory contribution permanent fund.

National governments have the option to direct the allocation of its Permanent Fund directly or it can outsource such management to a 3rd party firm. It is still allowed to manage its own fund is primarily because all of its assets will originate from foreign markets. Permitting it to manage the fund enables the government to employ the capital for strategic or political purposes when appropriate. With more and more countries developing Sovereign Wealth Funds this aspect of State Capitalism will become more and more prevalent. It is unlikely that protectionist measures will work considering the modern trends in capital flow. Most nations will refrain from such extracurricular uses as profits are generally more important but the option remains on the table. Sometimes it must react to other market (or non market) pressures and it is appropriate that they aren't constrained by a strict fiduciary relationship based on returns.

The national permanent fund within a Capitalocracy must preserve all contributions and profit from investments made in a savings (or rollover) account and is forbid from drawing on the account and using the moneys until the cycle has been completed. There may be extraordinary circumstances when commandeering permanent fund assets is warranted but cause must be demonstrated. The only acceptable reasons should be for relief after natural disasters or in defense of the nation. Even then, the money should be diverted only when there are dire circumstances and it should be repaid according to a reasonable schedule. Each cycle will based upon a time frame of 25 years. This accelerates the speed at which the fund matures and taxes are reduced. Twenty Five is not an extraordinarily long wait the tax relief considering the lifespan of residents and countries. It also keeps the budget lean. If profits were prematurely made available the public may vote themselves more government benefits or subsidies and grossly inflate the budget. This could trend to socialism and most ordinary people reject its principle tenants.

The proceeds of government investment must be applied to defray taxes even if it is in partial amounts. Once a Permanent Fund completes a cycle no more contributions are made and the interest or profits earned are applied to the budget. The assets located in the fund are not frozen and can continue to be managed but they may not be withdrawn. The principle will become a permanent source of income for the government. For future increases in budget subsidy additional permanent funds are necessary. This is expected. Once the first cycle is complete the proportion of taxes normally contributed will be free for use in a second permanent fund. Subsequent permanent funds can be employed to for other reasons (i.e. improving government benefits or producing dividends) but the assets located in the first fund should only be applied to the general budget if that was its intended purpose. Capitalocratic models almost exclusively use interest from their permanent funds for budget subsidy.

Most national governments have what are to be considered on budget and off budget expenditures. In the example of the United States its General fund is on budget and Social Security and Medicare are off budget. Off budget programs generally have their own tax revenues. In the Capitalocracy-minor there may be multiple simultaneous Permanent funds. One for each on budget and off budget tax, but the number should be kept at a minimum. Larger funds have certain advantages but it would otherwise be inefficient to mix assets when there are multiple sources for government outlays. In this form of commercial government the funds are centralized; authorized by the legislature and managed by the executive branch. Most of the collected taxes will still contribute to one primary Fund so that the executive branch can leverage its capital to the greatest effect.

The national permanent funds within a Capitalocratic-minor commercial government will have entitlements that produce the least potential for conflict of interests. It will only be able to invest in profit generating secondary market instrument (including commodities, CDO's, derivatives, etc) that originates from, or where the principle operation is in, a foreign jurisdiction and is restricted to at most a minority position in those companies or instruments. National permanent funds are similarly limited when using primary market securities. Almost every conceivable argument against national government investment is dispelled because it will not interact with companies from its own economy. The fact that they are still relegated to a minority position, despite the companies' foreign origins, will eliminate most criticisms for government involvement in the foreign economies.

Government sponsored securities and bonds the most conservative investments and are often used to balance riskier allotments. The bond market dwarfs the total asset value of the stock market and is many respects much more important. Of course the national government will also be able to invest in government bonds and securities but those instruments may not be offered by those governments part of its own infrastructure (unless part of a **public finance engine**, see chapter 5). This is meant to remove any potential for political coercion a national government could apply to lower governments. In the same respects they may only purchase corporate bonds from businesses operating principally in foreign jurisdictions. National governments will always have access to general fund money for stimulating an economy or fully funding constituent governments so there is less impetus for giving a national government authority to invest domestically.

Capitalocratic-minor national governments may also purchase both residential and commercial real estate for resale, renovation, development, and rental in any foreign jurisdiction. Real estate is a great foil to other more risky investments. It is also a tangible and fungible instrument that has intrinsic value, it is usually durable, and it generates substantial incomes. The fact that a national permanent fund can only own land in foreign countries eliminates many of the inherent risks involved with governments owning land for commercial reasons. Governments will always retain the option of purchasing property in its own administrative jurisdiction for conservation or park use but all of those transactions must rely on subsidy from the General Fund. Sovereign wealth funds own residential and commercial properties and there isn't a major concern over a perceived threat of colonization but it may become an issue if significantly more governments capitalize. One nation will never have territorial rights to the property despite the fact it may own it.

Considering the fact that most national governments print their own money they are prohibited from trading either domestic or foreign currency. Restricting such traffic is in the interests of all nations. Otherwise the value of a currency could be exploited by increasing the volume of currency, by manipulating interest rates, or by issuing or defaulting on public debt. In more complicated systems national government could be authorized to invest in any currency except their own but that requires more oversight and more acceptance. In certain systems the ability to traffic in currency will prompt the creation of a fiat standard to be applied to their own currency. Many nations already back their own currencies with other currencies but adapting fiat standard based on a multitude of different currencies will offer some competitive advantages. For simplicities sake the Capitalocracy-minor national government must refrain from all currency trades. It can still invest in companies that actively trade currencies for profit, such as banks, but there will be criminal regulations against government officials sharing information with companies they are vested in.

There are no restrictions on gross ownership or market share because it can't invest in the domestic economy. All of their assets will be located in foreign markets and restrictions are only placed on governments when there is an identifiable risk to its own economy. In this case the domestic economy is nearly completely isolated from political interference by its national government and therefore no regulation is necessary. It is the duty of other nations to determine how much state capital and foreign government ownership they want in their economy. Sovereign Wealth Funds from other countries (i.e. China, Norway, Arab Emirates, and Russia) already own substantial positions in American companies now and they are simply treated as competing commercial interests. This trend must be reinforced especially when State Capital becomes more and more common. Governments must be considered competing interests because there is little difference between the public owning shares in a national company and a city or state owning a large proportion of equity in the same company (especially if that country is democratic).

Dislocated shareholders are less responsible or accountable than residents of a particular jurisdiction. They care most about dividends and value and are almost entirely insulated from public scrutiny. If a company like Ford creates a superfund site from excessive pollution the executives are generally found culpable but the company's shareholders are not. There may be some damages awarded but most often the company will escape paying little out to remedy the disaster. Cities and states will conduct themselves at a higher standard than corporate boards or dislocated shareholders because political officials are terrified of scandal and will avoid business practices that could harm their reputations. When a superfund site is left over from industrialization it is often the responsibility of the state and its tax payers to clean it up.

Governments should recognize this hidden cost of commerce and reorganize their business methods. This will help reform how businesses act within domestic or foreign communities. Ownership is more diffuse in the Capitalocratic models of commercial government so this is less of a concern but in other more liberal configurations this becomes an important function of government investment.

The account attributes for Neo-Capitalist lower governments remain the same as its national government. This is a mandatory contribution system and every municipality, city, county, and state must initiate and fund their own permanent fund, lower governments still can decide whether or not to outsource management of the funds despite being able to own instruments originating from their own jurisdictions, they must all devote the proceeds of government investment to budget subsidy, rolling over the returns for a minimum of 25 years, and they all make contributions to a single permanent fund under centralized control. This configuration is the most efficient at concentrating public wealth, ensuring it is used correctly, and ultimately benefiting residents and citizens. These attributes will be ubiquitous to most versions of commercial government and will only deviate when its prerogatives changes as in the socialist incarnations of state capitalism.

The State and municipal governments will have considerably greater freedom in terms of the selection of investments it may make. This is primarily due to the fact that state governments already operate pension funds and a MCPFS is fundamentally equivalent in terms of the assumed risk from investment into private equities. They can invest in local companies but are restricted to marginal positions with respect to secondary markets instruments. Domestic investment strengthens the local economy and the fact that only marginal shares may be acquired minimizes the risk for government corruption or abuse. A marginal position also eliminates the concern that a government will employ a social or political agenda with its assets in its own administrative jurisdiction. By allowing limited government involvement more companies can be excluded from making campaign contributions and lobbying local officials. This is not only a byproduct of government investment but one of the strongest arguments for government investment.

Lower governments have the same entitlement as national governments and can maintain minority positions in overseas companies and instruments. Although minority positions are large in comparison to marginal positions the governments must still abide by diversification standards which will naturally limit the total amount of stock held in any single company or industry. It is fully expected that most positions will remain much lower than even the marginal threshold on most occasions. Governments will protect themselves against excessive losses by diversifying their portfolios. A full minority position will be a rare occurrence but acceptable in some extraordinary circumstances. Most minority positions don't predispose the government to too great a risk from loss and the influence it may gain from representation can only exerted through consensus. This protects the free market from government interloping.

Secondary market instruments only represent only a fraction of the total number of securities offered in the market and any MCPFS must consider ownership gained through the primary security markets. Primary security instruments encompass equity positions in otherwise privately owned companies. This makes most small and medium businesses accessible for government investment and involvement. The same prerogatives that govern investments in secondary instruments apply to primary security instruments. In regards to primary security market instruments of companies originating or operating in the local economy the government is relegated to a marginal position. For companies operating in foreign economies the government can acquire minority positions. Minority positions are a little riskier in terms of complicating an economy but they only occur in foreign economies so there should be no concern for the vesting governments.

When the Capitalocracies allow their lower governments to manage their own permanent funds they may apply a social agenda to their investment portfolios. A government could exclude from their portfolios tobacco manufactures, alcohol producers, excessive polluters, weapons manufactures, those companies that abuse labor, exploiters of natural resources, and any company that regularly causes scandal. If the electorate of a particular state or city disagrees with any primary or ancillary effect of manufacturing, marketing, or selling a specific product then that government can abstain from investing. Certain electorates will be more sensitive to environmental concerns (i.e. pollution), production (i.e. unions or slave labor), or social concerns (i.e. abortion, alcohol, tobacco, guns, etc) and their governments can represent the people's disposition in portfolio allocation.

But governments aren't restricted to only negative actions. Positive actions are also possible. In the same respect an electorate excludes certain industries they may be equally inclined to focus on others. They may be preoccupied with other more beneficial sectors; like defense, scientific research, banking, or green technology companies. Concentrating public wealth dollars into specific sectors can make them more competitive. It can lead to faster development of more services and better products, more capital for mergers and acquisitions, expansion, or reorganization. More consistent and stable rates of capitalization will make profound differences in how a company is managed. Specialization of investment will lead to more experience with those instruments and can translate to civic pride and purpose.

An even more visceral effect of government influence on commerce is representation and voting in public companies boards. Governments can forward their social agenda by participating in company votes and installing board members. This is an awesome tool for shaping commercial standards and practices. Consensus can be reached with other likeminded regional or local governments and the combined proportion of votes can be significant enough to cause action in agreement with their social agendas. The dampened corporate influence on politics is compounded with the increased representation of the plural on corporate boards. The convergence of interests and reversal in roles between corporations and government alters the fundamental prerogatives in a conventional capitalist democracy but to the effect of maximizing benefits to both constituents and resident businesses. If social norms outpace industry regulation then the public wealth can be used to reform domestic industry from within.

A government can bend to the public will and only enter into business contract and transaction with private or public companies that have favorable reputations and histories. This will reward private and public companies when they make socially redeemable decisions or take actions that earn profit while protecting the environment or protecting consumers. Governments will primarily be represented in companies operating in an opposing political jurisdictions but an agenda can have repercussions expressed within their administrative jurisdiction. By manipulating current trends in corporate governance, businesses operating within their jurisdiction may make favorable changes when industry standards are upgraded. Governments of similar sentiment may invoke initiatives within the corporate governance of companies operating within the administrative jurisdiction of the concerned government, or they may make regulatory changes that imitate their commercial-social agendas.

For higher governments there is more value in making changes that cause an immediate loss of profit because the government is also more likely to spend money rehabilitating or remediating a problem caused by dangerous or destructive products and processes. Bad loans require bail outs, chemical spillage requires cleaning up, pollution causes environmental damages and possibly catastrophes, non bio-degradable wastes occupies much needed space, and dangerous pharmaceutical or industrials can cause disability or death. In most instances it is the government that must spend money and resources containing or repairing the problems. Rather than burdening a commodity or industry with a green tax, governments can lobby companies from within. Immediate and gross changes will be probably be resisted but at least there will be momentum towards more sustainable processes or practices.

A government is also more likely to make riskier or more socially rewarding decisions because a government is guaranteed continued contributions into the fund and relies on a median average profit on investments for success. They will recuperate immediate losses with savings earned from less General Fund expenditures on managing pollution cleanup, environmental cleanup, or healthcare. Most governments would be concerned primarily with profits but would still be averse to scandal. They will not compromise their positions as elected or appointed officials over a comparably small proportion or margin of profit. This will introduce concerns of public welfare into corporate governance on a large scale for the first time in economic history. Ultimately companies will become responsible to both stock owners and voters. This byproduct of government investment will become more exaggerated in the more liberal incarnations of commercial government (i.e. Corporatocracies and Solocorporatocracies) but is still present in Capitalocratic models.

All Neo-Capitalist nations are dissected into competitive jurisdictions based on regional governments. The regional government has representation in the national government and can more easily protect their own interests. It also has a lot more capital at its disposal and can aggressively protect itself. Municipal and county governments are only represented within the same state and are rather limited in their contributions. If competitor jurisdictions were not separated by regional boundaries the municipal governments may compromise their neighbors by integrating themselves as business owners and competitors. When competitive jurisdictions are based upon state (or provincial) borders smaller governments are shielded from co-opting influences in their state. Competitor jurisdictions based upon municipal boundaries are generally only permitted in more mature commercial governments and in this book that just happens to be the Competitive Socialist and Neo-Populist systems.

Lower governments will be able to invest in both federal instruments (bonds and T-bills) and domestic instruments (municipal bonds) from any jurisdiction it deems reasonable. They can already invest in both primary and secondary market securities to a marginal degree within their administrative jurisdictions and it would be awkward to limit their ability to purchase bonds from the same companies. Corporate bonds instill no authority to influence corporate boards so there is less of a threat of compromise. All permanent funds will be required to diversify and this will prevent governments from investing too aggressively in companies heavily vested in their local economies. Trafficking in municipal bonds from governments within the same regional administrative jurisdiction can prove to be more useful than simply providing incomes to permanent funds and since they all are represented within the same legislature there is little risk of graft or abuse.

The state and local governments may purchase real estate for resale, renovation, development, or rental in foreign jurisdictions and competitor domestic jurisdictions. Real estate represents an extremely lucrative instrument that generally appreciates in value. It will often be used to temper the risk inherent in other instruments. They can take full advantage of real estate in competitor jurisdictions and must be satisfied with this limitation. In order to eliminate most concerns over potential abuse no Capitalocratic government is able to own properties located within their administrative jurisdictions. Unlike bonds, or minority positions in stock or private equities, owning property can easily be abused by municipalities or states with zoning regulations and imminent domain powers. The quickest and most certain way to cause public sentiment to turn away from government investment is to allow municipal governments profit from commercial or residential property ownership within their own jurisdictions.

The lower governments are not restricted in their sale of or purchase of either national or foreign currencies. It would take too long for the states or lower governments to coordinate manipulation of national currency. Currency trading is an exceptional opportunity to earn dividends on funds devoted to cash reservoirs. Currency is one of the most liquid instruments any institution can invest in. Local governments don't have tremendous influence on central banks (interest rates) and cannot authorize the printing of more money. The same regulations that criminalize purposefully leaking information regarding national economic policy to private companies will cover leaked information to permanent fund managers on the state or local levels. Economic policy must be release to both government money managers and private institutions at the same time. Speculation on partial information is always permitted but a central bank will give no forewarning to permanent fund managers at the exclusion of private money managers or private companies.

The intent of a Capitalocracy-minor is to maximize gains and minimize conflicts. In order to preserve free market conditions certain limitations will be enforced to protect against an oversaturation of domestic government investment in the domestic economy. The combined share of stock (primary and secondary markets) all domestic governments may hold must be less than 48% of the total outstanding stock from a domestic company. This is cumulative so the total proportion of all stock owned by all domestic governments must be in the minority (i.e. <48%). Governments will retain the rights and representation afforded by security ownership but never be in the majority. Thus private interests will always be in a dominant position when compared to government interests. This limitation ensures the free market continues to function properly.

The most sensible way a national government can enforce this limit is through maintaining a database all lower governments must use to manage their portfolios. This way when the threshold is reached the national government can immediately suspend all future government trades in excess of 47% gross ownership. Otherwise, they would have to rely on end of day reporting and calls for divestiture in the subsequent trading day (or reporting quarter). It is only a minor obstacle for trading governments but definitely necessary if a people are worried about excessive state ownership. Commercial governments must be comfortable with the idea of courts or regulatory agencies being able to force divestiture because there will be many instances where the act is necessary.

When a threshold is exceeded governments will be forced to relinquish ownership of the offending position and immediately sell it on an open market. There are a number of ways this can be enforced. The last government to make a trade can be forced to divest, or every vested government can be forced to sell a small part of their positions. The forced sale can be based on which government has the largest position so that no single government has overwhelming representation. There will also be instances when a private company enters a new market which will cause a vested government to exceed its entitlement. In this case too forced divestiture will be a solution. The most obvious use for forced divestiture is when a specific legislation or administrative law will make some companies more profitable and some less so. Whenever there is a conflict in interests forced divestiture will be used. Lawsuits for forced divestiture can be issued by private parties, competitive governments, or regulatory agencies and higher governments.

Local and regional governments must conform to the <48% rule when investing within its own nation but it has unfettered access to foreign markets. Although local and regional governments can have majority shares on their own they can combine for majority positions. Several states and large cities could easily purchase individual stakes that coalesce into a majority position and this must not be prevented. Obviously it is in the interests of the people for governments to be able to earn the highest dividends possible and unrestricted access in foreign markets is one way this can be affected. There is no reason another country would not interpret a local or regional government from another country as another ordinary competitor. Governments don't discriminate now and they should not begin to discriminate when state capital becomes more prevalent.

This is a fair system if one wants to keep government abuses in check, if they want to reasonably limit government ownership of companies, and if they want to minimize the risks of corruption or profiteering without compromising profits but some of the limitations are unnecessary. A more liberal configuration can concede to limiting ownership positions in domestic theatres while enhancing governments with more aggressive entitlements with foreign instruments. The Capitalocracy-major offers a balanced mix of entitlements that most populations will be comfortable with it.

Capitalocracy, major:

Code:
I;A.1, B.3.a, C.1, D.1.b, E.1.a.x, **II;A.3.x.iii, B.2.3.4.x**, C.2.a.b.x, D.1, **E.2.3.x.iii;** III.A.2.x, B.2.x

I.A.2.3, B.3.a, C.1, D.1.b, E.1.a.x, II;A.3.xxx.i**, A.3.xx(c).ii, A.3.x.iii,** B.2.3.xx(c).xxx, **B.2.3.4.x,** C.2.a.b.x.xx(c), D.3, E.3.xxx.i, **E.3.xx(c).ii**, **E.2.3.x.iii**, III; A.2.x, A.1.xx.xxx, B.2.x

Key:

I. **A.1** (national government), **B.3.a** (option to manage itself with social agenda), **C.1** (budget subsidy only), **D.1.b** (savings method with 25 year cycle), **E.1.a.x** (separate permanent funds for on and off budget expenses), **II. A.3.x.iii** (may invest in any secondary instrument to a majority degree in foreign jurisdictions), **B.2.3.4.x** (may invest in any form of debt be it public, corporate, or personal debt, in foreign jurisdictions), **C.2.a.b.x** (may utilize any residential or commercial real estate in foreign jurisdictions), **D.1** (currency trades prohibited), **E.2.3.x.iii** (may invest in venture capital or primary security instrument to a majority degree, including starting new businesses, but in foreign jurisdictions only), **III.A.2.x** (gross ownership is unrestricted in foreign jurisdictions), **B.2.x** (market share is unrestricted in foreign jurisdictions).

I. **A.2.3** (regional and local governments), **B.3.a** (option to self manage permanent funds with social agenda), **C.1** (budget subsidy only), **D.1.b** (savings method with 25 year cycle),

E.1.a.x (has multiple funds for on and off budget expenses), **II. A.3.xxx.i** (may invest in any secondary instrument to a marginal degree in their administrative jurisdictions), **A.3.xx(c).ii** (may invest in any secondary instrument to a minority degree within opposing domestic regional economies,), **A.3.x.iii** (may invest in any secondary instrument to a majority degree in foreign jurisdictions), **B.2.3.xx(c).xxx** (may use any form of public or corporate debt when it originates from opposing regional jurisdictions or their administrative jurisdictions), **B.2.3.4.x** (may invest in any form of debt be it public, corporate, or personal debt, in foreign jurisdictions), **C.2.a.b.x.xx(c)** (may purchase any residential or commercial real estate in foreign or opposing regional jurisdictions), **D.3** (may trade any currency), **E.3.xxx.i** (may invest in primary instruments up to a marginal degree in their administrative jurisdictions), **E.3.xx(c).ii** (may invest in primary security instruments, up to a minority degree in opposing regional jurisdictions), **E.2.3.x.iii** (may invest in venture capital or primary security instrument to a majority degree, including starting new businesses, in foreign jurisdictions only); **III. A.2.x** (gross ownership unrestricted in foreign theatres), **A.1.xx(c).xxx** (gross ownership is constrained to less than 48% in administrative and opposing regional jurisdictions), **B.2.x** (allowed unrestricted market share in foreign economies).

The **Capitalocracy-major** uses the template of account attributes and entitlements established in the minor variety but make two subtle changes. First, they expand permanent fund entitlements for investing in foreign economies. Second, they permit their regional and local governments to maintain minority degrees of ownership.

Within the national permanent fund **(I.A.1...)** the major variety substitutes;

- II.A.3.x.ii with **II.A.3.x.iii** (may invest in any secondary instrument to a majority degree within a foreign market),
- II.B.2.3.x with **II.B.2.3.4.x** (may invest in any public, corporate, or private debt instruments when they originate from a foreign economy),

- And II.E.3.x.ii is exchanged for **II.E.2.3.x.iii** (may invest in any primary securities, including venture capital and initiating new businesses, in foreign economies).

Within lower government permanent funds **(I.A.2.3....)** it substitutes the same entitlements;

- II.A.3.x.ii with **II.A.3.x.iii** (may invest in any secondary market instrument to a majority degree within a foreign market),
- II.A.3.xx(c).iv with **II.A.3.xx(c).ii** (may invest in any secondary market instrument to a minority degree within an opposing regional jurisdiction)
- II.B.2.3.x with **II.B.2.3.4.x** (may invest in any public, corporate, or private debt instruments when they originate from a foreign economy),
- II.E.3.x.ii is exchanged for **II.E.2.3.x.iii** (may invest in primary securities, including majority positions and initiating new businesses, when in foreign economies),
- And II.E.3.xx(c).iv with **II.E.3.xx(c).ii** (may invest in primary securities to a minority degree when they originate from opposing domestic jurisdictions).

The Capitalocracy-major model exploits the fact that there are far fewer inherent conflicts when investing in the economies of foreign nations. They can participate in every facet of commerce an ordinary business or individual is entitled to. No internal restrictions are placed on their involvement but other governments may certainly enact regulations or limitations on 3rd party nations becoming vested in their economy. Sovereign wealth funds generally have no restrictions placed on them to limit their interaction with foreign populations or commercial parties. This model of commercial government enables its permanent funds to operate nearly identical to Sovereign Wealth Funds in this respect but still reigns in domestic investment as a means to protect its own market economy from its own involvement.

Under these circumstances all permanent funds are allowed to acquire majority positions in any company operating principally in a foreign jurisdiction be it public stock or private equity. The government may even initiate and manage new businesses but they must function solely in foreign jurisdictions.

Foreign governments are generally treated as ordinary commercial parties and will be afforded no special benefits or powers. That is true now and it will be so in the future. Cities and states will not be able to leverage any significant political capital when operating companies in foreign countries because they individually have little influence over their won national government. If there is political coercion commercial parties including other governments can sue in international courts for remediation. Surely a foreign national government will rebuke the national government of the interloping state and cause the offense to end. Most well developed nations will protect themselves with adequate regulations so that foreign governments can't unfairly monopolize market share or dissuade competition.

New businesses must always remain competitive. If they are not earning a profit then they only have access to their own capital stores to remain solvent. If the owning government seeks to recapitalize the ailing company it must rely on purely conventional methods. It will either have to offer preferred or common stock for public consumption or it will have to apply to commercial banking institutions for loans. If neither of these options seem palatable it can involve private equity or venture capital firms. In all instances a government is strictly forbid from devoting more money from its permanent fund or general fund to strengthen the company. This pertains to any public company where the government assumes ownership through the purchase of common stock, and it is especially important when the government corporation is nonprofit. Using this mechanic will insulate capitalist leaning governments from socialization and it will help socialist states remain fluid.

The Capitalocracy-major enables participating governments to traffic in citizen debt through credit (retail or credit card), mortgages, personal or school loans, or past due amounts as long as all parties involved have sole citizenship outside the domain of the national government. This is an ordinary function of business and national governments should not be denied this entitlement when competing in foreign jurisdictions. This is in addition to the ordinary entitlements of purchasing foreign treasury securities, municipal bonds, and corporate bonds from foreign companies or governments. Mandatory diversification will ensure the national permanent fund does not over expose itself to risk involved with one type of instrument or product.

The last significant change is that regional and local governments in a Capitalocracy-major can now take more substantial positions in domestic companies: minority shares allow ownership of a maximum of 33% of outstanding shares or private equity. Although they have rights that protect their positions and can interact through shareholder votes and corporate board elections they do not have the authority to control companies outright. Any agendas they may have must be facilitated through coordination with private interests or through consensus with other governments. Despite the fact that lower governments can forward their interests the domestic economy should not be compromised. Most often these governments will be focused on generating profits and only exercise a social agenda when it saves them money that they would ordinarily pay out of their general fund.

The Capitalocracy-major will be the most successful model of commercial government if domestic involvement is still a concern of its citizens but when they are also comfortable the idea of their cities, states, and nations fully competing in foreign countries. There is only one more generic sample of the Capitalocratic class to discuss. Previously all gross ownership in domestic companies was limited to less than 48% but that can be relaxed so that lower governments are able to exercise social agendas through the corporate boards of publicly owned companies. No single government will have a majority position but a collection of vested government can lead through consensus. This format of commercial government is named Capitalocracy-general.

Capitalocracy, general:

Code:

I; A.1, B.3.a, C.1, D.1.b, E.1.a.x, II; A.3.x.iii, B.2.3.4.x, C.2.a.b.x, D.1, E.2.3.x.iii, III; A.2.x, B.2.x

I; A.2.3, B.3.a, C.1, D.1.b, E.1.a.x, II; A.3.xxx.i, A.3.xx(c).ii, A.3.x.iii, B.2.3.xx(c).xxx, B.2.3.4.x, C.2.a.b.x.xx(c), D.3, E.3.xxx.i, E.3.xx(c).ii, E.2.3.x.iii, III; **A.2.x.xx.xxx, B.1.xx.xxx**, B.2.x

Key:

I. **A.1** (national government), **B.3.a** (option to manage itself with social agenda), **C.1** (budget subsidy only), **D.1.b** (savings method with 25 year cycle), **E.1.a.x** (separate permanent funds for on and off budget expenses), **II. A.3.x.iii** (may invest in any secondary instrument to a majority degree in foreign jurisdictions), **B.2.3.4.x** (may invest in any form of debt be it public, corporate, or personal debt, in foreign jurisdictions), **C.2.a.b.x** (may utilize any residential or commercial real estate in foreign jurisdictions), **D.1** (currency trades prohibited), **E.2.3.x.iii** (may invest in venture capital or primary security instrument to a majority degree, including starting new businesses, but in foreign jurisdictions only), **III.A.2.x** (gross ownership is unrestricted in foreign jurisdictions), **B.2.x** (market share is unrestricted in foreign jurisdictions).

I. **A.2.3** (regional and local governments), **B.3.a** (option to self manage permanent funds with social agenda), **C.1** (budget subsidy only), **D.1.b** (savings method with 25 year cycle), **E.1.a.x** (has multiple funds for on and off budget expenses), **II. A.3.xxx.i** (may invest in any secondary instrument to a marginal degree in their administrative jurisdictions), **A.3.xx(c).ii** (may invest in any secondary instrument to a minority degree within opposing domestic regional economies,), **A.3.x.iii** (may invest in any secondary instrument to a majority degree in foreign jurisdictions), **B.2.3.xx(c).xxx** (may use any form of public or corporate debt, when it originates from opposing regional governments or their own administrative jurisdictions), **B.2.3.4.x** (may invest in any form of debt be it public, corporate, or personal debt, in foreign jurisdictions), **C.2.a.b.x.xx(c)** (may purchase any residential or commercial real estate in foreign or opposing regional jurisdictions), **D.3** (may trade any currency), **E.3.xxx.i** (may invest in primary instruments up to a marginal degree in their administrative jurisdictions), **E.3.xx(c).ii** (may invest in primary security instruments, up to a minority degree in opposing regional jurisdictions), **E.2.3.x.iii** (may invest in venture capital or primary security instrument to a majority degree, including starting new businesses, in foreign jurisdictions only); **III.A.2.x.xx.xxx** (gross ownership is unrestricted in all jurisdictions), **B.1.xx.xxx** (market share is restricted to less than 48% in opposing regional and administrative jurisdictions) **B.2.x** (allowed unrestricted market share in foreign economies).

The **Capitalocracy-general** shares all of the same account attributes and entitlements in the national permanent fund of the Capitalocratic-major system but make two adjustments to lower government entitlements.

Lower government permanent funds **(I.A.2.3)** substitute;

- III.A.1.xx.xxx with **III.A.2.xx.xxx** (gross ownership is unrestricted in opposing regional and administrative jurisdictions). This combines with III.A.2.x (unrestricted gross ownership in foreign theatres) which is already permitted.
- **III.B.1.xx.xxx** (market share is restricted to <48% in opposing regional and administrative jurisdictions) is added to complement the relaxation on gross ownership

This permits Capitalocratic governments to manage industry through consensus taking full advantage of representation on corporate boards and participating in shareholder votes but a majority of market share will always be owned by private industry. Those companies where government ownership exceeds 47% of the outstanding shares may not have more than 47% of market share in any industry. The total market share of all companies where government ownership exceeds 47% must be less than 48%. Governments may be involved with the private industry which owns a majority market share but their collective position must always be 47% or less. Any transgression in gross ownership or market share will be immediately dealt with by forced divestiture. This will ensure that government ownership doesn't eclipse private ownership and compromise the profitability of industry within the nation.

Nearly all of the reasonable options to limit a government's involvement in the domestic economy have been exhausted. Now it is time to situations where governments can own majority shares of stock or private equity within the domestic economy. Nations that see government ownership as an advantage and not a threat can choose to employ a wildly more aggressive incarnation of commercial government. For these people the Corporatic templates will offer the greatest opportunity for profit and for social advance as certain tiers of government are allowed to gain majority positions of ownership in private or public companies in competitive jurisdictions.

Corporatocracies *(aka Merchant Democracies)* compete for profits with private industry and other competitive government corporations. They can express themselves more effectively on corporate boards or in shareholder votes. Previous commercial governments relied on consensus for management decisions. These governments will be able to exert far more leadership and influence because they can be sole owners or majority owners in both private and public companies. There are two subclasses and each includes an incremental and cumulative expansion in entitlements. By far the least compromising is the Corporatocracy lesser: they give the lowest governments the most freedoms for competing in the domestic economy while still limited the larger and more responsible tiers of government. Municipalities and counties can pursue any legitimate commercial activity in any competitor jurisdiction within their own country as well as foreign economies

Corporatocracy, minor:

Code;

I; A.1, B.3.a, C.1, D.1.b, E.1.a.x, II; A.3.x.iii, B.2.3.4.x, C.2.a.b.x, D.1, E.2.3.x.iii, III; A.2.x, B.2.x

I; A.2, B.3.a, C.1, D.1.b, E.1.a.x, II; A.3.xxx.i, A.3.xx(c).ii, A.3.x.iii, B.2.3.xx(c).xxx, B.2.3.4.x, C.2.a.b.x.xx(c), D.3, E.3.xxx.i, E.3.xx(c).ii, E.2.3.x.iii, III; A.2.x.xx(c).xxx, B.1.xx(c).xxx, B.2.x

I; A.3, B.3.a, C.1.D.1.b, E.1.a.x, II, A.3.xxx.i, **A.3.x.xx(c).iii,** B.2.3.xxx, **B.2.3.4.x.xx(c),** C.2.a.b.x.xx(c), D.3, E.3.xxx.i, **E.2.3.x.xx(c).iii,** III;A.2.x.xx(c).xxx, B.1.xx (c).xxx, B.2.x

Key:

I. **A.1** (national government), **B.3.a** (option to manage itself with social agenda), **C.1** (budget subsidy only), **D.1.b** (savings method with 25 year cycle), **E.1.a.x** (separate permanent funds for on and off budget expenses), **II. A.3.x.iii** (may invest in any secondary instrument to a majority degree in foreign jurisdictions), **B.2.3.4.x** (may invest in any form of debt be it public, corporate, or personal debt, in foreign jurisdictions), **C.2.a.b.x** (may utilize any residential or commercial real estate in foreign jurisdictions), **D.1** (currency trades prohibited), **E.2.3.x.iii** (may invest in venture capital or primary security instrument to a majority degree, including starting new businesses, but in foreign jurisdictions only), **III.A.2.x** (gross ownership is unrestricted in foreign jurisdictions), **B.2.x** (market share is unrestricted in foreign jurisdictions).

I. **A.2** (regional governments), **B.3.a** (option to self manage permanent funds with social agenda), **C.1** (budget subsidy only), **D.1.b** (savings method with 25 year cycle), **E.1.a.x** (has multiple funds for on and off budget expenses), **II. A.3.xxx.i** (may invest in any secondary instrument to a marginal degree in their administrative jurisdictions), **A.3.xx(c).ii** (may invest in any secondary instrument to a minority degree within opposing domestic regional economies,), **A.3.x.iii** (may invest in any secondary instrument to a majority degree in foreign jurisdictions), **B.2.3.xx(c).xxx** (may use any form of public or corporate debt, when it originates opposing regional governments or their own administrative jurisdictions), **B.2.3.4.x** (may invest in any form of debt be it public, corporate, or personal debt, in foreign jurisdictions), **C.2.a.b.x.xx(c)** (may purchase any residential or commercial real estate in foreign or opposing regional jurisdictions), **D.3** (may trade any currency), **E.3.xxx.i** (may invest in primary instruments up to a marginal degree in their administrative jurisdictions), **E.3.xx(c).ii** (may invest in primary security instruments, up to a minority degree in opposing regional jurisdictions), **E.2.3.x.iii** (may invest in venture capital or primary security instrument to a majority degree, including starting new businesses, in foreign jurisdictions only); **III.A.2.x.xx.xxx** (gross ownership is unrestricted in all jurisdictions), **B.1.xx.xxx** (market share is restricted to less than 48% in opposing regional and administrative jurisdictions) **B.2.x** (allowed unrestricted market share in foreign economies).

I. **A.3** (municipal and county governments), **B.3.a** (option to self manage permanent funds with social agenda), **C.1** (budget subsidy only), **D.1.b** (savings method with 25 year cycle), **E.1.a.x** (has multiple funds for on and off budget expenses),

II. A.3.xxx.i (may invest in any secondary instrument, with their administrative jurisdictions to a marginal degree*)*, **A.3.x.xx(c).iii** (may invest in any secondary instrument in foreign countries and opposing domestic regional economies to a majority degree), **B.2.3.xxx** (may invest in public and corporate debt within its own administrative jurisdiction), **B.2.3.4.x.xx(c)** (may invest in any form of debt be it public, corporate, or personal debt, in foreign and opposing regional jurisdictions), **C.2.a.b.x.xx(c)** (may invest in any residential or commercial real estate in foreign or opposing regional jurisdictions), **D.3** (may trade any currency), **E.3.xxx.i** (may invest in primary instruments, up to a marginal degree in administrative jurisdictions), **E.2.3.x.xx(c).iii** (may invest in primary security instruments, up to a majority degree in foreign or opposing regional jurisdictions, and may even initiate new businesses), **III.A.2.x.xx(c).xxx** (gross ownership is unrestricted in all jurisdictions), **B.1.xx(c).xxx** (market share is restricted to less than 48% in opposing regional and administrative jurisdictions) **B.2.x** (allowed unrestricted market share in foreign economies).

The **Corporatocracy-minor** repeats the same account attributes and entitlements of the Capitalocratic-general model of commercial government within its national and regional permanent funds but municipal and county governments see their entitlements profoundly expanded.

The lowest governments **(I.A.3…)** substitute;

- II.A.3.xx.ii with **II.A.3.xx.iii** (may invest in any primary securities, including venture capital and initiating new businesses, in opposing regional jurisdictions),
- II.B.2.3.xx with **II.B.2.3.4.xx** (may invest in any public, corporate, or private debt instruments when they originate from opposing regional jurisdictions),
- And II.E.3.xx.ii with **II.E.2.3.xx.iii** (may invest in any primary securities, including venture capital and initiating new businesses, in opposing regional jurisdictions).

The Corporatocracy-minor allows its municipalities and counties to vest and fully compete within every jurisdiction except their own administrative jurisdictions. The lowest government's access to capital is limited and they are the least able of all governments to forward their agendas within the political superstructure of the nation. There is the least risk for political or economic compromises when the smallest governments are allowed majority ownership. They will be able to own any private or public company and initiate their own Competitive Government Incorporations. The trend is propagated by improving the entitlement governing government securities and bonds, corporate bonds, and personal debt. Now they can traffic in any form of debt in any competitive domestic regional jurisdiction. As a result municipal Competitive Government Corporations (C-G Corporations) will have most of the entitlements private industry has when it is concerned with any jurisdiction other than its administrative jurisdiction. This can make government incorporations formidable competition and be extremely lucrative for prudent but assertive counties, cities, and towns.

The usual protections against usurpation, uncompetitive business practices, or corruption are in play and these governments will simply represent independent competitive interests in those jurisdictions. There will never be an instance where a Corporatic government can invest to a degree greater than marginal when a company is headquartered in the administrative jurisdiction or when a company derives more than 5% of its revenue from the same region. Even the more liberal versions of Corporatism forbid this gross intersection of interests. Profits should never compromise the integrity of a town, city, county, state, or nation and relegating them to marginal positions almost guarantees the separation of industry and state. When governments do have the authority to interfere with competitive companies in their own administrative jurisdictions they are almost invariably restricted to nonprofit cooperatives providing low cost products and services to residents.

Allowing controlling shares and permitting governments to initiate and operate their own companies is an important landmark. They will now be able to create their own mutual funds, hedge funds, REITS, annuities, or index funds. This is important for managing their own wealth but it is more important because the can create financial instruments for consumption by the public or other governments. For an activity they would otherwise ordinarily be doing they can rake in significant profits. This can inadvertently exponentially increase their economic influence in local or foreign markets as they can now leverage their own considerable wealth with that of adventurous consumers. Although drastically more important in the Competitive State Capitalist systems, permanent fund managers can begin offering stock from their C-G Corporations back to their resident communities.

They need not conform to the <48% rule with respect to their controlling shares in companies in either competitive or administrative jurisdictions but may not collectively own greater than 48% of market share in any region or industry. This restriction on market share does not apply when the governments don't own a collective ownership share greater than 48% percent in individual companies. If government investment breeches the 47% threshold in a company that individually owns more than 47% market share than their collective position will be reduced to below 47% gross ownership. Forced divestiture will commonly be used to reinforce market share concentration limits in government owned companies if such transgressions can't be prevented by a less intrusive means. The only other alternative is to break up the company so that it no longer controls more than 48% market share but this is the act of last resort because it disrupts private investment. Non majority share interests pose little or no threat to private industry.

Like the other Neo-capitalist models, local governments need only conform to the laws of the foreign government in which they invest when the capital is exported to a foreign theatre. Forced divestiture is only permitted for instruments originating from foreign markets when there are national security concerns and an embargo is placed on the antagonistic country. Ordinary commercial interests are also subject to forced divestiture in this respect and governments don't earn any exemption because of their statuses. This should be a rare occurrence and most foreign instruments held in permanent funds will be safe from forced divestiture. Stability will promote more government investment and that will engender lower taxes for residents and citizens. Foreign investment will also play a key role in ensuring the domestic market is not over saturated with state capital from its own governments so it will be important to make such investment stable. Often foreign investment is preferable to domestic investment exactly for this reason.

Citizens must be comfortable with government investment within their country be it originating from foreign nations or domestic jurisdictions. A government represents its own interests and must be interpreted as such. The only difference between private commercial interests and government commercial interests is that market share is calculated differently. Not only is the gross market share of domestic government ownership guarded but each regional government assumes responsibility for the market share of its constituent parts. National governments assume the market share of all its subordinate governments even though it does not receive the profits. This is what is referred to as constructive market share. A higher government is a composite of interests from its constituent parts. This prevents the concentration of ownership of one sector or industry in one geographical region of the nation. It should also serve to limit concentration of ownership in the regional or national tiers of government which on its own is a serious concern. This pertains to the competitive government corporations of both domestic and foreign competitors.

In the same respects a national government includes both regional and local government public wealth in its tally of ownership, a regional government includes county and municipal wealth, and counties must include municipal wealth in their calculations. This also establishes a trend for when forced divestiture us used. Lower governments have a greater right to property ownership than higher governments and if government ownership exceeds the maximum allotment then the highest government must sell enough shares so the overall quotient of ownership becomes compliant. It moves from national, to state, to county, and finally to municipal property. Transgressions should always be avoided by careful monitoring of positions by a national government database so that new purchases do not cause an over accumulation any only occur when other factors cause the conflict. Only in those rare situations does forced divestiture occur in order from top down. Otherwise the new acquisition will simply be prohibited and no transgression will occur.

Nations can experiment with liberal entitlements by first empowering municipalities and counties so that they can develop the necessary regulatory apparatus before allowing regional governments to become fully vested in competitor jurisdictions. When the regulatory requirements are satisfied entitlements can be updated to allow regional government to compete on the same footing as local governments. Therefore regional governments in the Corporatocracy-major format adopt the same entitlements as municipal governments. This is the most liberal form of Neo-capitalist commercial governments as any further changes will as more progressive entitlements will cause the system to be categorized as Neo-populist or Competitive State Capitalist.

Corporatocracy, major:

Code;

I; A.1, B.3.a, C.1, D.1.b, E.1.a.x, II; A.3.x.iii, B.2.3.4.x, C.2.a.b.x, D.1, E.2.3.x.iii, III; A.2.x, B.2.x

I; A.2.3, B.3.a, C.1, D.1.b, E.1.a.x, **II; A.3.xxx.i, A.3.x.xx(c).iii, B.2.3.xxx, B.2.3.4.x.xx(c), C.2.a.b.x.xx(c), D.3, E.3.xxx.i, E.2.3.x.xx(c).iii,** III; A.2.x.xx(c).xxx, B.1.xx (c).xxx, B.2.x

Key:

I. **A.1** (national government), **B.3.a** (option to manage itself with social agenda), **C.1** (budget subsidy only), **D.1.b** (savings method with 25 year cycle), **E.1.a.x** (separate permanent funds for on and off budget expenses), **II. A.3.x.iii** (may invest in any secondary instrument to a majority degree in foreign jurisdictions), **B.2.3.4.x** (may invest in any form of debt be it public, corporate, or personal debt, in foreign jurisdictions), **C.2.a.b.x** (may utilize any residential or commercial real estate in foreign jurisdictions), **D.1** (currency trades prohibited), **E.2.3.x.iii** (may invest in venture capital or primary security instrument to a majority degree, including starting new businesses, but in foreign jurisdictions only), **III.A.2.x** (gross ownership is unrestricted in foreign jurisdictions), **B.2.x** (market share is unrestricted in foreign jurisdictions).

I. **A.2.3** (regional and local governments), **B.3.a** (option to self manage permanent funds with social agenda), **C.1** (budget subsidy only), **D.1.b** (savings method with 25 year cycle), **E.1.a.x** (has multiple funds for on and off budget expenses), **II. A.3.xxx.i** (may invest in any secondary instrument, with their administrative jurisdictions to a marginal degree*)*, **A.3.x.xx(c).iii** (may invest in any secondary instrument in foreign countries and opposing domestic regional economies to a majority degree), **B.2.3.xxx** (may invest in public and corporate debt within its own administrative jurisdiction), **B.2.3.4.x.xx(c)** (may invest in any form of debt be it public, corporate, or personal debt, in foreign and opposing regional jurisdictions), **C.2.a.b.x.xx(c)** (may invest in any residential or commercial real estate in foreign or opposing regional jurisdictions), **D.3** (may trade any currency), **E.3.xxx.i** (may invest in primary instruments, up to a marginal degree in administrative jurisdictions), **E.2.3.x.xx(c).iii** (may invest in primary security instruments, up to a majority degree in foreign or opposing regional jurisdictions, and may even initiate new businesses), **III.A.2.x.xx(c).xxx** (gross ownership is unrestricted in all jurisdictions), **B.1.xx(c).xxx** (market share is restricted to less than 48% in opposing regional and administrative jurisdictions) **B.2.x** (allowed unrestricted market share in foreign economies).

The **Corporatocracy-major** applies the entitlements previously earned by municipal and county governments in the (minor) variety to regional governments so that all lower governments have the same liberal entitlements.

Regional governments **(I.A.2…)** substitute;

- II.A.3.xx.ii with **II.A.3.xx(c).iii** (may invest in any primary securities, including venture capital and initiating new businesses, in opposing regional jurisdictions),
- II.B.2.3.xx with **II.B.2.3.4.xx(c)** (may invest in any public, corporate, or private debt instruments when they originate from opposing regional jurisdictions),
- And II.E.3.xx.ii with **II.E.2.3.xx(c).iii** (may invest in any primary securities, including venture capital and initiating new businesses, in opposing regional jurisdictions).

Every government within the nation will be able to own majority positions in both private and public companies in every jurisdiction except their administrative jurisdiction. There they will still be relegated to marginal positions. The Corporatocracy-major is the most aggressive form of commercial government but they may still not own majorities in market share. These protectionist measures are in place to protect the free market. Only Neo-populist and Competitive State Capitalist systems exceed the threshold of majority gross ownership and minority market share so that all of the means to production and distribution can be owned by the state (albeit predominantly managed for profit in a competitive market).

This format engenders the greatest amount of profit sharing (or wealth conservation) while maintaining the franchise of the owners' class. Regional jurisdictions join municipal jurisdictions and gain access to all of the normal business functions ordinary commercial institutions have when they operate in opposing regional jurisdictions. This includes secondary stock instruments, public, corporate, and personal debt instruments, commercial and residential real estate, currency trading, primary security instruments (equity) and new business creation. They are treated in every respect like commercial institutions in every jurisdiction except their own and no town, city, county, or state within the same nation can discriminate against them with protectionist measures. Neither will they be afforded any special benefits or exemptions from local laws. Paramount to the success of Corporatic models is the uniform application and enforcement of commercial regulations and laws. They are meant to protect consumers and providers alike not matter where there origination, operation, or residency.

Corporatic governments interact with private commerce at a much higher frequency and more businesses will be excluded from making campaign contributions or lobbying political officials. Not only are companies directly invested in excluded but so are businesses that perform transactions with competitive government corporations. Whenever there is an exchange of consideration between a C-G Corporation and a private company that company is forbid from political influence within the owning municipality or state. This compounds the fact that all C-G Corporations are naturally excluded from making campaign contributions or political lobby. There won't be many commercial interests left who are allowed to compromise local or regional politics but this will be tempered by government realignment of public welfare with profits. Most governments will naturally elect to create market conditions that reinforce competition and profitability because they will be reciprocated in other jurisdictions. At the same time they won't abandon efficient regulation and even handed enforcement.

THE NECRO-ECONOMICON

Chapter 4

Competitive State Capitalist
And Neo-Populist systems

It is assumed that after decades or centuries of government investment a majority of public and private companies will be owned by the many constituent governments of a nation. Normally, restricting government ownership to less than 48% of the market share for any one region or industry will protect against such accumulation but Solocorporatocracies (*aka Omnicorporatocracies*) remove these limits on gross ownership and market share. The final product of decades of concentrated government investment is Competitive State Capitalism. Competitive State Capitalism has some very fundamental differences with traditional socialism. Competitive State Capitalism interprets the socialist creed that government must control all means to production and distribution as meaning that government incorporation, as a whole, can control most means to production and distribution but those means will be limited to efforts of competing national, regional, and municipal governments. Competitive State Capitalism is not intended to create an egalitarian state. It is meant to enfranchise all segments of the population through superior wealth conservation. Wealth will no longer concentrate in a few individuals but rather contribute directly to a jurisdictions ability to depress taxes, create dividends for residents, or improve government sponsored benefits.

Its residents and citizens are not prevented from competing with small, medium, or large business owners but such private interests are protected only through the standard anti-trust and monopoly laws. A significant proportion of medium and large asset class corporations should now be under the locus of regional or municipal government managers. There is no coercion involved. The simple fact is that permanent funds will be flush with capital from decades of successful investment and governments can pay a premium for larger and larger shares of private or public companies. The transfer of ownership between individuals and governments is facilitated under free market conditions and not imminent domain. Solocorporatocracies do not usurp the wealth of their residents and citizens; everything is paid for in accord with fair market value and only when consent is legally offered. Unlike traditional socialist states class systems are preserved in the Competitive Socialist States. Every configuration requires the C-G Corporations owned by the many competing jurisdictions to return a significant portion of their stock back to residents. This will be the primary mechanism the wealth rich retain their franchise and the middle class maintain their wealth.

The proportion of government to private ownership grows at an exponential rate in periods of a decade. The growth is analogous to how algae can overcome a pond. After algae are introduced it will cover the entire surface area of the body of water after 30 days of reproduction. On the 29th day its volume will be exactly half of the available surface area of the pond. At some point a commercial government will reach a point equivalent to the 29th day of algae growth if it maintains a constant rate of domestic investment. The Solocorporatic models represent growth of government ownership passed the 29th day of exponential growth when the usual restrictions on gross ownership and market share are repealed. An eclipse of private ownership can be prevented but some populations will see the exceptional merits of the Sociocorporatocracy and its uncanny ability to conserve wealth in the lower and middle classes. The transition to Solocorporatocracy is gradual, not sudden, and it will be a priority to protect private wealth and maintain class differentiation. In fact, a Corporatocracy can relax gross market share accumulation without immediately turning into a Solocorporatocracy but the change will most likely be inevitable unless reversed.

Most of the competitive government incorporations will be public companies and a large proportion of its stock will be in private hands. When sales of private or (private) public companies occur there will be an exchange of stock resulting in private co-owners of predominantly government owned companies. Almost all of the government incorporations will be forced to offer stock to the public when they need to capitalize. This helps with class differentiation as richer individuals will continue to earn substantially more money than the working class. It is also a normal tendency for individuals to retain majority ownership of private or public companies despite continuing to sell shares to government investors. Private wealth is not compromised and mobility will be preserved. Private industry only becomes less likely because governments will have the necessary capital to cause transfer of ownership. The rich will still be wealthy and the lower classes will be hard working.

Competition is preserved by the introduction of tens of thousands of governments and government agencies as motivated investors and owners. The equity exchange between individual owners and governments will actually increase the rate at which new companies are created and help spur on competition. Competitive State Capitalist markets shouldn't compromise small businesses. The U.S. government identifies all businesses that make less than 150 million a year as "small Businesses". The fact is that real small business; barbers, convenience stores, bars and restaurants, law firms, dry cleaners, real estate companies, hardware stores, architecture firms are major employers in the economy. Local governments may compete with other small business owners in a limited capacity but city, state, and national governments will see no incentive in managing such businesses. In this respect the popular market provides the greatest benefit because small businesses will likely see higher profits when taxes are abbreviated and dividends inflate resident's disposable incomes.

Competitive State Capitalist economies are absolutely the most efficient systems in terms of conserving wealth; rather than the majority of equity being held by a slim minority, wealth aggregates in communities and states. Taxes will be displaced by permanent fund earnings making the wealthy wealthier while vastly improve the middle and lower classes lifestyles. Governments competing with other governments will drive up the prices of public stock and stockholders will reap considerable gains. The higher the profits earned by governments the lower the taxes and greater the dividend checks for residents. The more efficient distribution of equity among the general population will spur on real estate to appreciate and stock values to increase wildly. Consumption is, after all, the single greatest contributor to corporate profits and when they are substantially enhanced it spills over into all aspects of the economy.

Profit sharing conserves wealth because most of the proceeds from competition and investment will be used to depreciate the tax rate in the owning jurisdiction. This will make private small businesses operating within the owning government's jurisdiction more profitable. It will also make ordinary wage employee's salaries much more valuable. The same salary will be taxed less and further contribute to consumption within the jurisdiction. Competition for products and services may draw down their cost. The reduction in taxes will allow lower cost goods without decreasing the profitability of the companies. Yes this sounds like a deflationary trend but it will clearly benefit resident populations without causing businesses harm. When residents have more disposable wealth and products and services cost less, the average standard of living should appreciate to exceptional levels. The middle class will grow to an unprecedented proportion of the population, absorbing the poor, and encroaching on the rich.

Governments generally pay higher median wages than private employers and more competitive government corporations will result in more middle class wages. The lowest wage employees can expect to receive slightly higher wages with better benefits. The voting public will ensure Executives are paid salaries commensurate with their skill and ability but in parity with other employees. We should see an end to outrageous differences between ordinary employees and executives that plague our commercial infrastructure right now. More reasonable pay for executives will enable government businesses to employ more personnel at a higher wages. C-G Corporation may be able to attract more experienced employees from the private sector in order to consolidate their leadership position within industry. Lower unemployment will also contribute to stronger consumption making the economy generally more resilient and more profitable.

Most ordinary small and medium business owners will see higher revenues from their own low taxes and from much greater rates of consumption. Lower taxes, higher wages, large dividends will drive down resource costs, labor costs and equipment costs making all industries (both government and private) more competitive. Lower manufacturing costs equals higher export rates. Exports enable one economy to draw income away from another economy and the difference contributes to the strengths and weakness of the two nations. Countries that rely on imports generally have softer labor markets because there are significantly less manufacturing jobs. Those that export more than they import create wealth faster and are able to conserve that wealth more efficiently. All commercial governments bolster the countries' ability to export products and therefore produce a more sound economy.

The more conflict inherent in a system the more likely it will continue and flourish. A free market economy has more conflict than a social market economy, and for that reason free market economies are more elastic and durable. A Competitive State Capitalist market is an economy that has a larger concentration of government ownership than private ownership but they still employ a healthy amount of competition. They retain many of the successful characteristics of free markets but employ a more efficient means of conserving wealth. C-G Corporations have no advantage over private industry except for the fact that governments rely on taxes on private and government industries to grow their public wealth. Consumers will still be protected against monopoly and uncompetitive business practices despite the increase in government ownership.

When 51% or more of domestic industry is owned by the government they are likely to become Competitive State Capitalist but it really is market share that determines the categorization. A nation is only reclassified as Competitive State Capitalist when domestic C-G Corporations own 51% or more market share in 51% or more markets. Many Corporatic nations can relax limits on market share accumulation without becoming Competitive State Capitalist. In these instances private industry could resist buyout from domestic governments or foreign companies and governments can accumulate large swathes of ownership within the country. Ideal Competitive State Capitalist nations will have acquired most industry so that only truly small business survives as privately owned. This way nearly all profits earned by corporations are used to depress resident's income and property taxes or translated into dividends or government benefits or local amenities.

The Solocorporatocracy-minor is adapted from the Capitalocracy-general model and simply expands lower government's rights in acquiring majority market share with the companies they already manage through consensus (where gross ownership is greater than 47%). The Solocorporatocracy-minor actually rolls back the liberalized entitlements of the Corporatic models because constituent governments are still unable to own majority stakes. This combination allows for governments to begin managing most aspects of an economy through corporate board elections and shareholder votes but it displaces the ownership over a great many number of competitive governments. Like all Competitive State Capitalist commercial governments it is meant to raise the standard of living for the majority of its residents which will either be salaried employees or owners of small businesses.

Solocorporatocracy, minor:

Code:

I; A.1, B.3.a, C.1, D.1.b, E.1.a.x, II; **A.3.xxx.i,** A.3.x.iii, **B.2.3.xxx,** B.2.3.4.x, C.2.a.b.x, D.1, E.2.3.x.iii, **E.3.xxx.i, III; A.2.x.xxx, B.2.x.xxx**

I; A.2.3, B.1.a, C.1, D.1.b, E.1.a.x, II; A.3.xxx.i, A.3.xx(c).ii, A.3.x.iii, B.2.3.xx.xxx(c), B.2.3.4.x, C.2.a.b.x.xx(c), D.3, E.3.xxx.i, E.3.xx(c).ii, E.2.3.x.iii, III; A.2.x.xx.xxx, **B.2.x.xx.xxx**

Key:

I. **A.1** (national government), **B.1.a** (must manage its own permanent fund with option of applying social agenda), **C.1** (budget subsidy only), **D.1.b** (savings method with 25 year cycle), **E.1.a.x** (separate permanent funds for on and off budget expenses), **II. A.3.xxx.i** (may invest in any secondary instrument, with their administrative jurisdictions to a marginal degree), **A.3.x.iii** (may invest in any secondary instrument to a majority degree in foreign jurisdictions), **B.2.3.xxx** (may invest in public and corporate debt within its own administrative jurisdiction), **B.2.3.4.x** (may invest in any form of debt be it public, corporate, or personal debt, in foreign jurisdictions), **C.2.a.b.x** (may utilize any residential or commercial real estate in foreign jurisdictions), **D.1** (currency trades prohibited), **E.2.3.x.iii** (may invest in venture capital or primary security instrument to a majority degree, including starting new businesses, but in foreign jurisdictions only), **E.3.xxx.i** (may invest in primary security instruments to a marginal degree within their administrative jurisdictions) **III.A.2.x.xxx** (gross ownership is unrestricted in foreign and administrative jurisdictions), **B.2.x.xxx** (market share is unrestricted in foreign and administrative jurisdictions).

I. **A.2.3** (regional and local governments), **B.1.a** (must manage its own permanent fund with option of applying social agenda), **C.1** (budget subsidy only), **D.1.b** (savings method with 25 year cycle), **E.1.a.x** (has multiple funds for on and off budget expenses), **II. A.3.xxx.i** (may invest in any secondary instrument to a marginal degree in their administrative jurisdictions), **A.3.xx(c).ii** (may invest in any secondary instrument to a minority degree within opposing domestic regional economies,), **A.3.x.iii** (may invest in any secondary instrument to a majority degree in foreign jurisdictions), **B.2.3.xx(c).xxx** (may use any form of public or corporate debt, when it originates opposing regional governments or their own administrative jurisdictions), **B.2.3.4.x** (may invest in any form of debt be it public, corporate, or personal debt, in foreign jurisdictions), **C.2.a.b.x.xx(c)** (may purchase any residential or commercial real estate in foreign or opposing regional jurisdictions), **D.3** (may trade any currency), **E.3.xxx.i** (may invest in primary instruments up to a marginal degree in their administrative jurisdictions), **E.3.xx(c).ii** (may invest in primary security instruments, up to a minority degree in opposing regional jurisdictions), **E.2.3.x.iii** (may invest in venture capital or primary security instrument to a majority degree, including starting new businesses, in foreign jurisdictions only); **III. A.2.x.xx.xxx** (allowed unrestricted gross ownership in foreign and domestic economies), **B.2.x.xx.xxx** (allowed unrestricted market share in foreign and domestic economies).

The **Solocorporatocracy-minor** is a Competitive State Capitalist version of the Capitalocracy-general. It expands the national governments involvement in its own economy and allows all of its constituent government's unrestricted gross ownership and market share ownership.

Additions to national government **(I.A.1...)** entitlements include;

- **II.A.3.xxx.i** (may invest in secondary security instruments to a marginal degree within its administrative jurisdiction),
- **II.B.2.3.xxx** (may invest in any public and corporate debt instruments even when they originate from their own administrative jurisdiction),

- **II.E.3.xxx.i** (may invest in any primary securities to a marginal degree within its own administrative jurisdiction),
- **III.A.2.xxx** (gross ownership is unrestricted within their administrative jurisdictions)
- And **III.B.2.xxx** (government owned companies may acquire a majority in market share within their administrative jurisdictions).

The national governments substitute;

- I.B.3.a with **B.1.a** (must manage its own permanent fund with option of applying social agenda).

Solocorporatic-minor lower governments **(I.A.2.3...)** substitute;

- I.B.3.a with **B.1.a** (must manage its own permanent fund with option of applying social agenda),
- And III.B.1.xx.xxx with **III.B.2.x.xx.xxx** (government owned companies may acquire majorities in market share within foreign jurisdictions, opposing regional jurisdictions, and their own administrative jurisdictions).

All national, regional, and municipal governments must manage their own permanent funds in the Solocorporatic-minor system. Outsourcing management of the fund contradicts their fundamental purpose. They are supposed to represent a complete merger between government and competitive industry. Most public companies competing within the economy will already be owned by other domestic governments and each C-G Corporation takes on political characteristics. It is expected that by now government employees will have developed the necessary skills and habits to manage a portfolio of investment capital. Many will have a cadre of loyal representatives serving on corporate boards while others will rely on professional shareholder voters. Some will install their own trusted CFO's and CEO's and many will rely on auditors to pry over accounting ledgers.

Government will become synonymous with profitability and seamless business management. C-G Corporations are represented in state Assemblies or national legislatures because their resident-owners have direct representation. Most of the executives will be appointed by governors, mayors, and town or city council members. C-G Corporations will not be at a loss of political influence even though they are forbid from actively lobbying through donations to campaigns or political action committees. There would be very little use for marginal equity positions within companies operating within their administrative jurisdictions if a 3rd party money manger represented purely commercial interests on their corporate boards.

In many instances higher governments will commit permanent fund moneys to companies owned by other governments and operating within their administrative jurisdiction simply to gain some representation in how the company interacts with its residents or resident businesses. Solocorporatic-minor national governments employ marginal positions of both primary and secondary market securities within their administrative jurisdictions solely for the purpose of installing a very limited amount of government control on the companies which compete within their jurisdictions. They also gain access to bonds offered by constituent governments or those companies operating within their political boundaries. This is an ordinary function of investment but when coupled with entitlements to marginal positions it can add to the leverage a government can exert on industry competing within their own jurisdictions. If anything the limited equity stakes will give an administrative jurisdiction to proprietary information of foreign owned companies and they will be able to ensure that no uncompetitive business practices are authorized and that accounting frauds do not occur.

At this point in evolution of the commercial government most of the public companies will be owned by competitor jurisdictions and these marginal positions will create an interface between city or state governments with the national government. Economic policy can be forwarded through fiscal policy, tax policy, regulatory policy, and now through corporate governance. Although they cannot dictate company policy they can influence it. They can try to ensure that the company remains compliant with city, state, or national regulations. They can use their rights as shareholders to gain access to accounting information to create transparency.

None of the lower government can yet hold a majority degree of ownership so all of the public corporations must be governed through consensus. This places the national government on equal footing with its subordinate governments individually but not collectively. Thus antagonistic positions will not get them anywhere despite their political authority but laws not passed by the legislatures, and regulations set in administrative law but not enforced, can be enacted through industry standards and practices decided on by government sponsored corporate board members. This can have a dramatic impact on the court system as decisions are often determined by common practices and industry standards. Subsequent laws can be formed from the bottom up through consensual management.

Applying federalist measures of control on public wealth is another device that is available for Solocorporatic states. Unlike private wealth, public wealth can be legitimately manipulated. The higher concentration of public wealth in the domestic economy will translate to more efficient implementation of economic policies. Higher governments can require subordinate governments more money in simple savings accounts. This will flush the banking system with lending capital. They can require more money be applied to municipal bonds or treasury securities. This can soften bond rates and make government operation more cost effective. They can control inflation through manipulating tax rates to complement interest rate changes from the central bank. Higher government can even dictate the proportion of public wealth applied to domestic securities forcing some capital to flow out into competitor economies. With more control governments may be able to eliminate or suppress my bubbles and avoid more busts.

Higher governments won't be able to exert control over the management of companies owed by lower governments nor can they force unnecessary liquidation but higher governments can dictate the use of new contributions or the interest earned on current investments. Government officials and representatives are likely to apply more scrutiny to such measures when it involves their own city or state's public wealth. Thus unnecessary or reckless policies will likely be vibrantly resisted by governors, mayors, representatives, and senators. At this point some governments may object to other governments setting composition standards or dictating risk allocation but it must not be forgotten that the assets held in permanent funds are public. If a higher government can establish cause for a change in proportions then it is assumed it is for the benefit of the citizenry. In this respect state owned assets can be treated differently then municipal and county assets as multi-regional areas can be treated with different economic policies stemming from the federalist controls.

Marginal positions restrict the proportion of company stock they may own as well as the proportion of their permanent fund which is comprised of the stock. This will protect against political compromise because the proportions of gains earned through the company will be relatively small compared to the sum of all income earned from a national permanent fund's investments. There will be little incentive to endanger public welfare or fleece their residents. There are already huge incentives for politicians to bend to the will of commerce. We permit huge amounts of money to be donated to political campaigns. We allow our retired representatives to take jobs with companies they lobbied for while in office. We allow them to maintain their own personal wealth no matter what inherent conflicts may arise. If anything is true, government investment will secure the scrutiny that was always needed but was recklessly avoided.

Prior to this phase governments could own not own a majority of market share with any company principally owned by an individual government or collection of governments. This relegated C-G Corporations to an inferior position with respects to private industry. Solocorporatocracies unleash government ownership and competition in the domestic economy when market share limits are lifted. This is the delineating quality in a Solocorporatic format of commercial government. Solocorporatic governments are no longer limited to <48% gross ownership nor <48% markets share and thus their C-G Corporations can occupy a superior position to that of private industry. Government industry still has no inherent advantage over private industry. C-G Corporations continue to be regarded simply as additional competitive parties. All forms of commerce must conform to antitrust and monopoly laws, anti-collusion laws, and fair business practices legislation. Solocorporatic industries must also remain profitable and rely on conventional capitalization techniques to fund their companies or face bankruptcy or liquidation.

Whereas the Solocorporatocracy-minor still limits constituent governments to at most a minority degree of ownership the Solocorporatocracy-major combines unrestricted market share with entitlements of majority ownership. It is actually much closer in origins to the Corporatocracy as they share most attributes and entitlements but it of course expands allows majority ownership of market share. This is far more complicating in terms of managing monopoly and political hegemony but it is assumed the necessary regulatory and oversight apparatuses will already be institutionalized within the political and economic structure of the nation.

Solocorporatocracy, major:

Code;
I; A.1, **B.1.a,** C.1, D.1.b, E.1.a.x, II; **A.3.xxx.i,** A.3.x.iii, B.2.3.4.x, **B.2.3.xxxx,** C.2.a.b.x, D.1, E.2.3.x.iii, **E.3.xxx.i,** III; **A.2.x.xxx, B.2.x.xxx**

I; A.2.3, **B.1.a**, C.1, D.1.b, E.1.a.x, II; A.3.xxx.i, A.3.x.xx(c).iii, B.2.3.4.x.xx(c), C.2.a.b.x.xx(c), D.3, E.2.3.x.xx(c).iii, E.3.xxx.i, III; A.2.x.xx(c).xxx, **B.2.x.xx (c).xxx**

Key:
I. **A.1** (national government), **B.1.a** (must manage its own permanent fund with option of applying social agenda), **C.1** (budget subsidy only), **D.1.b** (savings method with 25 year cycle), **E.1.a.x** (separate permanent funds for on and off budget expenses); **II. A.3.xxx.i** (may invest in any secondary instrument, with their administrative jurisdictions to a marginal degree), **A.3.x.iii** (may invest in any secondary instrument to a majority degree in foreign jurisdictions), **B.2.3.4.x** (may invest in any form of debt be it public, corporate, or personal debt, in foreign jurisdictions), **B.2.3.xxx** (may utilizing public and corporate debt from companies and governments that originate from their administrative jurisdictions), **C.2.a.b.x** (may utilize any residential or commercial real estate in foreign jurisdictions), **D.1** (currency trades prohibited), **E.2.3.x.iii** (may invest in venture capital or primary security instrument to a majority degree, including starting new businesses, but in foreign jurisdictions only), **E.3.xxx.i** (may invest to a marginal degree using primary security instruments within their administrative jurisdictions); **III.A.2.x.xxx** (gross ownership is unrestricted in foreign and administrative jurisdictions), **B.2.x.xxx** (market share is unrestricted in foreign and administrative jurisdictions).

I. **A.2.3** (regional and local governments), **B.1.a** (must manage its own permanent fund with option of applying social agenda), **C.1** (budget subsidy only), **D.1.b** (savings method with 25 year cycle), **E.1.a.x** (has multiple funds for on and off budget expenses), **II. A.3.xxx.i** (may invest in any secondary instrument, with their administrative jurisdictions to a marginal degree), **A.3.x.xx(c).iii** (may invest in any secondary instrument in foreign countries and opposing domestic regional economies to a majority degree), **B.2.3.xxx** (may invest in public and corporate debt within its own administrative jurisdiction), **B.2.3.4.x.xx(c)** (may invest in any form of debt be it public, corporate, or personal debt, in foreign and opposing regional jurisdictions), **C.2.a.b.x.xx(c)** (may invest in any residential or commercial real estate in foreign or opposing regional jurisdictions), **D.3** (may trade any currency), **E.3.xxx.i** (may invest in primary instruments, up to a marginal degree in administrative jurisdictions), **E.2.3.x.xx(c).iii** (may invest in primary security instruments, up to a majority degree in foreign or opposing regional jurisdictions, and may even initiate new businesses), **III.A.2.x.xx(c).xxx** (gross ownership is unrestricted in all jurisdictions), **B.2.x.xx(c).xxx** (allowed unrestricted market share in foreign and domestic economies, including administrative jurisdictions).

Within the structure of the **Solocorporatocracy-major** all of its lower governments have the same liberal entitlement to majority ownership within competitor jurisdictions that Corporatocracy-major commercial government systems have but they also incorporate the Competitive State Capitalist characteristics where national governments can involve themselves within the local economy and all governments are granted the ability to maintain majority interests of market share.

Additions to national government **(I.A.1...)** entitlements include;

- **II.A.3.xxx.i** (may invest in secondary security instruments to a marginal degree within its administrative jurisdiction),
- **II.B.2.3.xxx** (may invest in any public and corporate debt instruments even when they originate from their own administrative jurisdiction),

- **II.E.3.xxx.i** (may invest in any primary securities to a marginal degree within its own administrative jurisdiction),
- **III.A.2.xxx** (gross ownership is unrestricted within their administrative jurisdictions)
- And **III.B.2.xxx** (government owned companies may acquire a majority in market share within their administrative jurisdictions).

The national government also substitutes;

- I.B.3.a with **B.1.a** (must manage its own permanent fund with option of applying social agenda).

Their lower governments **(I.A.2.3…)** substitute;

- I.B.3.a with **B.1.a** (must manage its own permanent fund with option of applying social agenda).
- And III.B.1.xx.xxx with **III.B.2.x.xx.xxx** (government owned companies may acquire majorities in market share within foreign jurisdictions, opposing regional jurisdictions, and their own administrative jurisdictions).

This system is by far the most efficient in terms of wealth conservation. It is expected that competing governments will now own the lion's share of private and public companies. This means that most of the profits earned by businesses within the country are now applied to reducing tax liabilities, producing dividends, or improving government sponsored benefits. Private competition is never discouraged and the higher wages, lower taxes, and dividends should promote more small business creation but when they prove themselves successful it is likely a government will at least offer to buy it out. Although class differentiation does exist the quality of living for most residents should be improved to middle class standards.

There should be no doubt that this configuration presents itself as an alternative to traditional capitalism but it is far from socialist: government still doesn't control all means to production and distribution in the traditional sense, commerce is still facilitated by competing interests each controlling only some aspects of manufacturing, distribution, or sales, but the industrial bases to start to aggregate within the larger states and cities.

Competition is still the dominant force in the economy regardless of whom or what constitutes the owner's class.

The most aggressive Competitive State Capitalist commercial government is the Solocorporatocracy-general. The first two Solocorporatocracies were focused on profit sharing. This version concentrates on interest bearing and its expanded entitlements are meant to allow higher government much more control over subordinate governments through their C-G Corporations. Solocorporatocracy-general systems allow for governments to invest up to a minority degree in those C-G Corporations operating or originating from within their administrative jurisdiction. This only applies if the company is majority owned (>51%) by one or more domestic governments. All private companies operating within the administrative jurisdiction are protected and the government is still relegated to marginal positions. The increased interface between government and industry resembles traditional socialism but is far less intrusive.

Solocorporatocracy, general:

Code;
I; A.1, B.1.a, C.1, D.1.b, E.1.a.x, II;A.3.x.iii, **A.3.xxx.ii**, B.2.3.xxx, B.2.3.4.x, C.2.a.b.x, D.1, E.2.3.x.iii, **E.3.xxx.ii**,
III; A.2.x.xxx, B.2.x.xxx

I; A.2.3, B.1.a, C.1, D.1.b, E.1.a.x; II.A.3.x.**xx(cc)**.iii, **A.3.xxx.ii,** B.2.3.4.x.**xx(cc)**, B.2.3.xxx, C.2.a.b.x.**xx(cc)**, D.3,E.2.3.x.**xx(cc)**.iii,**E.3.xxx.ii,** III;A .2.x.**xx(cc)**.xxx, B.2.x.**xx(cc)**.xxx

Key;

I. **A.1** (national government), **B.1.a** (must manage permanent fund itself with social agenda), **C.1** (budget subsidy only), **D.1.b** (savings method with 25 year cycle), **E.1.a.x** (separate permanent funds for on and off budget expenses), **II. A.3.x.iii** (may invest in any secondary instrument to a majority degree in foreign jurisdictions), **A.3.xxx.ii** (may invest in any secondary instruments to a minority degree within their administrative jurisdictions), **B.2.3.xxx** (may utilizing public and corporate debt from companies and governments that originate from their administrative jurisdictions), **B.2.3.4.x** (may invest in any form of debt be it public, corporate, or personal debt, in foreign jurisdictions), **C.2.a.b.x** (may utilize any residential or commercial real estate in foreign jurisdictions), **D.1** (currency trades prohibited), **E.2.3.x.iii** (may invest in venture capital or primary security instrument to a majority degree, including starting new businesses, but in foreign jurisdictions only), **E.3.xxx.ii** (may invest in primary securities to a minority degree in their administrative jurisdictions), **III.A.2.x.xxx** (gross ownership is unrestricted in foreign and administrative jurisdictions), **B.2.x.xxx** (market share is unrestricted in foreign and administrative jurisdictions).

I. **A.2.3** (regional and local governments), **B.1.a** (must manage permanent fund itself with social agenda), **C.1** (budget subsidy only), **D.1.b** (savings method with 25 year cycle), **E.1.a.x** (has multiple funds for on and off budget expenses), **II. A.3.xxx.ii** (may invest in any secondary instruments to a minority degree within their administrative jurisdictions), **A.3.x.xx(cc).iii** (may invest in any secondary instrument in foreign countries and opposing domestic economies to a majority degree, with opposing jurisdictions based on municipal boundaries), **B.2.3.xxx** (may invest in public and corporate debt within its own administrative jurisdiction), **B.2.3.4.x.xx(cc)** (may invest in any form of debt be it public, corporate, or personal debt, in foreign and opposing jurisdictions, based on municipal boundaries), **C.2.a.b.x.xx(cc)** (may invest in any residential or commercial real estate in foreign or opposing municipal jurisdictions), **D.3** (may trade any currency), **E.3.xxx.ii** (may invest in primary securities to a minority degree in their administrative jurisdictions), **E.2.3.x.xx(cc).iii** (may invest in primary security instruments, up to a majority degree in foreign or opposing jurisdictions, with opposing jurisdictions defined by municipal boundaries, and may even initiate new businesses), **III.A.2.x.xx(cc).xxx** (gross ownership is unrestricted in all jurisdictions), **B.2.x.xx(cc).xxx** (allowed unrestricted market share in foreign and domestic economies, including their administrative jurisdictions).

The **Solocorporatocracy-general** allows for the greatest involvement by governments within their administrative jurisdictions without succumbing to overtly socialist entitlements. It should employ federalist measures of control on the permanent funds of its constituent governments to help with any deficits in the competitive market caused by a large concentration of public wealth.

All of the constituent government permanent funds **(I.A.1.2.3....)** substitute;

- I.B.3.a with **I.B.1.a** (the government must manage its own fund and it can apply a social agenda with ownership positions),
- II.A.3.xxx.iv with **II.A.3.xxx.ii** (they may invest in any secondary market security to a minority degree within their administrative jurisdictions),
- II.E.3.xxx.iv with **II.E.3.xxx.ii** (they may invest in primary market securities to a minority degree within their administrative jurisdictions),
- And .xx(c) with **.xx(cc)** for all instruments in section II and limitations in section III (competitor jurisdictions are now based on municipal boundaries and not regional boundaries)

Allowing minority ownership of companies operating within or originating from their administrative jurisdictions gives higher governments more control over lower governments which have earned a higher degree of independence. Without question one of the principle ways a national government, or state government reigns in control over subordinate governments is by withholding tax rebates. When these lower governments have vast stores of public wealth at their disposal they can act out more because they have greater financial independence. In order to counteract this trend higher government can infiltrate the corporate boards of lower government's competitive incorporations. Stock ownership entails certain privileges and higher governments can leverage these rights within the court system to coerce cooperation or transparency. They can then use their wealth to forward political agendas or economic policies through the companies owned by their constituent governments.

Solocorporatic-general national governments are still unable to trade currency on the foreign currency exchange. This can be amended to authorize trades of foreign currencies while excluding trade of their national currency but this requires a level of trust that should not be easily gained. Nor can they profit from domestically located real estate. Although the national government is giving limited authority to own equity stakes in companies operating within its administrative governments this is primarily for political reasons, permitting a government to buy, sell, renovate, or develop real estate will compromise its ability to legitimately apply zoning laws, property taxes, and law enforcement. Transgression of this boundary is what separates Competitive State Capitalist commercial governments from Neo-Populist commercial governments. They permit governments to limited competition within their own administrative jurisdictions and that includes entitlements to equity positions, government and commercial bonds, private debt, and real estate located within their administrative jurisdictions.

In most versions of commercial government competitor jurisdictions are defined in terms of regional boundaries so that municipalities from the same state or province can't invest in or compete in their neighbor's jurisdictions. The Solocorporatocracy-general defines a competitive jurisdiction along municipal boundaries. Governments can now comingle economic gain with political favor by competing in opposing municipal jurisdictions within the same region. Ordinarily non competitive socialist states avoid this configuration because this configuration predisposes local governments to more political intersections and corruption but when governments are able to maintain minority positions in companies within their administrative jurisdictions there is less concern that a competing government will monopolize commerce within those jurisdictions.

There is only one trend left to describe in commercial government. It is a form of regression in that certain jurisdictions are authorized to own majority positions in companies and traffic in instruments that originate from or operate in their administrative jurisdiction. This must be a controlled experiment or it will most certainly compromise an economy. A government that seeks profit from residents within its jurisdiction will be more prone to corruption and abuse of those people but employing nonprofit commercial institutions can erase many of the horrible inequalities or injustices inherent in a capitalist economy. I-A Corporations are simply a platform for municipalities (states and nations) to offer government services partially funded by the government and partially paid for by the resident consumers. Proliferation of Intra-Administrative Corporations (I-A Corporations) within a state or nation will improve the standard of living for many of a locations poorest people and the rules governing them will ensure that private industry or C-G Corporations are not overly disadvantaged by the lower cost products offered.

Cooperatives are nonprofit organizations where members can receive products or services free of markup. I-A Corporations resemble privately incorporated cooperatives in every functional aspect except that the original funding comes the government and most private cooperatives don't receive tax breaks during their operation. Cooperatives perpetuate their own operation by charging just enough to pay for overhead and future gross inventory. In this respects I-A Corporations will sustain themselves from sales charges and will not cause their sponsoring governments to continue devoting tax revenues to the government benefits. Their reliance on sales incomes to overcome overhead introduces free market pricing pressures which is a much sounder practice for providing government benefits than a socialist market which depends solely on rationing. The fact that most cooperatives require membership conforms nicely to the fact the only residents should have access to subsidized goods and all regular consumers can be excluded from their markets.

Most contemporary socialist "Cooperatives" are state funded and are not required to price their products to recuperate costs. Nationalized industries provide no tax revenue and most conventional governments rely on taxes on private industry to fund all of their programs. As a result conventional socialist versions of cooperatives are unsustainable. Not only are they a constant drain of government resources but they impede ordinary market economy. They are generally monopolistic, stamping out all private competition. I-A Corporations are meant to co-exist with competitive private companies. There will always be alternatives to government sponsored services and products. Populist governments will be forced to balance their benefits versus tax revenue producing companies creating limits on subsidized lifestyles. Unlike conventional socialist cooperatives I-A Corporations can t operate at a loss with governments making up the difference between revenue and overhead. Populist cooperatives will fail if there is not adequate public support for their products.

All I-A Corporations are restricted in funding in the same way C-G Corporations are. Permanent Fund capital is applied only once and the I-A Corporation is expected to perform its role without future government subsidy. This will ensure that there is no dumping or uncompetitive pricing. It will have to charge enough money for products and services to fund its own operation. It will have to rely on conventional commercial loans to expand into new regions or float losses. This will result in higher cost products until the loan is repaid but the alternative would completely eliminate all aspects of a competitive market. This may cause more markups and erase the pricing differences between I-A Corporation and C-G Corporation or private industry. Governments can't simply subsidize the costs of the sponsored benefit. Allowing cash infusions from either the permanent fund or general fund will also drain resources and cause higher taxes. I-A Corporations will be allowed to keep a small percentage of profit to protect against insolvency but this will be closely monitored. They will be allowed to fail when mismanaged or rendered unnecessary by other market conditions.

There are two main mechanisms in an I-A Corporation's operation that will allow it to provide lower cost products to its residents. The first, or generic method, is simply not charging customers for profit. The I-A Corporation markup their products only so much as to compensate for rent costs, employee costs, and inventory costs. I-A Corporations will have to include all overhead into the price of their products so that they become self sufficient. Many I-A Corporations will still recapture a little profit from year to year to help defray unexpected expenditures or losses in future revenue and to avoid bankruptcy. Normally markup would produce profits for the business owners but since it is nonprofit there will be a net reduction of 10 or 15% in consumer cost. This may seem like a nominal amount but I-A Corporations focus on the needs of the poorest residents and 15% decrease in grocery or utility costs can be the difference between starving or suffering from hypothermia.

The second, or specific method, is gaining tax exempt status. Tax exempt status can only be gained by offering certain necessities such as food, clothing, shelter, or utilities, and even then only part of their total tax liabilities can be avoided. Municipal owned I-A Corporations will be exempt from their own property taxes but will continue to have to pay state income, payroll, and sales taxes. They will also be responsible for paying national income taxes, capital gains taxes if applicable, and of course payroll taxes. Regionally owned I-A Corporations will have to pay municipal property taxes as well as national income taxes but be exempt from their own sales or income taxes. No I-A Corporation will ever be exempt from payroll taxes, not even national I-A Corporations simply because the contribute revenue into specific social insurance programs.

Municipal I-A Corporations are the most efficient form of populist entitlement because tax exemption from property taxes will reduce overhead and that will directly affect product costs. In some extreme circumstances rent or real estate tax can represent 20-30% of overhead and this will translate to a significant advantage in price for the I-A Corporation's product. They can combine the 10 or 15% reduction as a nonprofit with the 20-30% reduction in price from tax exempt status. This will result in the cheapest pricing for I-A Corporation products. State and national I-A Corporation can gain tax exempt status on sales, income, or capital gains taxes from their own jurisdiction but this will barely move product pricing. I-A Corporations are nonprofit and the majority of those taxes are applied to revenues. With the benefits focused on municipal I-A Corporations every competitor jurisdiction can be assured that their capital investments won't be made superfluous by their transition to a Neo-Populist system.

Most regional and national I-A Corporations will therefore only be able to offer a discount of 10-15% on the products or services they offer. Regardless of the overall reduction in product costs the beneficial affects should not be underestimated. Most of the Neo-Populist states will have halted their budget subsidy programs and diverted public wealth into producing dividends. A slight discount on products combined with large dividend checks will provide the poorest residents with the help they need. Dividends applied to these products will simulate nearly completely subsidized government benefits. Despite I-A Corporations being slightly advantaged in terms of product pricing residents and citizens will have the opportunity to spend dividend checks on non I-A Corporation products. This promotes consumerism and protects selection.

Neo-Populist entitlements are staged so that I-A Corporations may be authorized for one type of government at the exclusion of another. Integrating I-A Corporations from multiple tiers of government makes higher government's I-A Corporations more useful for implementing more universal government benefits. When nonprofit municipal manufactures sell their low cost products to nonprofit regional retailers the effects of eliminating markup is compounded and an even lower cost product can be offered. This effect is exacerbated if it happens to be a necessity and the originating municipality has gained tax exempt status. An I.A.C. of one jurisdiction can sell products to an I.A.C. from another jurisdiction as long as it is a mutually beneficial partnership. A municipal I.A.C can manufacture and sell clothing to the I.A.C of its principle regional jurisdiction but not to a competitor I.A.C. in another state. Likewise, the municipal I.A.C. can sell products to a national I.A.C. retailer but not to I-A Corporations operating in foreign countries (unless integrating blocs).

I-A Corporations are regulated in how they may interact with non Intra-administrative Corporations. I-A Corporations can never sell reduced cost products to C-G Corporations or private industry regardless of whether or not it is a necessity or a luxury. A private retailer has no right buying reduced price goods from I-A Corporations, apply larger than usual markups and selling them back to residents or citizens. This would cause a gross imbalance in the competitive market economy and create rampant corruption. I-A Corporations can still retail or market products made from C-G Corporations or private industry within their administrative jurisdictions but they couldn't infiltrate competitor jurisdictions' economies. There is simply no incentive to do so and it would erode the other jurisdiction's ability to raise tax revenue.

Overall market share of I-A Corporations will be determined by a constructive scale adding lower level I.A.C. market share with higher government's I.A.C. market share so the combined market share does not have a monopolistic hold over any specific region or state. This is true of both the minor and major varieties of Monocorporatocracy and the Commucorporatocracy. It simulates the constructive market share schedule applied to C-G Corporations in the Competitive State Capitalist and Neo-populist systems. All I-A Corporations provide uncompetitive services so their tally should directly oppose the total market share of competitive industries. The balance should always favor private industry and C-G Corporations. Maintaining a large number of competitive governments operating within the national economy is necessary to perpetuate government funding and employment. Higher government will retain authority to force divestiture of any assets compromising local economies including nonprofit cooperatives.

When a government purchases a majority-partial position in a multi-national or multi-regional company that competes heavily within their principle jurisdiction then that company must continue to offer products at comparable prices within competitor jurisdictions or comparable prices to competitor's products within the same jurisdiction. Other shareholders have the right to protect their interests and by mandating competitive pricing it ensures losses won't be purposefully caused. They cannot earn tax exemption and they cannot perform the service as a nonprofit I.A.C. would. Products and services from public profit corporations can't be commandeered for the purpose of offering subsidized government benefits. The regulatory agencies of higher governments will provide oversight and the courts will address complaints from residents, shareholders, and competitors. The simplest solution to this conundrum is having the assets concerned with their administrative jurisdiction spun-off after a third party audit and sold separately to the jurisdiction so it can convert the service to a government sponsored benefit.

If the government purchasing all outstanding shares of a multiregional company it can appropriate those operations within its jurisdiction for use as an I-A Corporation. Although it is in essence one company it separates profit seeking operations from nonprofit. Nonprofit operations follow the ordinary I-A Corporation formula and must fund themselves adequately enough through service charges on residents to continue its operations. In all other jurisdictions it can lawfully pursue profits and its primary agenda does not change. Governments can appropriate complete equity shares in companies operating solely in their administrative jurisdiction with the sole intent to transmute the service into a government benefit. In this situation it is especially important that it earns enough from sales to justify continued operations. Richer jurisdictions will no doubt to translate profits into better recreational, entertainment, wealth management, banking and insurance benefits and they can accomplish this primarily through I-A Corporations with residency necessary for membership to the cooperative.

The purpose of authorizing I-A Corporations is to create a system of government entitlement without completely usurping market share or eliminating competition. Private Industry will always be there to offer alternative products and services. I-A Corporations should only be used as alternatives to government benefits directly subsidized by taxes and not as ordinary commerce because they still cause harm to the tax base. They displace other small businesses that would normally be taxed on their revenues. If too many I-A Corporations were operating within a single jurisdiction then the government would see a deficit in tax revenue. This would jeopardize funding for the government if its permanent fund doesn't cover all regular expenditures during a year. The startup capital for I-A Corporations comes from the permanent fund and since they are all nonprofit the permanent fund would already see depreciated returns on its principal. The third disadvantage of a market economy over-saturated with I-A Corporations is that they can extinguish the profits from C-G Corporations operating in competitor jurisdictions thus resulting in tremendously more losses for a permanent fund.

Taxes would then have to increase for the dramatically fewer non I-A Corporations (i.e. private industry and C-G Corporations) predisposing a local economy to financial crises. When the permanent funds earn lower revenues dividend production will have to be cut straining consumers and business owners alike even more. Inflation can spiral out of control unless balance is reasserted between I-A Corporations and competitive corporations. The dangers are many but so are the benefits. A city could take charge of its healthcare needs by sponsoring a health insurance company. A county could protect its natural resources by aggregate control of water and electricity utilities. A small town could even provide its own banking and mortgage services to residents. There is no doubt that larger population bases will benefit a great deal more from I-A Corporations because food and shelter can be cheaply administered to deserving residents. Organizing cooperative can benefit governments of all sizes and be targeted at one demographic at the expense of the others.

At this stage it is a purely academic to discuss whether or not government benefits can be improved with proceeds; the local governments can actively subsidize necessities (food, shelter, clothing, or utilities) through their holdings and operations. The delineating quality in commercial governments that makes a system Neo-Populist is its ability to own and maintain Intra-Administrative Corporations that account for a significant portion of market share. They complement I-A Corporations by diverting public wealth from budget subsidy to dividend production. The combination of low cost products and large dividends will enfranchise the poorest residents with access to basic necessities like cheaper food, clothing, utilities, and shelter. Neo-Populism retains many of the advantages of a capitalist economy but combines such with lower cost products and services for the least economically successful segments of the population.

Neo-Populism offers an alternative to conventional socialism that still achieves the many positive aspects of government intervention without completely eliminating a competitive market. Neo-Populist states do not limit private consumerism and property ownership. In fact they promote such in order to sustain its operations of a government. Private wealth will remain protected be it involved with domestic competitive government incorporations, private industry, or ownership of foreign companies and their securities. Competitive State Capitalism remains monetized which is a substantial difference with conventional socialism. Except for coordinated I-A Corporations all commerce is facilitated by competitive interests.

There is no monopoly of a central bank. There is no usurping of agriculture and manufacturing under single government management. Local economies should still be dominated with small businesses and professional services. There will certainly be some large companies independently owned that refuse to sell interests to governments. Competitive State Capitalism, and more specifically Neo-Populism, disagree with almost every central tenant of conventional socialism and should coalesce to form a more perfect system of economy and entitlement.

All of the Neo-populist configurations use the Solocorporatic-general template so they are entitled to invest up to a minority degree within their administrative jurisdictions. This is a natural check on I-A C. proliferation because governments will have more of a vested interest in keeping local markets competitive. They will have an opportunity to profit while keeping most corporate or business decisions within the control of private individuals or competitor jurisdictions. If representatives are skeptical about allowing governments to invest to a minority degree within their own administrative jurisdictions then they can adapt Solocorporatic-minor and Solocorporatic-major templates to permit I-A Corporations. The resulting systems are still Neo-populist but all intra-administrative investment has a ceiling in that only marginal degrees are allowed. These residents can be better assured that their governments won't exploit them through minority positions in local companies.

Entitlement to operate I-A Corporations does not have to be authorized for all governments immediately. It can be staged so that only specific governments can manage cooperatives. This can ensure that the market economy is not overwhelmed by nonprofit cooperatives. The Monocorporatic-minor model of commercial government limits government interference to the local economies of municipal and county governments.

Monocorporatocracy, minor:

Code;

I; A.1, B.1.a**,** C.1, D.1.b, E.1.a.x, II;A.3.x.iii, A.3.xxx.ii, B.2.3.xxx, B.2.3.4.x, C.2.a.b.x, D.1, E.2.3.x.iii, E.3.xxx.ii, III; A.2.x.xxx, B.2.x.xxx

I; A.2, B.1.a, C.1, D.1.b, E.1.a.x, II; A.3.x.xx(cc).iii, A.3.xxx.ii, B.2.3.xxx, B.2.3.4.x.xx(cc), C.2.a.b.x.xx(cc), D.3, E.2.3.x.xx(cc).iii, E.3.xxx.ii, III;A.2.x.xx(cc).xxx, B.2.x.xx(cc).xxx

I; A.3, B.1.a, **C.2, D.2**, E.1.a.x, **II; A.3.x.xx(cc).xxx.iii, B.2.3.4.x.xx(cc).xxx,C.2.a.b.x.xx(cc).xxx,**D.3, **E.2.3.x.xx(cc).xxx.iii,** III; A.2.x.xx(cc).xxx, B.2.x.xx(cc).xxx

Key:

I. **A.1** (national government), **B.1.a** (must manage permanent fund itself with social agenda), **C.1** (budget subsidy only), **D.1.b** (savings method with 25 year cycle), **E.1.a.x** (separate permanent funds for on and off budget expenses), **II. A.3.x.iii** (may invest in any secondary instrument to a majority degree in foreign jurisdictions), **A.3.xxx.ii** (may invest in any secondary instruments to a minority degree within their administrative jurisdictions), **B.2.3.4.x** (may invest in any form of debt be it public, corporate, or personal debt, in foreign jurisdictions), **B.2.3.xxx** (may utilizing public and corporate debt from companies and governments that originate from their administrative jurisdictions), **C.2.a.b.x** (may utilize any residential or commercial real estate in foreign jurisdictions), **D.1** (currency trades prohibited), **E.2.3.x.iii** (may invest in venture capital or primary security instrument to a majority degree, including starting new businesses, but in foreign jurisdictions only), **E.3.xxx.ii** (may invest in primary securities to a minority degree in their administrative jurisdictions), **III.A.2.x.xxx** (gross ownership is unrestricted in foreign and administrative jurisdictions), **B.2.x.xxx** (market share is unrestricted in foreign and administrative jurisdictions).

I. **A.2** (regional), **B.1.a** (must manage permanent fund itself with social agenda), **C.1** (budget subsidy only), **D.1.b** (savings method with 25 year cycle), **E.1.a.x** (has multiple funds for on and off budget expenses), **II. A.3.xxx.ii** (may invest in any secondary instruments to a minority degree within their administrative jurisdictions), **A.3.x.xx(cc).iii** (may invest in any secondary instrument in foreign countries and opposing domestic regional economies to a majority degree), **B.2.3.xxx** (may invest in public and corporate debt within its own administrative jurisdiction), **B.2.3.4.x.xx(cc)** (may invest in any form of debt be it public, corporate, or personal debt, in foreign and opposing regional jurisdictions), **C.2.a.b.x.xx(cc)** (may invest in any residential or commercial real estate in foreign or opposing regional jurisdictions), **D.3** (may trade any currency), **E.3.xxx.ii** (may invest in primary securities to a minority degree in their administrative jurisdictions), **E.2.3.x.xx(cc).iii** (may invest in primary security instruments, up to a majority degree in foreign or opposing regional jurisdictions, and may even initiate new businesses), **III.A.2.x.xx(cc).xxx** (gross ownership is unrestricted in all jurisdictions), **B.2.x.xx(cc).xxx** (allowed unrestricted market share in foreign and domestic economies, including administrative jurisdictions).

I. **A.3** (local governments), **B.1.a** (must manage permanent fund itself with social agenda), **C.2** (dividend production), **D.2** (defrayment method), **E.1.a.x** (has multiple funds for on and off budget expenses), **II. A.3.x.xx(cc).xxx.iii** (may invest in any secondary instrument to a majority degree in both foreign and domestic economies including their administrative jurisdictions, and opposing jurisdictions defined by municipal boundaries. Unless the equity is used to form an I-A Corporation it is still relegated to a minority position within its administrative jurisdiction), **B.2.3.4.x.xx(cc).xxx** (may invest in any form of debt be it public, corporate, or personal debt, in foreign and domestic economies including their administrative jurisdictions, opposing jurisdictions defined by municipal (local) political boundaries), **C.2.a.b.x.xx(cc).xxx** (may invest in any residential or commercial real estate in any jurisdiction including their administrative jurisdictions, opposing jurisdictions defined by municipal boundaries), **D.3** (may trade any currency), **E.2.3.x.xx(cc).xxx.iii** (may invest in primary security instruments, up to a majority degree in both foreign and domestic economies including their administrative jurisdictions with opposing jurisdictions defined by municipal boundaries, and they may even initiate new businesses. Unless the equity is used to form an I-A Corporation it is still relegated to a minority position within its administrative jurisdiction), **III.A.2.x.xx(cc).xxx** (gross ownership is unrestricted in all jurisdictions), **B.2.x.xx(cc).xxx** (allowed unrestricted market share in both foreign and domestic economies).

The **Monocorporatocracy-minor** uses the Solocorporatocracy-general template but the entitlements permitted by municipal and county governments allow for majority control of companies within their administrative jurisdictions for the purposes of creating government sponsored benefits. Majority control of companies operating or originating from administrative jurisdictions is the delineating characteristic of Neo-Populist systems.

Municipalities and counties **(I.A.3….)** substitute;

- I.C.1 with **I.C.2** (public wealth must be diverted to producing dividends for residents and citizens),
- I.D.1.b with **I.D.2** (they switch to a defrayment method so that funds are immediately made available for dividends)
- II.A.3.xxx.ii with **II.A.3.xxx.iii** (they may invest in any secondary security instrument to a majority degree within their administrative jurisdictions when used to form I-A

Corporations, otherwise they are relegated to minority degrees of ownership),

- II.B.2.3.xxx with **B.2.3.4.xxx** (may invest in any form of debt be it public, corporate, or personal within their administrative jurisdictions),
- And II.E.3.xxx.ii with **II.E.2.3.xxx.iii** (may invest in primary security instruments, up to a majority degree within their administrative jurisdictions and they may even initiate new businesses (for I-A Corporations, otherwise minority degree only).

Additions to municipal government **(I.A.1...)** entitlements include;

- **II.C.2.a.b.xxx** (may purchase, rent, and renovate both residential and commercial real estate within their administrative jurisdictions).

Combining the authority to manage Intra-administrative Corporations with the prerogative of producing dividends with public wealth is an overt characteristic of Neo-Populist commercial governments. Dividends are complementary to Intra-Administrative Corporations as it makes the already low cost products or services even cheaper for the poorest citizens and residents. This will escalate the standard of living of indigent and despondent residents without compromising an otherwise healthy free market economy. Dividends promote consumer selection and the distributed money can be used to purchase any I-A Corporation, C-G Corporation, or private industry products. I-A Corporations present the only viable alternative to increased spending on government benefits as too many government benefits will usurp the free markets and cause pricing and supply crises. The combination of I-A Corporations and dividends produces an economic system that protects those least able to support themselves while preserving a market economy to reward those best able to support themselves.

This is the first time account attributes deviate from the traditional configuration of purpose and method being restricted to budget subsidy and savings in cycles of 25 years. It takes into account the fact that Solocorporatocracy-general models evolve from earlier versions of commercial governments and several cycles should have already been completed enabling the state to maintain minimal taxes. The most efficient combination of account attributes for Neo-Populist states includes the prerogative of creating dividend checks for residents and combines it with utilizing a defrayment method to disseminate the checks. Dividends would be bigger if a savings method was used to accumulate wealth before the fund paid out but a people would have to wait longer before they were compensated. It is expected that dividends will be immediately be made available to legitimize authorizations for I-A Corporations. The change in purpose and method to dividend production and defrayment also allows for governments to immediately start subsidizing more and more government benefits for residents and citizens through Intra-Administrative Corporations.

The critical entitlement that makes the Monocorporatic-minor system Neo-Populist is enabling local governments to maintain I-A Corporations that assume more than 30% market share in more than 51% of their markets. Municipalities or cities can begin to offer subsidized amenities or necessities as an alternative to products and services offered by private industry or C-G Corporations. A town could own and operate its own low cost laundries, bakeries, gymnasiums, and supermarkets. It could even offer wealth management, banking, and insurance products. More importantly it can assume ownership of properties for low income housing in the jurisdiction or bargain for control of local utilities. If a necessary product or service was absent in the town then the town could organize an establishment to offer the services through an I-A Corporation.

The Monocorporatocracy-minor balances localized socialization with the limited facility and capability of local government. They generally do not have enough capital resources to eliminate private interests competing within their jurisdictions and thus can't disrupt the competitive market. I-A Corporations will have to be balanced against revenue producing private industry so that the tax base is protected. State laws still have supremacy to their subordinate lower governments and local governments have no direct representation in national government. Since government sponsored benefits through I-A Corporations will not be uniform throughout a state or region local governments will compete with each other based on the availability of amenity, subsidy, or product. They will serve as competitive advantages for businesses and residents to relocate to that area which can be overtly capitalist despite the creation of I-A Corporations.

A less reserved Monocorporatic state allows regional governments to complicate their administrative jurisdictions by competition in the regional economy. Only the national government is left to apply oversight over the state governments' use of I-A Corporations. Regional governments represent a concentration of capital which can far more easily marginalize competitive industry within its jurisdiction. More uniform amenities and government benefits are indicative of socialist governments and a Monocorporatic-major system conforms to this precondition. There is still significant deviation from a planned economy but many of the difference begin to erode from the competitive socialist market economy. Even more care must be applied to balance I-A Corporations with C-G Corporations and the few privately owned companies still remaining so that there are enough jobs for residents and so that government funding through taxes and competitive industry is not compromised.

Monocorporatocracy, major:

Code;

I; A.1, B.1.a, C.3, D.2, E.1.a.x, II; A.3.x.iii, A.3.xxx.ii, B.2.3.4.x, C.2.a.b.x, D.1, E.2.3.x.iii, E.3.xxx.ii, III; A.2.x.xxx, B.2.x.xxx

I; A.2.3, B.1.a, **C.2, D.2,** E.1.a.x, **II; A.3.x.xx(cc)..xxx.iii, B.2.3.4.x.xx(cc).xxx, C.2.a.b.x.xx(cc).xxx,** D.3, **E.2.3.x.xx(cc).xxx.iii,** III; A.2.x.xx(cc).xxx, B.2.x.xx(cc).xxx

Key:

I. **A.1** (national government), **B.1.a** (must manage permanent fund itself with social agenda), **C.1** (budget subsidy only), **D.1.b** (savings method with 25 year cycle), **E.1.a.x** (separate permanent funds for on and off budget expenses), **II. A.3.x.iii** (may invest in any secondary instrument to a majority degree in foreign jurisdictions), **A.3.xxx.ii** (may invest in any secondary instruments to a minority degree within their administrative jurisdictions), **B.2.3.4.x** (may invest in any form of debt be it public, corporate, or personal debt, in foreign jurisdictions), **B.2.3.xxx** (may utilizing public and corporate debt from companies and governments that originate from their administrative jurisdictions), **C.2.a.b.x** (may utilize any residential or commercial real estate in foreign jurisdictions), **D.1** (currency trades prohibited), **E.2.3.x.iii** (may invest in venture capital or primary security instrument to a majority degree, including starting new businesses, but in foreign jurisdictions only), **E.3.xxx.ii** (may invest in primary securities to a minority degree in their administrative jurisdictions), **III.A.2.x.xxx** (gross ownership is unrestricted in foreign and administrative jurisdictions), **B.2.x.xxx** (market share is unrestricted in foreign and administrative jurisdictions).

I. **A.2.3** (regional and municipal governments), **B.1.a** (must manage permanent fund itself with social agenda), **C.2** (dividend production), **D.2** (defrayment method), **E.1.a.x** (has multiple funds for on and off budget expenses), **II. A.3.x.xx(cc).xxx.iii** (may invest in any secondary instrument to a majority degree in both foreign and domestic economies including their administrative jurisdictions, and opposing jurisdictions defined by municipal boundaries. Unless the equity is used to form an I-A Corporation it is still relegated to a minority position within its administrative jurisdiction), **B.2.3.4.x.xx(cc).xxx** (may invest in any form of debt be it public, corporate, or personal debt, in foreign and domestic economies including their administrative jurisdictions, opposing jurisdictions defined by municipal (local) political boundaries), **C.2.a.b.x.xx(cc).xxx** (may invest in any residential or commercial real estate in any jurisdiction including their administrative jurisdictions, opposing jurisdictions defined by municipal boundaries), **D.3** (may trade any currency), **E.2.3.x.xx(cc).xxx.iii** (may invest in primary security instruments, up to a majority degree in both foreign and domestic economies including their administrative jurisdictions with opposing jurisdictions defined by municipal boundaries, and they may even initiate new businesses. Unless the equity is used to form an I-A Corporation it is still relegated to a minority position within its administrative jurisdiction), **III.A.2.x.xx(cc).xxx** (gross ownership is unrestricted in all jurisdictions), **B.2.x.xx(cc).xxx** (allowed unrestricted market share in both foreign and domestic economies).

The **Monocorporatocracy-major** uses the Monocorporatocracy-minor template but expands intra-administrative majority ownership to state (or provincial) governments.

Regional governments **(I.A.3....)** substitute;

- I.C.1 with **I.C.2** (dividend production to complement regional I-A Corporation deployment)
- I.D.1.b with **I.D.2** (A defrayment method allows government subsidy to be immediately applied to regional I-A Corporations)
- II.A.3.xxx.ii with **II.A.3.xxx.iii** (they may invest in any secondary security instrument to a majority degree within their administrative jurisdictions when forming I-A Corporations),
- II.B.2.3.xxx with **B.2.3.4.xxx** (may invest in any form of debt be it public, corporate, or personal within their administrative jurisdictions),
- And II.E.3.xxx.ii with **II.E.2.3.xxx.iii** (may invest in primary security instruments, up to a majority degree within their administrative jurisdictions and they may even initiate new businesses when they are non profit).

Additions to regional government **(I.A.1...)** entitlements include;

- **II.C.2.a.b.xxx** (may purchase, rent, and renovate both residential and commercial real estate within their administrative jurisdictions).

The two versions of Monocorporatocracy are almost identical except that the liberties granted to local governments are extended to regional governments in the second evolution. Now, both regional and local tiers of government substitute a limit to minority shares with unrestricted ownership for both primary and secondary stock instruments with the intent of creating I-A Corporations within their own administrative jurisdictions. The same trend applies to trafficking in government bonds and securities, personal debt, and real estate. All regional and local governments have unrestricted use of these instruments regardless of where they originate. Regional government can start consolidating industry and property for use as state-wide government benefits. They are still limited to a minority degree in C-G Corporations and a marginal degree in private or foreign companies. If another country has formed a Competitive Socialist BLOC with another company than investment into their C-G Companies is increase from marginal to minority positions.

All of the Neo-Populist states have markedly more competitive markets than ordinary communist nations although they are nowhere near as efficient as free markets. I-A Corporations can cause serious drag on an economy but are really used only in last resort. Their real purpose is to reduce the tax liabilities of residents by creating a semi-market economy for government benefits. Rather than a government subsidizing the whole cost of some amenity on a perpetual basis it makes a single capital investment with the intent of having those residents interested in the benefit pay for it. This way the state absorbs some of the cost and the residents absorb some of the costs. It should be more cost effective than simply giving tax deductions or direct cash subsidy because the government can offer the goods or services at a reduced cost instead of the subsidy being redirected to profits for private business owners.

It is important to note the differences between a socialist market and a popular market economy. The most significant difference is that the popular market is a monetized system that still protects individual's property rights. Even in Neo-Populist versions of commercial government there is no gross usurpation of industry. I-A Corporations may erode the profitability of some industries but they don't assume complete market share. When a regional government has privileges to be involved within its own administrative jurisdiction it cannot discourage the other local or regional government from competing in that market. Monopolies will not be tolerated on the regional and national levels. This compels participation by municipalities, state governments, and national governments in the economy as competitors through C-G Corporations. The same is true for its citizenry. They too will be able to compete in the local and national economies with their individually owned businesses. Citizen industry will be far less frequent when most medium and large private businesses are transmutated into C-G Corporations but it will not be prohibited.

C-G corporations and private industry will be able to offer alternatives of equal or superior quality to I-A products and services. Commerce is already redundant. Often there are multiple restaurants, barbers, lawyers, delicatessens, retailers, doctors, and specialty businesses all competing within the same town or city. Redundancy is what we call competition and even if a product or service was offered by an I-A Corporation there certainly would be plenty of competition from private small business owners or C-G Corporations. It is very likely that the impoverished will depend primarily on I-A products while the middle and upper classes will strive on competitive products. In this respect the Neo-Populist state can protect its least viable residents while not inhibiting its more successful residents. No government could reasonably monopolize all commerce within its jurisdiction. It would simply tax its permanent fund to heavily depreciating the amount of budget subsidy it receives while also decimating the tax base supporting the government.

Most government benefits are not universally implemented in Neo-Populist systems. Higher governments won't be able to dictate how the lower governments use their public wealth so most municipalities and states will offer different amenities than the others. Some will focus on rental controlled apartments and cheaper food products, others will concentrate on subsidized public utilities and recreation, while a few may specialize in banking and insurance products. Even when similar amenities are offered they will charge different prices. Some will charge more and others less. Variety in government sponsored benefits is a competitive aspect of the economy as long as it is well balanced with income generating commerce. There will always be private alternatives to I-A Corporations thanks to a persistent competitive market. This is a drastic contrast to traditional socialist market economies as there is absolutely no deviation from national wide standards and absolutely no alternatives.

Although dividend production is compatible with any of the Competitive State Capitalist and Neo-Capitalist systems but it is used most effectively in the Neo-Populist systems. When dividends are applied to I-A Corporation products the residents have the most purchasing power and their standard of living can be increased a significant amount more. For this reason all of the Neo-Populist systems couple dividend production with I-A Corporation entitlements. It is also expected that most nations will only acquiesce to the allure of Neo-Populism and I-A Corporations when they have progressed through the earlier stages of commercial government. The nation should have already completed many cycles of budget subsidy and built up an extensive network of public wealth and C-G Corporations. With taxes already depressed to a manageable level the nation can focus on public welfare through dividend production. Of course this is true of any mature commercial government but much more likely in Neo-Populist or Competitive Socialist systems.

A very important quality of all Competitive State Capitalist and Neo-Populist configurations is that their C-G Corporations are securitized. This means that most industry operating within the country will offer stock for public consumption. This is a stark contrast to traditional socialist industry where there was no profit sharing or public representation on corporate boards. Every company where a single government is the principle owner (>51% equity stake) must be made a public stock company. For efficiency's sake companies can be organized around larger holding companies (competitive authorities) but ultimately they must be public. Domestic C-G Corporations must then offer some of the stock for public consumption. The percentage will increase as the government becomes more progressive in entitlements.

The only Competitive State Capitalist model not mandated to return a portion of their C-G Corporation stock is the Solocorporatic-minor but only because none of their companies will be exclusively owned. Solocorporatic-major C-G Corporations must return at least 25% of their total stock back to residents. Solocorporatic-general must relinquish 30% and Monocorporatic-minor systems must release at least 35% of its stock to residents or other C-G Corporations. Monocorporatic-major systems must relinquish 40% and Commucorporatic systems must release a minimum of 45% to other parties. Only the permanent funds will not offer stock: they remain under complete control of the owning jurisdiction. Communal ownership produces several very important advantages.

Securitization ensures that profits from business don't aggregate within one jurisdiction or one population base. Of course there will still be anti-trust protections but this helps legitimize the high concentration of government ownership. In each case a significant portion of a C-G Corporation will be owned by citizens or other competitor jurisdictions. It will ensure that more scrutiny is applied to the operation of I-A Corporations as they will impact more shareholders and more permanent funds. Making residents partial owners in securitized C-G Corporations gives them incentive to support government competition. The uncompetitive aspect of intra-administrative involvement must be held in check by shared commercial interests. If residents are hurt by the propagation of I-A Corporations there incidence will be less frequent and the competitive economy can be better preserved. One of the most important reasons to securitize is that residents will be guaranteed representation on the corporate boards of government owned businesses. This will keep C-G Corporations honest in their dealings with other C-G Corporations and their customers.

When Competitive State Capitalist industry is securitized it helps with class distinction as different residents from the same jurisdiction will have different combinations and proportions of C-G Corporate stock. These stocks will always have to pay dividends. When C-G Corporate stock dividends are complemented by dividends paid by permanent funds it will produce different classes and maintain previous class distinctions within the quasi-socialist state. Those formerly rich from ownership of large or medium businesses will see that wealth replaced with C.G.C. stock (an exchange occurring at market rates). This stock should be of equal value then as it was when managed by private interests. It will be just as fungible and produce nearly the same dividends. Professionals and small business owners will strive in the environment rife with large dividends and low taxes. Better yet, working class and poorer people will have an opportunity to grow their wealth through warrants on C.G.C. stock offered by the jurisdictions they have residency in.

When the government incorporation offers stock and dividends it permits foreign governments and their citizens to retain partial ownership of the nation's industries. As long as returns are being generated by those investments foreign investors will not suffer a loss when private and public companies are transferred to the competing domestic governments. Protecting a foreign citizen's investments helps ensure a smooth transition to Competitive State Capitalism because foreign governments will be less motivated to prevent socialization. Disrupting foreign ownership of assets located within the country can cause severe antagonism and would otherwise isolate the changing state. Markets within the CSC state are still competitive and open to foreign competitors. When foreign assets are protected and open markets are preserved the Competitive Socialist nation should then be able to preserve its relations with other Neo-Capitalist or Competitive State Capitalist nations.

Securitization of nationalized (and municipalized) industries also lends itself to reversing the trend to communism. The socialization of industry occurred in transactions conforming to free market pricing dynamics. This trend can simply be reversed. Each share will already have an intrinsic value and much of it will already be in private hands. If nationalized industries are to be dissolved then the remaining stock can be sold directly to members the public, auctioned off to certain residents, or disseminated by lottery to citizens. If necessary the vast stores of foreign instruments held as public wealth by the various constituent governments can be transferred to the public.

When the Soviet Union collapsed its industry was hastily valued and sold off and a mechanism for returning socialized industry to private hands was not in place. Competitive State Capitalist industry is already valued and conventional stock markets can be employed in its dissemination of industry. Even Neo-Populist I-A Corporations can be updated into profit yielding organizations which can be sold to competitors. Thus Competitive State Capitalist states can be reformed with relative ease which makes their instantiation less of a threat to global economics.

An exchange of public stock between two competitive socialist nations or governments can signal merger and a competitive socialist economic bloc can be formed. Assimilation is more a process of profit sharing than it is an aggressive or hostile takeover when a comparative value in stock can be found between the constituent C-G Corporations to facilitate an even exchange. Stock ownership imparts representation on the corporate boards of C-G Corporations providing integration of the political systems. The nations are still dissected into competitive jurisdictions so the merger of two nations will not create extraordinary conflicts when the entitlements are still dependent on eligibility requirements. Consensus to merger is still required because C-G Corporations are only involved in competing jurisdictions and this introduces a third party which must offer consent to make the operation work. When the process of mutable boundaries is employed different jurisdictions can merge actually causing a change in territorial borders. This is the most profound expression for forming economic blocs because the most complete political and economic integration occurs. In these instances permanent funds are assumed by the consuming jurisdictions along with all of their normal government responsibilities.

The one similarity Neo-Populism has with Communism is that dividends produced by public wealth can go a long way to create a welfare state when combined with the low cost of Intra-Administrative Corporation's products and services. If ever the value of dividends produced by public wealth and C-G Corporations were greater than the base cost of living then the state would have to conscript people into the labor force. In most likelihood prices and taxes can be raised to maintain pressure on the labor force. Although this situation is highly unlikely, and even if so easily fixed, but if it were to occur then the welfare state would coexist with a competitive state within the same nation.

Although the poorest are likely to live in highly subsidized lifestyles and be conscripted into labor pools (for I-A Corporations, government administration, and even rented to C-G Corporations), the middle and upper classes will be gainfully employed in C-G corporations, professional services, privately owned small businesses, or be independently wealthy and have access to a wide variety of higher quality goods and luxury items. This is possible only because public welfare is not tied into government expenditures. Their subsidies do not result in higher taxes applied to the middle and upper classes.

Most I-A Corporations are self-perpetuating and most governments can sustain their own operations through their permanent funds. This limited socialization will not disrupt the competitive labor and product markets available to more motivated or ambitious residents. I-A Corporate products are not free and this will maintain pressure for citizens to be productive. Dividends aren't used exclusively to purchase I-A Corporate products so the poor will likely continue to consume some private or competitive products adding durability and flexibility to the function of competitive economy. By this stage of commercial government the middle class should be the largest segment of the population and very capable of supporting its own production and consumption. High economy (superior products, luxuries, or exotica) will support itself by employing its own consumers. In this respect a welfare state can co-exist with a competitive economy erasing most of the defects in capitalism and not condemning itself to the stagnation of a completely socialist economy.

There is only one more generic class of commercial government to describe. It is the Commucorporatic model and there are virtually no restrictions on government investment and involvement. National governments can completely immerse themselves in the commerce of competitor jurisdictions (C-G Corporations) as well as their own administrative jurisdictions (I-A Corporations). It can employ its own I-A Corporations and coordinate with lower government to create a network of near universal government sponsored benefits. As long as monopoly laws aren't infringed on they can assume large swathes of market share for nonprofit utility.

Competitive industries must be still balanced with non-competitive industries for this system to survive, but more of its public wealth will be located in foreign theatres providing incomes regardless of how compromised their local economy becomes. Most governments will be intertwined politically and economical with each other through partially ownership of the nation's constituent network of C-G Corporations and the Commucorporatocracy will almost certainly need to employ federalist measures of control over the public wealth of subordinate governments in order to tease and whip the economy into fluid function.

Commucorporatocracy (aka Competitive Communist)

Code;
I.A.1.2.3, B.1.a, **C.2**, D.2, E.1.a.x; II.**A.3.x.xx(cc).xxx.iii, B.2.3.4.x.xx(cc).xxx, C.2.a.b.x.xx(cc).xxx, D.3, E.2.3.x.xx(cc).xxx.iii;** III.A.2.x.xx(cc).xxx, B.2.x.xx(cc).xxx

Key:
I. **A.1.2.3** (national, regional, and local governments), **B.1.a** (must manage permanent fund itself with social agenda), **C.2** (dividend production), **D.2** (defrayment method), **E.1.a.x** (has multiple funds for on and off budget expenses), **II. A.3.x.xx(cc).xxx.iii** (may invest in any secondary instrument to a majority degree in both foreign and domestic economies including their administrative jurisdictions, and opposing jurisdictions defined by municipal boundaries. Unless the equity is used to form an I-A Corporation it is still relegated to a minority position within its administrative jurisdiction),

B.2.3.4.x.xx(cc).xxx (may invest in any form of debt be it public, corporate, or personal debt, in foreign and domestic economies including their administrative jurisdictions, opposing jurisdictions defined by municipal (local) political boundaries), **C.2.a.b.x.xx(cc).xxx** (may invest in any residential or commercial real estate in any jurisdiction including their administrative jurisdictions, opposing jurisdictions defined by municipal boundaries), **D.3** (may trade any currency), **E.2.3.x.xx(cc).xxx.iii** (may invest in primary security instruments, up to a majority degree in both foreign and domestic economies including their administrative jurisdictions with opposing jurisdictions defined by municipal boundaries, and they may even initiate new businesses. Unless the equity is used to form an I-A Corporation it is still relegated to a minority position within its administrative jurisdiction), **III.A.2.x.xx(cc).xxx** (gross ownership is unrestricted in all jurisdictions), **B.2.x.xx(cc).xxx** (allowed unrestricted market share in both foreign and domestic economies).

The **Commucorporatocracy** uses the Monocorporatic-major template but expands intra-administrative majority ownership to national governments.

National governments **(I.A.1....)** substitute;

- II.A.3.xxx.ii with **II.A.3.xxx.iii** (they may invest in any secondary security instrument to a majority degree within their administrative jurisdictions),
- II.B.2.3.xxx with **B.2.3.4.xxx** (may invest in any form of debt be it public, corporate, or personal within their administrative jurisdictions),
- And II.E.3.xxx.ii with **II.E.2.3.xxx.iii** (may invest in primary security instruments, up to a majority degree within their administrative jurisdictions and they may even initiate new businesses).

Additions to national government **(I.A.1...)** entitlements include;

- **II.C.2.a.b.xxx** (may purchase, rent, and renovate both residential and commercial real estate within their administrative jurisdictions).

The Commucorporatocracy extends the privileges earned by Monocorporatic states to compete in their own administrative jurisdictions to the national tier. Now local governments, state governments, and the national government can all buy, sell, or own majority positions of primary and secondary security instruments in any jurisdiction it deems as profitable or advantageous. They may traffic in any public, commercial, or personal debt instruments originating from domestic sources or foreign markets. There are no exclusions in regards to which commercial or residential property it chooses to buy, sell, or manage, and it can trade in any currency, even its own. More importantly they can coordinate I-A Corporations across every jurisdiction and in every tier of government. There may be no principle regulator which can safeguard private property rights and settle commercial disputes without at least some bias but this should be mitigated by the fact that a large proportion of C-G Corporation stock must be owned by residents or resident businesses.

Most socialist nations employ planned economies which are generally rife with usury, manipulation, corruption and inefficiency. Populist economies are not yet planned but are heavily managed. Managed economies are similar to planned economies but the majority of commerce will still be facilitated by C-G Corporations so many free market dynamics are still present. The Commucorporatocracy nearly fully depends on federalist control over constituent government's permanent funds to smooth out the wrinkles caused by excessive infiltration of those I-A Corporations which can combine products and services across all tiers of government. Public wealth is employed to facilitate focused capitalization of certain C-G sectors, to manipulate credit markets through cash reserves, to bolster demand through dividends, and to manipulate inflation through different income and sales taxes. The proliferation of I-A Corporations will almost certainly disrupt the ordinary fluid mechanics of an otherwise competitive market sustained by C-G Corporations and a managed market helps defray the inefficiencies caused.

Public wealth will be important to ensure the limited market economy is not replaced with planned or socialist economy. Even Commucorporatocracies must carefully balance I-A Corporations with the commercial base so as to not disrupt public funding or disenfranchise C-G Corporations from its constituent governments. Lower governments are likely to resist the usurpation of market share by national I-A Corporations as most of the competitive businesses will be owned by municipalities and states. Foreign investment and competition will still play an important role in Commucorporatic economies. Most citizens will work for either government incorporations originating from a competitive jurisdiction or privately owned small businesses and therefore have widely varying incomes. This will of course be adjusted by how much in dividends a resident earns from their governments or from C.G.C stock and foreign instruments. Conventional free market pressures will still dictate most product pricing and labor costs making Commucorporatism superior to communism is almost every imaginable way but still lend franchise to its most impoverished citizens.

I-A Corporations can be even be applied in Capitalocratic and Corporatic systems so that governments are still limited in terms of gross ownership and market share but government sponsored benefits can be given to residents. Being able to offer government sponsored benefits through I-A Corporations is one outlet for excess revenue generated by very successful commercial governments. They can make residency more competitive with citizens vying for those locations with the least taxes and best services. These systems would not be Neo-populist because unless I-A Corporations accounted for more than 30% of market share in more than 51% of markets. If these proportions are breached in Neo Capitalist systems then they can be re-categorized as Popular Neo-Capitalist states.

Even very successful commercial governments may suffer from crisis of labor shortages, hyperinflation of domestic currencies, complete collapse of the MCPFS, or if government debt is ignored until it overtakes the nation. Communism may be the result of such catastrophe. There is any number of unpredictable causes for crisis. There are even more predictable causes but they are almost always ignored until it is too late. Commercial governments are as susceptible to economic crisis as traditional capitalist countries and it would not be the first time demagoguery enfranchises miscreants with inordinate political power. Communism is never an ideal state; it is an unfortunate product of bad social engineering. Historically poorly treated people make bad decisions. So do elected officials when no other reasonable solution presents itself. Formerly commercial governments will present opportunity for a new class of traditional communist state to emerge. This new class of Communism will be rife with public wealth concentrated in foreign instruments.

Unless the value of the assets held in the MCPFS collapse every municipal, county, state, and national government will have vast stores of foreign government treasury securities, municipal bonds, stock from foreign and domestic competitive government corporations, and stock or bonds from foreign or domestic private-public industry. This is markedly different from most cases where a nation submits to communism. Even if their internal economic system abolishes private property (or it is assumed by the communist government) public wealth will provide extra capital to barter for necessary resources and products not found within the nation. The nation could acquire the resources and equipment necessary to run a communist state and prolong its survival. Even more insidious is that the communist state can infiltrate another nation through real estate, government debt, ownership of industry, and other normally capitalist operations so to undermine it or assimilate it. When the communist nation preserves its public wealth it could use it to integrate itself within other sympathetic or antagonistic countries.

The penultimate Capital State is a nation whose constituent governments will have transferred most of their equity positions into foreign assets so that all of its government expenditures can be offset while maintaining near maximum proportions of Intra-administrative Corporations. The system will still be monetized and personal wealth will not be assumed but monopoly laws will obviously be suspended. Most C-G Corporations and private small businesses will be relegated to offering luxuries and exotica. Disposable income will be provided for by the dividends produced by public wealth (foreign investments). If necessary, labor forces can be rotated in and out of service for government administration and staff for I-A Corporations. The **Neo-Communist** system may be an evolution of commercial government but it is definitely not the intended effect. Excess wealth can be as destructive as pervasive poverty and the most successful nations may have to learn restraint or otherwise succumb to uncompetitive market economies and conscripted labor forces.

THE GRIS GRIMOIRE

Chapter 5

Traditional entitlements, Departmental capitalization,
Profit seeking I-A Corporations, and
other variations in commercial government

If there is significant gravity to government ownership but equally powerful reservations are still held concerning the impact of government involvement in the local economies then any commercial government class can be required to outsource management of their permanent funds to professional managers. This eliminates most of the concerns one would have with commercial government theory and practice. Third party money managers will never employ social or political agendas because of the requirements of the fiduciary relationship. They will be compelled to earn the greatest amount of profits with the least amount of risk. Government money is still involved in the economy so they are still classified as Competitive State Capitalist nations but there will be very little interference on corporate boards and in shareholder votes. Instead professional money managers will be their surrogates.

All of the ordinary Competitive State Capitalist and Neo-Capitalist sample systems can be converted into a Traditional class of commercial government. The only difference is that Traditional versions must include a mandate for management of their permanent funds to be outsourced to 3rd party money managers **(I...B.2).** All of the original themes in commercial government still apply to Traditional configurations. Some states will fear government ownership of company and relegate themselves to Traditional Capitalocratic entitlements. Others will be slightly more confident and allow majority ownership but still protest to majority market shares owned by C-G Corporations. They will maintain Traditional Corporatic entitlements. Many will see the merits of fully vested and competitive Traditional Solocorporatic systems. Overtly capitalist societies may acquiesce to the allure of Traditional Monocorporatic and Traditional Commucorporatic systems as insulating themselves with money managers and business managers may very well justify their unfettered competition within administrative jurisdictions. The efficacy of outsourcing management of permanent funds is lost in more progressive or socialist classes primarily due to most private businesses being replaced by C.G. Corporations from opposing jurisdictions but this could be one mechanism for profit and power sharing between city and state governments.

Traditional commercial governments imbue all government investment and competition with more legitimacy due to reinforcing the separation of Industry and State. This does not mean vested governments will have no oversight over their permanent funds. Outsourcing can be dependent on performance reviews where successful managers are rewarded with subsequent contracts. Reviews can be based on quarters, years, and even daily reports but both the managers and the politicians will be forbid from applying any agenda other than profits. This should mitigate any fears of government coercion of private industry while guaranteeing the best possible returns on government investments. Mandating governments to outsource management of their permanent funds will change the dynamics of a free market the least. Private commercial interests will dictate over all decisions made for pricing, supply, transport, and marketing.

If the mayor or governor prescribes to the belief that bigger is better than the entire permanent fund can be managed by one firm or individual. If necessary they could appoint members to the board providing oversight. But governments need not select only one professional manager. They can dissect their public wealth into any number of independent reservoirs of capital. Each reservoir can be allotted to a different manager or investment firm. Assets can be organized around function or purpose and imbedded within the same fund. If the fund is large enough to a construction company, an architectural firm, a lumber yard, and a equipment rental company then they can all be put under the locus of one manager. Likewise, the same government could organize its assets around class and separate different instruments into different funds managed by different firms. Allotment to different 3rd party managers can be related to past performance so that more experienced managers are responsible for more money than recently contracted firms or managers. Having multiple money managers can insulate a commercial government from economic catastrophe a great deal. Not only will each manger be forced to diversify their positions, but there will be variety in the strategies employed by each of the managers.

Outsourcing relieves the government of needing to employee a wide variety of specialized workers. If it were to manage its own wealth it would need its own analyst, brokers, fund managers, executives, and administrators. The government that outsources management may have to pay fees associated with the service but will not need to pay salaries, contribute to pension plans, maintain employee benefits. Third party money managers can be replaced, quickly swapped out, and their contracts terminated but employees have can't be easily fired. It would take government years of practice to become adequate at managing portfolios or businesses. The large investment brokers already have experience earning high yields and balancing low risk. Serious consideration should be given to Neo-Capitalist governments first contracting out management of their permanent funds so they can gain the necessary personnel and experience to manage larger allotments of money. Outsourcing management can depress the costs of maintaining permanent funds and lower taxes is the primary goal of commercial government. The two are complementary.

The concept of Traditional versions of commercial government should be easy to understand. Governments are allowed to earn revenue from investment capital but they can't be directly involved within the economy. Every class and model previously described can be converted to a Traditional format. Some will be more effective than others. However, there is one class in particular that is fundamentally changed by outsourcing permanent fund management. The Solocorporatic classes' theme is that the concentration of government ownership surpasses that of private industry and that the mode of economy is changed from capitalist to Competitive State Capitalist in accord with the direct involvement of governments within the local national economy. These traits are dramatically changed when the government can no longer legitimately manage its own funds. There will still be an overwhelming concentration of government ownership but it will be private business managers and private wealth management firms controlling the movement of capital.

The Traditional Solocorporatocracy-major is adapted from normal Solocorporatic-major template but it makes one simple substitution. A mandate to outsource the management of their permanent funds to 3rd party firm **(I.B.2)** replaces the option governments previously had to direct allocation of funds and manage the operation of their assets **(I.B.1.a).** In all other respects to is identical to the Solocorporatic-major template. Governments may own the majority of industry but they don't directly control it. Governments can't employ social or political agendas. They can't decide which employees to hire, or which vendors to contract with. All of the decisions that go into day to day operation will be made by private business managers. The composition of their permanent funds will be determined by mercenary parties. Governments will receive most of the proceeds from investment and competition but not be predisposed to the ethical pitfalls or temptation a government would otherwise be exposed to if it managed its own permanent fund and C-G Corporations.

Traditional Solocorporatocracy, major:

Code;

I.A.1, **B.2** C.1, D.1.b, E.1.a.x; II.A.3.xxx.iv, A.3.x.iii, B.2.3.4.x, B.2.3.xxxx, C.2.a.b.x, D.1, E.2.3.x.iii, E.3.xxx.iv; III.A.2.x.xxx, B.2.x.xxx

I.A.2.3, **B.2**, C.1, D.1.b, E.1.a.x, II; A.3.xxx.iv, A.3.x.xx(c).iii, B.2.3.4.x.xx(c), C.2.a.b.x.xx(c), D.3, E.2.3.x.xx(c).iii, E.3.xxx.iv; III.A.2.x.xx(c).xxx, B.2.x.xx (c).xxx

Key:

I. **A.1** (national government), **B.2** (must manage its own permanent fund with option of applying social agenda), **C.1** (budget subsidy only), **D.1.b** (savings method with 25 year cycle), **E.1.a.x** (separate permanent funds for on and off budget expenses); **II. A.3.xxx.iv** (may invest in any secondary instrument, with their administrative jurisdictions to a marginal degree), **A.3.x.iii** (may invest in any secondary instrument to a majority degree in foreign jurisdictions), **B.2.3.4.x** (may invest in any form of debt be it public, corporate, or personal debt, in foreign jurisdictions), **B.2.3.xxx** (may utilizing public and corporate debt from companies and governments that originate from their administrative jurisdictions), **C.2.a.b.x** (may utilize any residential or commercial real estate in foreign jurisdictions), **D.1** (currency trades prohibited), **E.2.3.x.iii**

(may invest in venture capital or primary security instrument to a majority degree, including starting new businesses, but in foreign jurisdictions only), **E.3.xxx.iv** (may invest to a marginal degree using primary security instruments within their administrative jurisdictions); **III.A.2.x.xxx** (gross ownership is unrestricted in foreign and administrative jurisdictions), **B.2.x.xxx** (market share is unrestricted in foreign and administrative jurisdictions).

I. **A.2.3** (regional and local governments), **B.2** (must manage its own permanent fund with option of applying social agenda), **C.1** (budget subsidy only), **D.1.b** (savings method with 25 year cycle), **E.1.a.x** (has multiple funds for on and off budget expenses), **II. A.3.xxx.iv** (may invest in any secondary instrument, with their administrative jurisdictions to a marginal degree*)*, **A.3.x.xx(c).iii** (may invest in any secondary instrument in foreign countries and opposing domestic regional economies to a majority degree), **B.2.3.xxx** (may invest in public and corporate debt within its own administrative jurisdiction), **B.2.3.4.x.xx(c)** (may invest in any form of debt be it public, corporate, or personal debt, in foreign and opposing regional jurisdictions), **C.2.a.b.x.xx(c)** (may invest in any residential or commercial real estate in foreign or opposing regional jurisdictions), **D.3** (may trade any currency), **E.3.xxx.iv** (may invest in primary instruments, up to a marginal degree in administrative jurisdictions), **E.2.3.x.xx(c).iii** (may invest in primary security instruments, up to a majority degree in foreign or opposing regional jurisdictions, and may even initiate new businesses), **III.A.2.x.xx(c).xxx** (gross ownership is unrestricted in all jurisdictions), **B.2.x.xx(c).xxx** (allowed unrestricted market share in foreign and domestic economies, including administrative jurisdictions).

All governments (I.A.1.2.3) substitute;

- I.B.1.a with **B.2** (must outsource management of their permanent funds and C-G Corporations).

The changes made in account attributes of the **Traditional Solocorporatocracy-major** will predispose most C-G Corporations to management by private 3rd party business managers. If all private industry has been extinguished this serves an important role in intersecting government interests with more government interests. Those governments with the highest concentration of ownership will have to contract with governments who own no market share. The wealthiest states won't be able to monopolize power and resource at the expense of smaller less capital intensive governments. Transparency is necessary so that governments can't combine their C-G Corporation market share with that of any C-G Corporation market share that they manage for another government. The same rules that exclude political influence should be applied to 3rd party management so that uncompetitive contracts and exchanges are kept at a minimum. This will be a delicate balance but the thousands of competitive municipal, county, city, state, and national governments will make it viable.

Mandating outsourced management does not have to be uniform. For simplicities' sake the example given included the account attribute requiring outsourcing for all of its governments but more complicated systems can include both methods of operation. It is obviously more prudent for national or regional governments to outsource management than county or municipal governments. Very few conflicts will arise when allowing local governments to manage their own funds. They have dramatically less capital to leverage into majority ownership positions. They naturally need fewer managers because the size of their funds is much smaller. Private commercial influence on politics should be dramatically abbreviated by government investment and it would be appropriate to eliminate an advantage C-G Corporations may gain. State governments are directed represented in the national theatre of politics with Senators and Representatives and this can give C-G Corporations too much political influence. National governments can gain a lot of trust by outsourcing their permanent funds. They may be otherwise viewed with suspicion when making significant purchases or striking certain trade agreements.

Combining forced outsourcing **(I...B.2)** common to the Traditional formats of commercial government with the defrayment method **(I....D.2)** common to Competitive Socialist formats and unstructured purpose **(I...C.4.d)** produces a model that simulates modern government budgetary practices and offers the greatest protection to free markets. As soon as profits are made the interest can be applied to current government expenditures and projects. Not only would the permanent fund be operated by commercial non-governmental managers but public wealth would grow more slowly when compared to funds utilizing savings or rollover methods for wealth accumulation. This can discourage or prevent the nation from evolving into more progressive systems, like the Solocorporatic model, and completely evade evolution into any of the Populist State systems. It is unlikely that the government employing these account attributes will develop more responsible spending and management habits because budgets can be inflated with investment proceeds but in the event governments don't learn these skills at least the people won't be too overwhelmed with excessive taxes.

There is one configuration that preserves a government's prerogatives for managing their own permanent fund money but eliminates many of the concerns that government involvement in the economy may ruin it. Governments can be restricted to broad spectrum instruments like mutual funds, hedge funds, index funds, REITS, or other collective investment instrument. Not only does this predispose funds to the greatest amount of diversification but it also marries government management to private sector management. The full gambit of professionally managed funds will be available and governments can judiciously decide on which funds to allocate money to. They would be free to move their money from one fund to another without being constrained to burdensome performance contracts. This translates to absolutely no government sector influence on private sector corporate governance. No doubt a great many skeptics of commercial government will be placated by maintaining the traditional roles of government and industry. Federalist measures on control can still be employed on public wealth but the variety of mechanisms able to be employed is reduced.

Broad-Capitalocratic

Code:
I.A.1.2.3, B.3.a, C.1, D.1.b, E.1.a.x, **II.A.2.x.xx(c).xxx**,
B.2.3.x.xx(c).xxx, C.2.a.b.x.xx(c), D.3 (national permanent fund is naturally excluded), **E.1.x.xx(c).xxx**;
III. A.1.x.xx.xxx, B.1.x.xx.xxx

Key:
I. **A.1.2.3** (all governments; national, regional, and local), **B.3.a** (option to manage itself with social agenda), **C.1** (budget

subsidy only), **D.1.b** (savings method with 25 year cycle), **E.1.a.x** (permanent funds for both on and off budget expenses), **II. A.2.x.xx(c).xxx.ii** (may invest in any broad spectrum instrument originating from any jurisdiction), **B.2.3.x.xx(c).xxx** (may use any form of public or corporate debt, regardless of where it originates), **C.2.a.b.x.xx(c)** (may purchase any residential or commercial real estate in foreign or competitor (regional) jurisdictions), **D.3** (may trade any currency, the national government can be excluded from making trades), **E.1.x.xx.xxx** (may not invest in any primary market securities, no private equity, and may not initiate new businesses); **III.A.1.x.xx.xxx** (gross ownership is constrained to less than 48% in all applicable jurisdictions), **B.1.x.xx.xxx** (market share is constrained to less than 48% in all applicable jurisdictions).

The **Broad Capitalocratic** model of Traditional commercial government is based on the Capitalocratic-minor template but substitutes;

- **(I.A.1.2.3, II.A.2.x.xx(c).xxx.ii)** for (I.A.1, II.A.3.x.ii) and (I.A.2.3, II.A.3.x.xx(c).ii) (all governments are empowered to invest in any broad spectrum instrument originating from or operating in any jurisdiction),
- And **(I.A.1.2.3, II.E.1.x.xx(c).xxx)** for (I.A.1, II.E.3.x.ii) and (I.A.2.3, II.E.3.x.xx(c).ii) (no government can invest in any primary market securities regardless of what jurisdiction they originate or operate in).

Government architects could reasonable install a limitation on stock ownership without limiting the use of any other instrument. Real estate is already restricted to competing regional jurisdictions so the entitlements will be similar to other nontraditional Competitive State Capitalist models. Public and corporate debt entitlements impart no representation on corporate boards and entail no voter participation so there limited use will still be available. It would be completely unreasonable to create artificial limitations on currency trades because there are virtually no abuses that can arise from even excessive trafficking. The only other major change is that private equity is eliminated as a possible investment alternative. Primary market securities are even more intrusive than stock ownership and a government overly concerned with government involvement will quickly exclude them from eligible investments. It should be stressed that even this ultra-conservative configuration can accomplish the intended goal of budget subsidy rather quickly.

Legislatures can easily substitute broad spectrum instruments for any domestic entitlement while still allowing minority or majority ownership in foreign markets. This limits government interference in the domestic theatre while promoting government involvement in foreign theatres. Although this configuration is not enumerated and explicated it is of equal value to the more adequately explained versions of commercial government. The entitlements chosen will always be situation specific. If government ownership of real estate is anathema to the public's code of ethics than that can reasonably be excluded with no debilitating effect on profits. The most significant point to take away from this sample configuration is that commercial governments do not have to begin installing corporate boards or participating in share holder votes to earn incomes. The separation of state and industry can remain intact without compromising a government's ability to attain solvency and guarantee its sovereignty.

Financing governments with private equities is not a perfect model: The Alaskan's Permanent Fund is subject to wild fluctuations in the value of their assets. This is a major deficit in private finance of governments. Even if managed well and adequately diversified their Permanent Fund is likely to produce diminishing returns in a depressed market. Crashes can erase years of dutiful contributions. The Alaskans will likely be forced to compensate for raising capital through bonds, suspending their dividend, or for the first time in their history levy state income or sales taxes. The crashing markets could set Alaska back for years or decades depending on how fast the general economy recovers. Despite this inherent danger private equity finance of governments is still much more efficient than our conventional public finance system based solely on taxes and bonds.

Alaskans certainly don't consider themselves Communists even though they are practicing a variation on State Capitalism. It is a fact that the State of Alaska owns significant shares of public and private companies and that is pretty close to the socialist model of governance. Socialism would indeed be the product if every other government in the U.S. had Permanent Funds of their own in proportional sizes. That is in fact the obvious theme of the Solocorporatic models of commercial government but it is not appropriate for all people. Think of how large California's Permanent Fund would need to subsidize their whole budget (nearly a trillion dollars) and imagine if it and Texas, and New York, and the other 47 states were also vested in private equities. Now think of how commerce could be impacted by state governments voting in synchronicity for corporate board elections or shareholder votes. And what if municipality, city, and county governments also competed for private equity, a huge proportion of wealth would be transferred to the public sector.

The proliferation of State Capital in a free market may produce fundamental changes; the residents would find themselves persisting under a popular market economy or the country may be reclassified as a Competitive State Capitalist nation. Vested governments can circumvent government interference by outsourcing management of their funds, and this alleviates many concerns of socialization, but the fact remains government money is in play in the domestic economy. If governments vested in private equities seems to risky or is a little too close to socialism the government can still accomplish its goals of budget subsidy by investing solely in municipal bonds, state bonds, and treasury bills issued by either domestic or foreign governments. Public Finance Corporations provide an important and non controversial method to replace private equity financing.

Every municipal, county, state, and national government can imitate Alaska in the formation of a Permanent Fund but devote it completely devoted to public debt. Public debt takes the form of municipal bonds, public authority bonds, state bonds, and Treasury Bills. Rather than incorporating a standard Permanent Fund they will incorporate a Public Finance Corporation and accompany that with a Public Finance Exchange. Public Finance Corporations will have all of the same advantages of Permanent Funds but none of the defects; the twists and tumults of private equity will be avoided and governments will still be able to reliable and generous incomes for budget subsidy (or dividends). Public Finance Exchanges will dictate the proportions of tax revenue which must be applied to municipal bond consumption which must occur within the state or province, and decide how much to apply to national debt products as well as foreign government public debt.

Public Finance Engine:

Code;
I. A.1.2.3, B.3.a, C.1.b, D.1, E.1.a.x; II.A.1, **B.2.x.xx.(cc).xxx**, C.1, D.1, E.1; III, A.2.x.xx.xxx, B.2.x.xx.xxx

Key:
I. **A.1.2.3** (all governments; national, regional, and local), **B.3.a** (option to manage itself with social agenda), **C.1** (budget subsidy only), **D.1.b** (savings method with 25 year cycle), **E.1.a.x** (permanent funds for both on and off budget expenses), **II.A.1.x.xx.xxx** (no government may buy or sell any stock, option, commodity, derivative, or other applicable secondary market instrument), **B.2.x.xx(c).xxx** (may use any form of public debt, be it national treasury security or municipal bond, regardless of where it originates), **C.1** (may not purchase any residential or commercial real estate regardless of the jurisdiction), **D.1** (may not trade any currency), **E.1.x.xx.xxx** (may not invest in any primary market securities, may not initiate new businesses); **III.A.2.x.xx.xxx** (there are no particular limitations on gross ownership), **B.2.x.xx.xxx** (there is no applicable market share inherent in bond ownership).

Nations employing a **Public Finance Engine** will be relegated to trafficking exclusively in government bonds. It is an example of an atypical Traditional commercial government. Regardless of the theatre of the economy every local, regional, and national government can be limited to the equivalent of U.S. treasury securities, state, and municipal bonds (including those originating from public authorities like the PANYNJ and MTA). In addition to endowing all governments with reliable incomes separate from taxation creating an exchange should reduce the future bond liabilities of participating governments making public finance wildly more efficient. A public finance exchange would also ameliorate the many deficits, or inequalities, in our public financing system by creating a system where larger cities or states could buy back national or state funds devoted to the exchange through bond sales.

Trafficking in government bonds does not engender the same risks as being vested in stock or commodities markets. It doesn't produce the high rate of return conventional investments do but they are much more conservative and not subject to rapid depreciation in value. Each asset will be backed taxes raised by the issuing government. This almost guarantees repayment of the bond and protects the original investment of the consuming government. Only very rarely does a municipal, state, or national government default on its bond payments. With a well diversified portfolio of domestic and foreign public debt The Private Finance Corporation's revenue will be almost as reliable as the government's own ability to raise money through taxes. Well balanced governments, those that don't maintain large deficits will be able to secure revenue above and beyond its normal tax revenue (or bond revenue).

One town could apply its contributions to purchase bonds offered by other towns or cities within the same state, it could choose to buy bonds from its own state government, towns in other states, other state's bonds, treasury securities from its national government, or even bonds and securities offered by other nation's central, provincial, or municipal governments. Any public debt instrument is an eligible investment for a Public Finance Corporation. Governments will become the primary consumers of other government's debt. Local governments will likely be the most voracious consumers of bonds. They don't carry the same levels of public debt as large cities and state governments and will benefit the most from the incomes generated by the purchases. Conversely, large cities and state or national governments will benefit most from decreased bond liabilities. They truly stand to save millions or billions from increased competition for public finance instruments.

The increased availability of public wealth for purchasing public debt will cause competitive downward pressure on bond rates. This will initially be offset by private consumption but later in the exchange's development there should be a net reduction in bond rates. If every government set aside 7% of their general fund for contribution to a Public Finance Corporation, and the average proportion of general fund moneys that are raised through bond sales were 5 or 6%, then there would be more money available for bond purchases than there are bonds to purchase. Participating governments could then reduce the rates offered by their bonds.

Even a single point drop in bond rates will produce a 20% reduction in future liabilities.

If only a few tenths of a point are shaved off the governments still stand to save 5 or 10% on bond payments. State and national governments are accruing massive amounts of public debt. Even a slight reduction in bond rates can save them countless millions or billions. These savings are unlikely to occur in the first few years of operation but if contributions are consistently made to P-F Corporations and the capital involved in them continue to be reapplied, then after 10 or 20 years enough money will be devoted to bond consumption to create a net reduction in bond rates and liabilities. If governments run deficits they are likely to be upwards of 10 or 20% of the total tax revenue for that year but after 20 years even a 3% contribution rate will overtake the demand for public assistance through bond sales.

Bond rates won't fall precipitously even after several decades of participation by local and regional governments. Without adequate bond revenues there is little incentive for governments to participate. There will always be an outlet for governments to find more competitive rates. Government capital will flow out of one state and into another when the original location is too saturated. There will definitely be enough circulating money to bring down the rates a little bit, which is one purpose of the Public Finance Exchange, but other national, or international rates will produce more attractive rates and this will satisfy the Public Finance Corporations other purpose of budget subsidy. The reductions in bond rates will only slightly affect the incomes of vested governments. P-F Corporations will be similar to permanent funds in that there revenues remain untaxed. This will make even degraded bond rates much more attractive than comparable commercial instruments. If the current bond rate is 5.5% that will earn an equivalent return as an instrument providing 7.5% interest in the private markets. Even if bond rates are adjusted downward by 25%, which would be an extraordinary amount, a 4% bond is still equivalent to an instrument producing 5.5% interest, or a 3% bond rate is still as good as a 4% rate when compared to private institution profit rates.

In order to make this process much more efficient each region and nation would create an exchange to moderate capital flows. They could dictate how much of the P-F Corporations much be spent on bonds from within the same county, state, or nation.

This is obvious a mechanism for public finance and being such falls under the scrutiny and oversight of those governments concerned. Both small and large cities and states will participate and an equilibrium can be reached between suppressing bond liabilities and maintain bond rates that support budget subsidy. Exchanges can also facilitate actions to support foreign policies by donating capital to the public finance markets of foreign nations. In this respect an act of charity can produce returns and satisfy everybody's needs. The most successful structure for Public Finance Exchanges will most likely be similar to that of the Federal Reserve so that each jurisdiction is represented on a regional board which votes on interest rates and can control money supply. Each regional board will then coordinate with other regional boards and form a national Public Finance Exchange.

If a national government were to devote even a small percentage of its tax revenue to consuming municipal bonds it would go a long way to flood the market. Participating in the Public Finance Engine can work as an ordinary function of rebating money back to the states or local governments. Money is always rebated back to taxpayers through government programs for residents and government subsidies. There are many reasons that this reimbursement is not evenly distributed to the states but there can be no doubt that Federalist tax policy inadvertently favors less developed and less populated states. Larger states like NJ and NY contribute the most tax dollars but get the least back; NJ has the third largest GDP and donates the third most in tax dollars but ranks 50th on reimbursement. NJ residents only see 61 cents on every dollar they send to D.C. It can't be described as anything other than a welfare system when certain other states earn upwards of $2.00 on every dollar their residents pay in federal taxes. The Public Finance Exchange can be a method for these states to buy back more revenue than which would normally be available.

The very same states that are forced to rely on bonds for public financing because less federal money is made available, such as NY, CA, MA, and NJ, would pay less in bond liabilities and have ample funding for their government services. The donator states could raise more money by bonds because they pay lower rates on those bonds. If bond rates are reduced by 25% then they can issue 1.25 as many bonds and raise 1.25x as much money while paying 25% less in bond payments. Those states with more concentrated populations and larger budgets would stand to be gain a lot more than the sparsely populated and poorer states. The majority of federal government expenditures can continue to be spent on the smaller jurisdictions while the PFE would depress bond liabilities in larger jurisdictions. This is hardly a substitute for fair distribution of federal contributions or subsidies but it can erode the blatant disparities.

Public Finance Corporations can easily be implemented on all levels of government and their proliferation will make public finance more efficient from the consumer's and issuer's perspectives. The end product of this improved public finance system is lower taxes for all residents and resident businesses be it produced by lower bond liabilities or higher bond revenues. Having a variable simultaneous municipal bond rate would allow for governments to cancel out the bond liabilities they accrue with bond revenue they earn. Most bond rates within the same state or nation are of an equal value so a government would need to devote an equal amount of money to investment as it gains in bond sales for it to break even. This is not true if variable municipal bond rates are offered for instruments with the same proportions of risk. If a government issued 4% of its budget in low interest municipal bonds (at a rate of 5.5%) for extra revenue and simultaneously conserved 3% of its budget for investment in foreign government bonds (achieving a 7.5% rate) the two would nearly balance. Bond liabilities would increase the money supply for government finance but not impact future budget expenditures because the interest paid and earned cancel.

Public Finance Corporations can even be integrated into an MCPFS by devoting a percentage of taxes for public finance within their permanent funds. This way Capitalocractic, Corporatic, Solocorporatic, Monocorporatic, and Commucorporatic systems can all take advantage of community public finance. Governments could issue bonds to accommodate 5% of their general fund and pay a rate of 3% while taking the same 5% investing that in private equity and earn a 10% rate. The leveraged assets would then produce a net gain of 7% interest. Long after the bond liabilities were exhausted their investments would continue to earn dividends and even more revenue would be captured. There should be no doubt that a properly administered Public Finance Engine could complement every Traditional, Competitive State Capitalist, Neo-Populist, and Neo-Capitalist variation of commercial government.

In the same respect commercial governments can specialize in public finance they can restrict their entitlements to other areas of fiscal or monetary policy. Many countries peg their national currency to an international currency like the dollar. Well the very same countries can authorize their constituent governments to begin trading in currencies as a means to earn extra revenue. Not only will they capture profits from trading but the sum total of all their currency assets can be used as a fiat reserve for their own currency. In more complicated systems a nation could even manipulate the value of their currency by changing the portfolio of currencies they own in the **Foreign Currency Reserve.** The Reserve is not likely to have enough foreign currency to back their national currency from the start but after 25 or 50 years of making contributions and rolling over interest the reserve should have some useable proportion of equity to back the currency. The same countries that are likely to relegate themselves to Public Finance Engines are likely to use Foreign Currency Reserves and the two can in fact be used simultaneously.

Commercial governments can employ other strategies to make public finance more efficient. Rather than each government making contributions to a single permanent fund, the constituent government agencies and departments making up that specific tier of government can apply an increase to their specific budget. An agency could petition for 3% more funding than what is necessary and then apply the difference to securities, commodities, real estate, bonds, and currencies within their own agency specific permanent fund. If only government agencies are capitalized it will result in a gross budgetary increase less than what is caused by an ordinary MCPFS focused on central governments. A significant portion of a budget is devoted to industry tax breaks, farm subsidy, dislocated projects (like congressional research), repaying bond liabilities (public debt), and emergency funding of all sorts. Agency capitalization does not include many of these expenditures so if agencies overcharge by 3%, total government expenditures may only rise 2%.

The capitalization of departments and agencies allows for a government to maximize entitlements when the potential for conflicts is low and to minimize entitlement when the potential is high. For example, a regulatory agency will be forbid from investing in stock of the companies it has specific authority over. The FDIC can be forbid from investing in any domestic foreign banks. A state Department of Banking and Insurance can be excluded from investing in or doing business with all insurance carriers and banking institutions operating within their administrative jurisdictions. Restrictions don't have to be specific. A national regulatory agency like the SEC can be excluded from making any stock purchase and the FTC can be excluded from trading in futures and commodities. These trends conform to the normal prerogative for commercial government to limit or eliminate conflicts of interests. In no way is the agencies' ability to earn profits for budget subsidy compromised because a wide variety of instruments are still available.

Agencies will generally have the same entitlements afforded by the specific class of commercial government employing the MCPFS but each permanent fund can be tailored around the specific exclusion corresponding to the department or agency capitalized. In Capitalocratic departmentalized capitalization most agencies will be relegated to at most a minority degree ownership (II...A.3.x.xx.ii) when vested in competitor jurisdictions and marginal degrees (II...A.3.xxx.i) when vested in their administrative jurisdictions. The rules are listed not the exceptions. If the agency happened to the NJ Department of Banking and Insurance than it would naturally be excluded from purchasing bonds or securities from banking, insurance, and real estate companies operating within their administrative jurisdictions. Their positions in competitor jurisdictions would otherwise be uncompromised. It would be too cumbersome to list which departments or agencies were excluded from what investments so only the most liberal entitlements are presented in the explications. The other classes of commercial government will described in a likewise fashion.

Capitalizing constituent government agencies eliminates some concern over governments interfering with commerce. State Capital is divided among many competitive parts and cannot be combined easily into majority positions. There are tens of thousands of competing agencies and departments within a nation. Each will have a capital allotment far smaller than if the nation were divided into competitive jurisdictions. The sum of all capitalized departments will have less of an impact on the general economy than would capitalized central governments. For many this will be an important advantage over allowing the principle government to invest in private equities. Central governments can leverage their permanent funds much more efficiently and this could be disruptive to a free market. By only allowing departmental capitalization a people can neutralize state capital being employed in social or political agendas. Departments will focus on the public finance aspect of capitalization rather than the political aspect of state capital.

Giving limited financial independence to government departments and agencies improves the national financial security of the nation. These departments will be less prone to drastic cuts in government spending due to changes in the economy. Despite a central government becoming insolvent and bankrupt, the departments and agencies will be able to continue providing emergency and necessary services. More importantly it serves to insulate a department from politicized budget processes. Often a program or department can fall out of favor when a new political party comes into office. Having its own semi-permanent funding will allow it to ride out antagonistic or mismanagement. If the returns are applied to budget subsidy they can make the whole government more efficient by maintain service levels and cutting taxes. Department specific financing can also be the primary means that services produced by the agency are improved by expanded staff, improved equipment, or additional resources.

If agency capitalization is the preferred method for government investment than the account attributes for the MCPFS can be updated so that departmentalized capitalization **(I...E.2.a)** replaces centralized capitalization (I...E.1.a.x). This authorizes agencies to overcharge for funding and apply the difference to their agency specific permanent fund. Those countries that rely solely on departmental capitalization can elect to maintain budget subsidy as their main prerogative for government investment and competition. Departmental capitalization is a less effective means to full budget subsidy because not all government expenditures are accounted for and less money is applied to each of the constituent agency permanent funds than would if contributions were made to one centralized permanent fund. Significant budget subsidy is still possible, especially after a series of cycles are completed, and it should not be overlooked because of the slight decrease in effectiveness.

A Fractal Capitalocracy-general is one of the most applicable configurations of commercial government. The prefix Fractal is attached to the title in order to designate it as departmental capitalization with the appropriate update in account attributes.

It accentuates the primary characteristics of the base model by displacing government ownership across a huge number of departments and agencies rather than a smaller group of central governments. Considering that majority market share is still unattainable by C-G Corporations this model still relies on private industry to dictate industry standards and pace of innovation. The Fractal Capitalocracy-general combines some of the advantages of the Corporatic mode of commercial government but augments the restraint of a Capitalocratic mode by splaying public wealth across a wider number and variety of government organization.

Fractal Capitalocracy, general:

Code:

I.A.1, B.3.a, C.1, D.1.b, E.2; II.A.3.x.iii, B.2.3.4.x, C.2.a.b.x, D.1, E.2.3.x.iii; III.A.2.x, B.2.x

I.A.2.3, B.3.a, C.1, D.1.b, E.2; II.A.3.xxx.i, A.3.xx(c).ii, A.3.x.iii, B.2.3.xx(c).xxx, B.2.3.4.x, C.2.a.b.x.xx(c), D.3, E.3.xxx.i, E.3.xx(c).ii, E.2.3.x.iii; III.A.2.x.xx.xxx, B.1.xx.xxx, B.2.x

Key:

I. **A.1** (national government), **B.3.a** (option to manage itself with social agenda), **C.1** (budget subsidy only), **D.1.b** (savings method with 25 year cycle), **E.2** (only departments and agencies within the government are capitalized), **II. A.3.x.iii** (may invest in any secondary instrument to a majority degree in foreign jurisdictions), **B.2.3.4.x** (may invest in any form of debt be it public, corporate, or personal debt, in foreign jurisdictions), **C.2.a.b.x** (may utilize any residential or commercial real estate in foreign jurisdictions), **D.1** (currency trades prohibited), **E.2.3.x.iii** (may invest in venture capital or primary security instrument to a majority degree, including starting new businesses, but in foreign jurisdictions only), **III.A.2.x** (gross ownership is unrestricted in foreign jurisdictions), **B.2.x** (market share is unrestricted in foreign jurisdictions).

I. **A.2.3** (regional and local governments), **B.3.a** (option to self manage permanent funds with social agenda), **C.1** (budget subsidy only), **D.1.b** (savings method with 25 year cycle), **E.2** (only departments and agencies within the government are capitalized), **II. A.3.xxx.i** (may invest in any secondary instrument to a marginal degree in their administrative jurisdictions), **A.3.xx(c).ii** (may invest in any secondary instrument to a minority degree within opposing domestic regional economies,), **A.3.x.iii** (may invest in any secondary instrument to a majority degree in foreign jurisdictions), **B.2.3.xx(c).xxx** (may use any form of public or corporate debt, when it originates from opposing regional governments or their own administrative jurisdictions), **B.2.3.4.x** (may invest in any form of debt be it public, corporate, or personal debt, in foreign jurisdictions), **C.2.a.b.x.xx(c)** (may purchase any residential or commercial real estate in foreign or opposing regional jurisdictions), **D.3** (may trade any currency), **E.3.xxx.i** (may invest in primary instruments up to a marginal degree in their administrative jurisdictions), **E.3.xx(c).ii** (may invest in primary security instruments, up to a minority degree in opposing regional jurisdictions), **E.2.3.x.iii** (may invest in venture capital or primary security instrument to a majority degree, including starting new businesses, in foreign jurisdictions only); **III.A.2.x.xx.xxx** (gross ownership is unrestricted in all jurisdictions), **B.1.xx.xxx** (market share is restricted to less than 48% in opposing regional and administrative jurisdictions) **B.2.x** (allowed unrestricted market share in foreign economies).

The **Fractal Capitalocracy-general** shares all of the same account attributes and entitlements in the Capitalocratic-general major system but make one simple adjustment to all of its constituent government's account attributes.

All government permanent funds **(I.A.1.2.3)** substitute;

- I.E.1.a.x with **I.E.2** (only departments and agencies are capitalized).

Any typical sample system can be updated into a fractal system. When the primary mode of capitalization is split among departments there is greater diversity in public wealth. This can insulate against terrific losses in the stock or real estate markets. Every ten or twenty years it seems there is some economic catastrophe but pension funds have survived them all. Most permanent fund managers, private or government, will naturally seek to maximize gains will minimizing risk. Departmental capitalization makes proper diversification much more likely. In the Case of the Fractal Capitalocracy-general their abridged entitlements will also be the cause of significantly more diversification than typical Corporatic or Solocorporatic models. Majority degrees of ownership can be more profitable than minority positions but there is definitely a lot more risk involved because of the concentration of wealth. Budget subsidy is much more important in times of crises and diversification will protect income revenue sustained from stock, bonds, currency trades, real estate, and private equity.

Often a commercial government will augment their centralized budget subsidy programs with the capitalization of their composite departments and agencies so that both budget subsidy and increased efficiency are achieved. In these instances the purpose of their permanent funds will be updated to improve those government benefits specific to their expertise or charter **(I...C.3 or .C.4.c)**. The departments also switch over to a defrayment method so they gain access to the interest earned on investments and can immediately begin improving their performance or services **(I...D.2)**. Capitalization will occur simultaneously within the central government and between all of its constituent agencies so that taxes can be depressed while improving the quality to government services. If applied correctly, the subsidy fund will have a vanishing contribution tax (hybrid wealth accumulation method) so that when the departments are authorized to make investments, possibly in a subsequent cycle, the aggregate increase to taxes is still a negligible amount (or the original amount of the increase). Government will become infinitely more efficient with the implementation of a mixed capitalization project.

This update in account attributes can be applied to any sample system listed. Take for example Corporatic departmental capitalization. The prefix Fractal is attached to the title in order to designate it as departmental capitalization. It is also noted that this configuration is supplemental because it is most often used in coordination with central capitalization. All of its liberal entitlements are applied to departments and agencies rather than a central permanent fund. It is nearly identical to the Corporatic model already described except it makes the aforementioned change to account attributes.

Supplemental **Fractal Corporatocracy, greater:**

Code;

I; A.1, B.3.a, **C.4.c**, **D.2**, **E.2**, II; A.3.x.iii, B.2.3.4.x, C.2.a.b.x, D.1, E.2.3.x.iii; III. A.2.x, B.2.x

I; A.2.3, B.3.a, **C.4.c**, **D.2**, **E.2**, II; A.3.xxx.i, A.3.x.xx(c).iii, B.2.3.xxx, B.2.3.4.x.xx(c),C.2.a.b.x.xx(c),D.3,E.3.xxx.i, E.2.3.x.xx(c).iii; III; A.2.x.xx(c).xxx, B.1.xx (c).xxx,B.2.x

Key:

I. **A.1** (national government), **B.3.a** (option to manage itself with social agenda), **C.4.c** (budget subsidy or improved government benefits),**D.2** (defrayment method), **E.2** (only the constituent departments and agencies are capitalized), **II. A.3.x.iii** (may invest in any secondary instrument to a majority degree in foreign jurisdictions), **B.2.3.4.x** (may invest in any form of debt be it public, corporate, or personal debt, in foreign jurisdictions), **C.2.a.b.x** (may utilize any residential or commercial real estate in foreign jurisdictions), **D.1** (currency trades prohibited), **E.2.3.x.iii** (may invest in venture capital or primary security instrument to a majority degree, including starting new businesses, but in foreign jurisdictions only), **III.A.2.x** (gross ownership is unrestricted in foreign jurisdictions), **B.2.x** (market share is unrestricted in foreign jurisdictions).

I. **A.2.3** (regional and local governments), **B.3.a** (option to self manage permanent funds with social agenda), **C.4.c** (budget subsidy or improved government benefits),**D.2** (defrayment method), **E.2** (only the constituent departments and agencies are capitalized), **II. A.3.xxx.i** (may invest in any secondary instrument, with their administrative jurisdictions to a marginal degree*)*, **A.3.x.xx(c).iii** (may invest in any secondary instrument in foreign countries and opposing domestic regional economies to a majority degree), **B.2.3.xxx** (may invest in public and corporate debt within its own administrative jurisdiction), **B.2.3.4.x.xx(c)** (may invest in any form of debt be it public, corporate, or personal debt, in foreign and opposing regional jurisdictions), **C.2.a.b.x.xx(c)** (may invest in any residential or commercial real estate in foreign or opposing regional jurisdictions), **D.3** (may trade any currency), **E.3.xxx.i** (may invest in primary instruments, up to a marginal degree in administrative jurisdictions), **E.2.3.x.xx(c).iii** (may invest in primary security instruments, up to a majority degree in foreign or opposing regional jurisdictions, and may even initiate new businesses), **III.A.2.x.xx(c).xxx** (gross ownership is unrestricted in all jurisdictions), **B.1.xx(c).xxx** (market share is restricted to less than 48% in opposing regional and administrative jurisdictions) **B.2.x** (allowed unrestricted market share in foreign economies).

The supplemental **Fractal Corporatocracy-major** applies the entitlements previously earned by the Corporatocracy-major to the semi-independent departments and agency making up the corresponding tiers of government.

All governments **(I.A.1.2.3...)** substitute;

- I.E.1.a.x with **I.E.2** (only departments and agencies within the tier of government are capitalized),
- I.C.1.b with **I.C.4.c** (budget subsidy or improved government benefits),
- I.D.1 with **I.D.2** (defrayment method).

Every department within a specific government will be able to own majority positions in both private and public companies in every jurisdiction except their own administrative jurisdiction. There they will still be relegated to marginal positions. Departments or agencies from municipalities and states join gain access to all of the normal business functions ordinary commercial institutions have when they operate in opposing regional jurisdictions. This includes secondary stock instruments, public, corporate, and personal debt instruments, commercial and residential real estate, currency trading, primary security instruments (equity) and new business creation. None of the competing agencies in the Fractal Corporatocracy-major may own majorities in market share. This is meant to preserve the dominant position of private industry despite the accumulation of public wealth within the various competing states and cities. If a people are secure with the idea of unrestricted government competition they can always commit to a Fractal Solocorporatic-major government model.

They are treated in every respect like commercial institutions in every jurisdiction except their own. They will never assume nonprofit and charity responsibilities nor will they be able to coordinate with another jurisdiction to offer low cost subsidized products and services. This is true when they operate within their administrative jurisdiction and when they operate within competitor jurisdictions. Their interaction with profit yielding companies from their own administrative jurisdictions will be closely guarded with oversight from antagonistic agencies within the same government, regulatory agencies from higher governments, and of course courts from other jurisdictions. No town, city, county, or state within the same nation can discriminate against them with protectionist measures. They will they never be afforded any special benefits or exemptions from local laws when other commercial interests do not receive the same benefit. Paramount to the success of Fractal Corporatic models is the uniform application and enforcement of commercial regulations and laws. They are meant to protect consumers and providers alike not matter where there origination, operation, or residency.

The fact that a department may not represent the sentiments of the other constituent agencies or parts of the same government does not mean that the traffic between the two will be unregulated. Fractal Corporatic governments interact with private commerce just as typical Corporatic governments do and businesses will continue to be excluded from making campaign contributions or lobbying political officials when money or favor is exchanged between them and their C-G Corporations.. All Fractal C-G Corporations are likewise excluded from making campaign contributions or political lobby with respect to competitor jurisdictions. Considering that there are a great deal more government agencies than central governments and thus a great deal more C-G Corporations each making their own contracts, political influence coming from the private sector should be much more effectively diminished. As a result there shouldn't be many commercial interests left who are allowed to compromise local or regional politics.

Departmental capitalization complements the current trend of privatization being brought on by the private finance initiative. The private finance initiative is concerned with outsourcing government services to private vendors. Capitalization enables governments to expand as private vendors in competitive jurisdictions with the proceeds of agency investment. Agencies can, through its stock assets, gain influence on corporate governance or access financial records of those private vendors their centralized government outsources work to. These measures are in addition to the oversight provided by performance payments and legislative hearings. If the private finance initiative takes a firm root in government funding, and it looks as though it will, then departmental capitalization will be required in order to insure compliance and to compensate for the increase costs.

State or city C-G Corporations can assume responsibility for some of the more sensitive duties normally outsourced in the private finance initiative. The same accounting principles are in play as when private vendors win contracts but C-G Corporations can be held to a higher standard. National government should prefer outsourcing State Department security to a regional government's security firm rather than a private vendor. Other governments are more accountable in their actions. Their political managers are subject to public pressures and their employees are less likely to behave badly or become corrupt. A national government could apply more oversight to a C-G Corporation than a private corporation. Sensitive data can be passed more securely. It makes tremendously more sense that C-G Corporations are used in substitution to private vendors when the details concern national security. Profit is still the main intent of the C-G Corporations so there will be competition between the public vendors for pricing and quality of service.

Budget subsidy is a fundamental goal for commercial governments but definitely not an exclusive focus. Dividend production was previously relegated to Neo-Populist systems simply to augment their subsidy of government benefits but it can easily be converted for use in Competitive Sate Capitalist or Neo-Capitalist systems. Whole nations can convert their permanent funds for dividend production **(I...C.2).** This overwhelmingly benefits residents with lower incomes because they will see the absolute largest increases in their disposable incomes but the increase consumption will also engorge industry with profits but one should not overlook the benefits it has for business owners. Consumption is the engine that drives 75 percent of the economy and rapidly inflating disposable incomes will bolster consumerism and provide the economy long term stability. This is quickly cause businesses earning to skyrocket with a corresponding sharp increase in valuations of their public stock. Trickle-up economics is the soundest economic strategy because it strengthens the fundamentals of an economy which will produce more permanent changes. The owners' class is already benefiting from the increased availability of government money for capitalization so there should be little argument against implementing a dividend production strategy within its MCPFS.

A dividend production strategy can be combined with either a rollover or defrayment method for wealth dispersal. Saving contributions and interest for a future payout day will obviously produce much larger dividends. The defrayment method obviously makes funds immediately available for public consumption. Using a savings method for budget subsidy or dividend production will greatly enhance the efficacy of those programs but can predispose the local economy to too great a concentration of government ownership. In order to slow this trend a government can adopt a defrayment method for wealth accumulation **(I....D.2).** Since only future contributions add to the current concentration of government ownership, and all interest earned on the government investment is applied immediately to budget subsidy, dividend production, or improving government benefits, the Corporatic nation can concede the lion's share of market share to private industry for a much longer period. There should be less government ownership to challenge the limitations on market share and this will mitigate many fears of socialization.

In lieu of I-A Corporations Competitive Socialist governments can simply increase their dividends and allow that to substitute for direct subsidy. Residents earning significant dividends from every tier of government (i.e. municipal, county, state, and national governments) can expect to be able to subsidize a large part of their lifestyles. Those residents earning the least from ordinary employment would still be able to buy enough food and clothing to support themselves and their families with dividends. Those with more comfortable lifestyles will simply become better consumers spending the money on recreation and luxury items. When nonprofit I-A Corporations are eliminated most dividends will be applied to private industry and C-G Corporations thus protecting the free market. Integrating dividend production with the private finance initiative simulates government benefits without actually devoting any permanent fund assets or general fund revenue.

Often producing a dividend will be more compelling than creating a nonprofit I-A Corporation simply because it protects the commercial tax base. Nor does it endanger permanent fund assets and jobs tied up in C-G Corporations (private sector). If a majority of governments are dependent on a combination of commercial taxes and C-G Corporation profits for public finance it makes sense that the country does not compromise itself or others with nonprofit I-A Corporation proliferation. In this respect Capitalocracies and Corporatocracies can provide for the welfare of their most disadvantaged residents without compromising the integrity of their economies with nationalized government benefits. Solocorporatic configurations switched to dividend production can maintain a more precise balance between welfare and competition all the while conserving wealth through its C-G Corporations. All of the competitive political configurations will benefit from the increased consumption and improved living standards associated with dividend production.

Production Solocorporatocracy-general:

Code;
I.A.1, B.1.a, **C.2, D.2,** E.1.a.x; II.A.3.x.iii, **A.3.xxx.ii**, B.2.3.xxx, B.2.3.4.x, C.2.a.b.x, D.1, E.2.3.x.iii, **E.3.xxx.ii**; III.A.2.x.xxx, B.2.x.xxx

I.A.2.3, B.1.a, **C.2, D.2,** E.1.a.x; II.A.3.x.**xx(cc)**.iii, **A.3.xxx.ii,** B.2.3.4.x.**xx(cc)**,B.2.3.xxx,C.2.a.b.x.**xx(cc)**,D.3, E.2.3.x.**xx(cc)**.iii, **E.3.xxx.ii;** III.A.2.x.**xx(cc)**.xxx, B.2.x.**xx(cc)**.xxx

Key:
I. **A.1** (national government), **B.1.a** (must manage permanent fund itself with social agenda), **C.2** (dividend production), **D.2** (defrayment method), **E.1.a.x** (separate permanent funds for on and off budget expenses), **II. A.3.x.iii** (may invest in any secondary instrument to a majority degree in foreign jurisdictions), **A.3.xxx.ii** (may invest in any secondary instruments to a minority degree within their administrative jurisdictions), **B.2.3.xxx** (may utilizing public and corporate debt from companies and governments that originate from their administrative jurisdictions), **B.2.3.4.x** (may invest in any form of debt

be it public, corporate, or personal debt, in foreign jurisdictions), **C.2.a.b.x** (may utilize any residential or commercial real estate in foreign jurisdictions), **D.1** (currency trades prohibited), **E.2.3.x.iii** (may invest in venture capital or primary security instrument to a majority degree, including starting new businesses, but in foreign jurisdictions only), **E.3.xxx.ii** (may invest in primary securities to a minority degree in their administrative jurisdictions), **III.A.2.x.xxx** (gross ownership is unrestricted in foreign and administrative jurisdictions), **B.2.x.xxx** (market share is unrestricted in foreign and administrative jurisdictions).

I. **A.2.3** (regional and local governments), **B.1.a** (must manage permanent fund itself with social agenda), **C.2** (dividend production), **D.2** (defrayment method), **E.1.a.x** (has multiple funds for on and off budget expenses), **II. A.3.xxx.ii** (may invest in any secondary instruments to a minority degree within their administrative jurisdictions), **A.3.x.xx(cc).iii** (may invest in any secondary instrument in foreign countries and opposing domestic economies to a majority degree, with opposing jurisdictions based on municipal boundaries), **B.2.3.xxx** (may invest in public and corporate debt within its own administrative jurisdiction), **B.2.3.4.x.xx(cc)** (may invest in any form of debt be it public, corporate, or personal debt, in foreign and opposing jurisdictions, based on municipal boundaries), **C.2.a.b.x.xx(cc)** (may invest in any residential or commercial real estate in foreign or opposing municipal jurisdictions), **D.3** (may trade any currency), **E.3.xxx.ii** (may invest in primary securities to a minority degree in their administrative jurisdictions), **E.2.3.x.xx(cc).iii** (may invest in primary security instruments, up to a majority degree in foreign or opposing jurisdictions, with opposing jurisdictions defined by municipal boundaries, and may even initiate new businesses), **III.A.2.x.xx(cc).xxx** (gross ownership is unrestricted in all jurisdictions), **B.2.x.xx(cc).xxx** (allowed unrestricted market share in foreign and domestic economies, including their administrative jurisdictions).

The **Production Solocorporatocracy –general** imitates the Solocorporatocracy-general template but updates all of their constituent governments account attributes with characteristics generally found only in Neo-Populist systems. Despite these changes it remains categorized as Competitive State Capitalist.

All governments **(I.A.1.2.3....)** substitute;

- I.C.1 with **I.C.2** (public wealth must be diverted to producing dividends for residents and citizens),
- I.D.1.b with **I.D.2** (they switch to a defrayment method so that funds are immediately made available for dividends)

This configuration does not cede market share to nonprofit I-A Corporations but a sophisticated welfare system is created by integrating the private finance initiative with C-G Corporations and profit sharing through dividends. In the same respects a Monocorporatic or a Commucorporatic system relies on profit sharing with residents through a maximum equity position the Production Solocorporatocracy requires C-G Corporations to release a minimum of 25% equity owned in C-G Corporations back to residents and other C-G Corporations. Like the most commercial governments C-G Corporate stock can be returned to specific citizens through stock warrants based on residency. This should ensure that even poorer residents receive a healthy mix of dividends from government permanent funds and C-G Corporations.

Ordinarily when a system's entitlements permit majority ownership within its constituent government's administrative jurisdictions this only allows them to operate nonprofit Intra-administrative corporations. Governments can traffic in real estate but not profit from it. Its use is constrained to provide partially subsidized residential areas. Likewise commercial loans and personal loans can be made but only as part of special low cost programs primarily for the resident's benefit. True it can profit from trading public and commercial bonds that originate from their administrative jurisdictions but this is common to most commercial governments. Despite being able to create or commandeer I-A Corporations they are still limited to minority degrees of ownership in profit yielding stock and equity positions in companies originating from or operating in their administrative jurisdictions. Simply put, it is usually far too risky to allow governments to profit off of their own citizens. Lower governments could conspire with higher governments for lax oversight, judges can be corrupted, and regulatory agencies can be coerced creating an environment dangerous to commerce. If they were able to profit from such instruments they could be more appropriately described as slave states.

The threat of economic compromise is not nearly as prevalent in departmentalized capitalization. Entitlements generally reserved for Neo-Populist systems can be applied without authorizing nonprofit I-A Corporations. In non Neo-Populist systems of departmentalized capitalization all of the entitlements apply to ordinary profit generating instruments. They can purchase, sell, develop, or renovate any piece of real estate for profit. They can traffic in any public, corporate, or personal debt with the intention of sustaining an income. They can own majority equity positions in any profit generating company operating within their administrative jurisdictions. This is possible because those departments and agencies will be naturally excluded from trafficking in instruments they have responsibility over regulating. Each agency provides a check on the others. The courts will remain autonomous and the voting public will have remedy against usurpation or coercion. Public pressure exerted on an executive branch can cause immediate remediation.

By now many of the competing national agencies and largest states or cities will have attained greater financial independence from the larger nation-state. This will translate into greater political or legal freedoms which will all balance against each other and coalesce to form an economy based on construction competition and cooperation. Competitive business laws, anti-monopoly, anti-collusion laws, and ordinary anti-corruption laws will apply to profit I-A Corporations and C-G corporations alike. These will combine with the natural exclusion caused by department charter to create an environment where consumers and competitive business owners are protected from usury, usurpation, coercion, and corruption. Legislation can be the most important check to the greater influence and independence of national departments, agencies, cities, and states and the people will always be able to exert their will through voting on their national Representative and Senators.

On occasion a fractal configuration with entitlements for profit seeking I-A Corporations is appropriate. This should be rare but it creates an interesting intersection of interests. National military branches like the Army, Navy, and Air force, or the

Department of Treasury, Department of Justice, and the Federal Reserve can all become significant owners-competitors within the domestic economy. Only the C-G Corporations from the largest cities and states will rival them. The Commutary configuration combines Commucorporatic account attributes and entitlements with departmental capitalization and profit seeking I-A Corporations. This of course sets precedent for the national military branches and most powerful national departments and agencies to involve themselves within the domestic economy. State and city C-G Corporations are still a dominant theme as they will be the primary mechanism by which state and city governments earn revenues to reduce taxes or improve performance but they will be tempered by competition by the national agencies.

Commutary (aka Auto-Colonial)

Code;
I.A.1.2.3, B.1.a, **C.4**, D.2, E.2, II; **A.3.x.xx(cc).xxx.iii,** B.2.3.4.x.xx(cc).xxx, C.2.a.b.x.xx(cc).xxx, **D.3, E.2.3.x.xx(cc).xxx.iii,** III; A.2.x.xx(cc).xxx, B.2.x.xx(cc).xxx

Key:
I. **A.1.2.3** (all governments; national, regional, and local), **B.1.a** (must manage permanent fund itself and apply social agenda), **C.4** (unstructured), **D.2** (defrayment method), **E.2** (departmental capitalization), **II. A.3.x.xx(cc).xxx.iii** (may invest in any secondary instrument to a majority degree in any economy including their administrative jurisdictions with opposing jurisdictions defined by municipal boundaries), **B.2.3.4.x.xx(cc).xxx** (may invest in any form of debt be it public, corporate, or personal debt, in foreign and domestic economies including their administrative jurisdictions with opposing jurisdictions defined by municipal boundaries), **C.2.a.b.x.xx(cc).xxx** (may invest in any residential or commercial real estate in any jurisdiction including their administrative jurisdictions with opposing jurisdictions defined by municipal boundaries), **D.3** (may trade any currency, although national permanent fund can still be excluded from trafficking the national tender), **E.2.3.x.xx(cc).xxx.iii** (may invest in primary security instruments, up to a majority degree in any

jurisdiction, with opposing jurisdictions defined by municipal boundaries, and may even initiate new businesses), **III.A.2.x.xx(cc).xxx** (gross ownership is unrestricted in all jurisdictions), **B.2.x.xx(cc).xxx** (allowed unrestricted market share in all jurisdictions).

The **Commutary** resembles the Commucorporatocracy except that its governments are not authorized to create nonprofit I-A Corporations but rather compete for profits in their respective administrative jurisdictions. Generally only fractal structures can sustain Competitive I-A Corporations because there would be too many significant conflicts in interests if only the central government was capitalized. Competition between the departments helps ensure resident populations aren't taken advantage of.

Changes to local, regional, and national governments' **(I.A.1.2.3...)** account attributes include;

- I.E.1.a.x with **I.E.2** (only departments and agencies are authorized to invest in and compete with other commercial parties),
- I.C.2 with **I.C.4** (departments and agencies can use investment proceeds to subsidize their own budgets, they can produce dividends for residents, or they could improve their charted function).

Expansions of all government **(I.A.1.2.3...)** entitlements include;

- II.A.3.x.iii with **II.A.3.x.xx.xxx.iii** (departments and agencies may assume majority positions in any stock, commodity, derivative, or fund to produce income regardless of from where the instrument originates or where its principle area of operation is),
- II.E.2.3.x.iii with **II.E.2.3.x.xx.xxx.iii** (departments and agencies can purchase any controlling shares in primary securities or equities in any theatre including their administrative jurisdiction and may even initiate new business but none can be nonprofit and gain tax exclusions- no nonprofit I-A Corporations).

The success of a Commutary system revolves around the independence of the vested departments and agencies. It would be incredibly dangerous to allow profit seeking I-A Corporations to be manage by central governments but it is possible when they are combined with Traditional entitlements. Even with the separation provided between government administrators and business managers by forced outsourcing the system would take on attributes that resemble a communist market economy more than a free or manage market economy but under some dire circumstances even that may be warranted.

These **Sociocorporatic** configurations are staged exactly like the Monocorporatic and Commucorporatic systems and have all of the same entitlements but includes mandated outsourcing of fund managers **(I.B.2)** to their account attributes. They would most likely specialize in profit seeking I-A Corporations (C.I-A Corporation) but ordinary nonprofit I-A Corporations could continue to be managed by government officials. There is a slight threat of compromise between private managers and interloping government officials but before a people elect to tread on this path there will probably be ample discussion and debate on how to adequate insulate both parties. The system can develop similarly to how a Traditional Solocorporatic does in that other governments are charged with manage both the C-G Corporations and I-A Corporations. It should be slightly easier to reign in political business managers than private money managers and at least institutionalize enough severe consequences against graft and corruption.

Most current Sovereign Wealth Funds and Permanent Fund are set up to allow unrestricted access to intra administrative ownership positions. Their saving grace is that most are outsourced to quasi private authorities and government does not gain direct access to economy. This always remains an option but it is unwise. It dramatically increases the potential for corruption and abuse. There is always too much incentive for government managers to manipulate commerce in their own jurisdictions for other than monetary gains. It remains unsettling even when profits remain the principle goal. Governments were never meant to grow rich from selling products and services to their residents. The entire hierarchy and organization of governments is meant to mitigate this dangerous tendency. Still there are natural occurring patterns in commercial government theory that tickle the concept and they should be address.

Most of the sample systems are simple in construction and based upon a single theme. This is done primarily to highlight the most significant differences between entitlements. For instance the Commutary emphasizes the fact that departmental capitalization authorizes profit seeking within administrative jurisdictions. Monocorporatic systems emphasize the use of nonprofit intra-administrative corporations to enhance public welfare. Traditional configurations can eliminate most government interloping and typical configurations can always limit gross ownership and market share. One nation can acquire the characteristics of different themes within its different tiers of government.

This is also true of capitalization modes. One tier can have a fractal mode of capitalization while the others remain centralized. Fractal and Traditional account attributes in one tier can certainly be used to complement centralized or political configurations (i.e. any of the ordinary sample systems) in other tiers if the need arises. Different tiers of government have different responsibilities. Government investment and competition definitely carries different risks depending on which tier of government becomes involved in the economy. Allowing the mix matching of themes and modes allows for a nation to adapt its own entitlement to very real economic and political realities. Governments can also accommodate multiple modes of capitalization working in subsequent cycles or simultaneously. This results in many remarkable and useful combinations.

Take for example regional governments in the U. States. They could have a Traditional PFE (Public Finance Engine) configuration with centralized capitalization but supplement this with Capitalocratic entitlements located in state departments and agencies. Most of the risk is mitigated without suppressing potential revenues. Many will see the merits of both and want to take advantage of the two modes simultaneously rather than waiting for a cycle to be completed. Those governments can simply fund each mode at a lower rate so the two combined equal a contribution rate they would normally apply to a single mode. Any tier can always be prohibited from capitalizing. Most often this would be the national tier, but states and counties can be excluded as well to concentrate the wealth on the municipal level, or both municipal and federal tiers can be excluded to concentrate public wealth in the regional or state governments.

The last example of commercial government offered in this book is the Poliplutocratic model and it combines attributes from the Traditional theme, the Political theme, and the Fractal theme.

Poliplutocracy

Code;

I.**A.1.2.3,** B.1.a, C.1.b, D.1, E.**1.a.x;** II.A.1, B.2.x.xx.(cc).xxx, C.1, D.1, E.1; III, A.2.x.xx.xxx, B.2.x.xx.xxx

I.**A.1,** B.3.a, C.4, D.2, **E.2;** II.A.3.xxx.i, A.3.x.iii, B.2.3.xxx, B.2.3.4.x, C.2.a.b.x, D.1, E.2.3.x.iii, E.3.xxx.i; III.A.2.x.xxx, B.2.x.xxx

I.**A.2.3,** B.1.a, C.4, D.2, **E.2;** II.A.3.xxx.i, A.3.xx(c).ii, A.3.x.iii, B.2.3.xx.xxx(c), B.2.3.4.x, C.2.a.b.x.xx(c), D.3, E.3.xxx.i, E.3.xx(c).ii, E.2.3.x.iii; III.A.2.x.xx.xxx, B.2.x.xx.xxx

Key:

I. **A.1.2.3** (all governments; national, regional, and local), **B.3.a** (option to manage itself with social agenda), **C.1** (budget subsidy only), **D.1.b** (savings method with 25 year cycle), **E.1.a.x** (permanent funds for both on and off budget expenses), **II.A.1.x.xx.xxx** (no government may buy or sell any stock, option, commodity, derivative, or other applicable secondary market instrument), **B.2.x.xx(c).xxx** (may use any form of public debt, be it national treasury security or municipal bond, regardless of where it originates), **C.1** (may not purchase any residential or commercial real estate regardless of the jurisdiction), **D.1** (may not trade any currency), **E.1.x.xx.xxx** (may not invest in any primary market securities, may not initiate new businesses); **III.A.2.x.xx.xxx** (there are no particular limitations on gross ownership), **B.2.x.xx.xxx** (there is no applicable market share inherent in bond ownership).

I. **A.1** (national government), **B.1.a** (must manage its own permanent fund with option of applying social agenda), **C.4** (unstructured), **D.2** (defrayment), **2** (departmental capitalization), **II. A.3.xxx.i** (may invest in any secondary instrument, with their administrative jurisdictions to a marginal degree), **A.3.x.iii** (may invest in any secondary instrument to a majority degree in foreign jurisdictions), **B.2.3.xxx** (may invest in public and corporate debt within its own administrative jurisdiction), **B.2.3.4.x** (may invest in any form of debt be it public, corporate, or personal debt, in foreign jurisdictions), **C.2.a.b.x** (may utilize any residential or commercial real estate in foreign jurisdictions), **D.1** (currency trades prohibited), **E.2.3.x.iii** (may invest in venture capital or primary security instrument to a majority degree, including starting new businesses, but in foreign jurisdictions only), **E.3.xxx.i** (may invest in primary security instruments to a marginal degree within their administrative jurisdictions) **III.A.2.x.xxx** (gross ownership is unrestricted in foreign and administrative jurisdictions), **B.2.x.xxx** (market share is unrestricted in foreign and administrative jurisdictions).

I. **A.2.3** (regional and local governments), **B.1.a** (must manage its own permanent fund with option of applying social agenda), **C.4** (unstructured), **D.2** (defrayment), **E.2** (departmental capitalization), **II. A.3.xxx.i** (may invest in any secondary instrument to a marginal degree in their administrative jurisdictions), **A.3.xx(c).ii** (may invest in any secondary instrument to a minority degree within opposing domestic regional economies,), **A.3.x.iii** (may invest in any secondary instrument to a majority degree in foreign jurisdictions), **B.2.3.xx(c).xxx** (may use any form of public or corporate debt, when it originates opposing regional governments or their own administrative jurisdictions), **B.2.3.4.x** (may invest in any form of debt be it public, corporate, or personal debt, in foreign jurisdictions), **C.2.a.b.x.xx(c)** (may purchase any residential or commercial real estate in foreign or opposing regional jurisdictions), **D.3** (may trade any currency), **E.3.xxx.i** (may invest in primary instruments up to a marginal degree in their administrative jurisdictions), **E.3.xx(c).ii** (may invest in primary security instruments, up to a minority degree in opposing regional jurisdictions), **E.2.3.x.iii** (may invest in venture capital or primary security instrument to a majority degree, including starting new businesses, in foreign jurisdictions only); **III. A.2.x.xx.xxx** (allowed unrestricted gross ownership in foreign and domestic economies), **B.2.x.xx.xxx** (allowed unrestricted market share in foreign and domestic economies).

The **Poliplutocracy** combines a centralized Public Finance Engine configuration with Fractal Solocorporatic-minor entitlements. This meshes Traditional and political themes with Uniform and Fractal themes. The Plutopolitocracy uses all of the usual account attributes and entitlements afforded to both templates it borrows characteristics from. Central governments can only traffic in government bonds and securities eliminating their ability to compromise free markets. Consensus is still required for departments to impact corporate governance because their maximum positions are still restricted to minor degrees of ownership. The reduced bond liabilities produced by a PFE complements revenues earned by mutually owned C-G Corporations making it one of the most efficient and reasonably conservative models of commercial government.

The political landscape of one nation can include several variations of commercial government within the structure of its constituent governments. For example, within the U. States the Northeast could employ Monocorporatic entitlements, the Northwest could employ Corporatic versions of departmental capitalization, The South could employ Traditional configurations like the public finance engine, and the Midwest could employ simple Capitalocratic entitlements. For simplicities sake they are grouped by region but this may not necessarily be true. It should not be uncommon that a large population base, like San Francisco, employ the I-A Corporations allowed by monocorporatic entitlements while the more significant California state government remains conservative with capitalocractic entitlements. Some states or cities will be more courageous than others and some more rational than the others, regardless of location or proximity. Many city governments have different agendas than their state governments.

Most national permanent fund entitlements remain constant so its constituent governments can run the full gambit of commercial government account attributes and entitlements without compromising an entire economy. Different regions within the nation will have different economic pressures and will respond uniquely this is especially true when the composite governments have rights such as in the United States and their State's Rights. It may be even more complicated when some states employ defrayment methods while other savings methods, and when some states or cities only use proceeds of government investment for budget subsidy while others produce dividends. A single purpose can be maintained indefinitely or a government could alternate between completed cycles. As already suggested more progressive entitlements can be authorized as the government matures so a state government that once felt reservations and employed a Traditional configuration may find itself employing Solocorporatic entitlements at a future date.

Although the argument for an MCPFS is forwarded as the main premise of the book simultaneously developing a network of permanent funds within all of a nation's constituent governments may be awkward. A commercial government could sprout from a combination of individual initiatives based on the part of motivated and ambitious legislatures. This is obvious in that the Alaskan state within the U.S. has its own permanent fund while the national government is without its own Sovereign Wealth Fund. The United States as a whole is certainly not a commercial government, but the state of Alaska is. Likewise, the Chinese manage several large Sovereign Wealth Funds on the national tier but none of its lower level governments actively compete in economy. A nation should not be categorized as commercial until a substantial portion of its governments have funds or if a few have substantially capitalized funds but those constituent governments with funds should be categorized as commercial.

All governments already have the right to manage permanent funds vested in private equities, own corporations intent on earning profits, and operate nonprofit authorities acting within their administrative jurisdictions. Without exception they all manage public pension funds for their government employee and some already own Sovereign Wealth Funds. Precedent has already been set and the incentive is there. Only confidence is needed. The sample systems offered in previous chapters merely establish guidelines for their implementation and emphasize those trends in commercial government theory that can easily be isolated. There are certainly many less obvious combinations that can be adapted to specific circumstances. Political architects can manipulate any configuration offered in this book and even create their own based on new attributes and entitlements. There is no reason that if some other important quality needs to be emphasized in their characteristics that they are simply amended to include such.

LEXIS NEXUS

Chapter 6

Rules & Regulations

Commercial governments will require a dizzying array of administrative laws and legislative laws to properly allay concerns of exploitation or corruption. Even the most conservative configurations of commercial government will require additional protections to be in place in regards to incorporating their permanent funds, managing their permanent funds, and private campaign financing. When majority ownership is allowed even more, more important, rules need to be implemented to ensure C-G Corporations don't have an advantage over private industry. For the most part these regulations are the same regulations that exist today but some have been adapted to the changing relationship between government and industry. Like the sample systems these are only suggestions. In all likelihood if a nation were to commit to commercial government it would need to prepare many more regulations than are offered in this section but they are a start to the process.

I. Every government has the inalienable right to own financial instruments, equity positions, real estate, and currencies for the purpose of earning profits but a higher government may limit such instruments and vehicles based on origin, operation, function, and degree of ownership (marginal, minority, and majority), and other mitigating factors.

Every government has a fundamental right to own any interest bearing or profit generating instrument as long as conflicts in interests are mitigated by proper regulation and oversight. Lower governments have a significantly stronger right to private property than higher governments due to the decreased probability of conflicts and thus are given much more liberal entitlements. The more responsible a government is and the degree with which it is charged with regulation and oversight the weaker its property rights are and the fewer entitlements it will have. When cause can be shown that there are absolutely no conflicts in interests then all governments have a right to own property. The specific property in question is stocks, bonds, currency, and real estate. It is even conceivable that no government suffers under any limitation as long as reasonable oversight is applied. The Alaskan Permanent Fund, the Australian Future Fund, and Russia's Oil Stabilization Fund are all relatively unregulated compared to the themed systems offered in this book. Nobody knows how a country will be transformed by creating a permanent fund system in all of its constituent municipal, county, state, and national governments so an appropriate amount of restraint was applied.

If ever there is an occasion where conflict arises then governments will forfeit their property. This is true when imposing gross ownership limits, market share limits, when enacting ne legislation or ordnances, and even when accepting bids for government contracts. One solution is forced divestiture being applied on a regular business. That is effective but intrusive. The best solution is eliminating the concern by applying conservative entitlements. Realistically speaking it will be a combination of both that provides the necessary legal precedent to allow fully vested governments. In almost every case where rights are involved certain mitigating factors change its entitlements. In the U. States citizens have the right to bear arms and own guns but felons and mentally ill people are justly prohibited from possession. Rights are always set against circumstance. Governments have a right to property but each class of instrument and jurisdiction entails different responsibilities and entitlements must be weighed against them.

II. Forced divestiture is applied in a cascading order of eligibility.

Forced divestiture is a mainstay of commercial governments. It is used in situations where conflicts of interests are present or become present, when too large of a position is acquired, when a combination of government's market share becomes too large, or even when the incidence of C-G Corporations over saturates the domestic economy. Regardless of the cause it is always facilitated by the courts. The courts enforce legislation so Assemblies and Congresses have authority and regulatory agencies can impose fines and sanctions but in contested matters courts with higher jurisdiction can force compliance. In matters where multiple governments have interests, higher governments always lose equity first. Lower governments have greater rights to income generating property simply because there are less inherent conflicts in their ownership of assets. Forced divestiture should be viewed as normal mechanism of commercial government but in most circumstances it can be avoided by governments simply relinquishing their positions before the conflict arises or when they occur.

III. Permanent fund managers have a fiduciary duty to earn the greatest returns possible with the least exposure to risk.

Unless marked otherwise permanent fund managers and business managers are obliged by the fiduciary duty to earn the most revenue while exposing residents to the least risk. This should align most C-G Corporations and permanent funds with traditional commercial interests in their zeal for profit seeking. They can't sacrifice revenue for social and political agendas unless already authorized to do so but even in those situations there are calculations that govern decision making. Managers must weigh the potential for loss of revenue in their permanent fund versus the loss of revenue in their general fund. If the state of California is expected to suffer 100 billion dollars over the next decade to land erosion cause by global warming then it has a financial incentive to coordinate its C-G Corporations and to vote its shares in a way that will minimize future losses due to economic forces.

The savings earned by environmentally friendly initiatives can offset the decrease in profitability of their assets. In every case where nonfinancial gains are sought with their assets Permanent fund managers must be careful that their C-G Corporations remain independently solvent because they will face bankruptcy or a change in ownership if the initiatives cause excessive losses. In the same respect a company can vote their shares for nonfinancial gains they can also pursue political agendas. Permanent fund managers could insist that every company that does business with their company uses union labor or they could use their venture capital to forward projects that only included union labor. Other lawful agendas include environmental conservatism or urban development and it is assumed that governments can pursue these nonfinancial goals without compromising their returns.

IV. Permanent Funds are incorporated in the owning jurisdiction but its authorities and C-G Corporations must be incorporated within a different state.

Permanent funds can be incorporated in the owning government's principle regional jurisdiction so that it doesn't suffer from an unnecessary tax on its revenue. The frequency of court cases involving the permanent fund being heard in the owning jurisdictions should be low enough so that governments can be exploitative. All of its authorities and C-G Corporations must be incorporated in opposing regions so that if they are legally contested then the matter will be heard in a court not associated with the owning government. Trust is essential to commerce and if governments begin to compete within the economy, or interact with companies through investment, then everybody must be satisfied that no exploitation will occur through government processes. Even the illusion of impropriety must be dispelled and the easiest way to do this is by eliminating the possibility that the owning governments legislations, regulations, and courts may interfere with citizen's and other government's rights.

V. The vested government has sole right to decide whether income from investment is used for budget subsidy, dividends, or government benefits.

No government may impose its will on another government and dictate how permanent fund moneys are used. This applies to income derived from completed cycles and when defrayment methods are implemented. It is up to the individual vested government to apply its permanent fund income to budget subsidy, dividends, or government sponsored benefits. Higher governments have certain liberties to manipulate subordinate government's wealth, and although it is called public wealth, it is the exclusive property of a specific community. It can in fact switch from budget subsidy one year to dividend production the next as long as the principal in the fund remains intact. This book offers format suggestions not absolute axioms by which all commercial governments must be abide. Each of the themes relies on consistency to maximize benefits. Haphazardly splitting revenue among random uses will eliminate their beneficial effects. Property rights reign supreme and even if a jurisdiction is forced to liquidate some of its assets it will retain all of the proceeds from its sales. This makes the administrative action of forced divestiture excusable even if it liberally used to preempt conflicts or eliminate them after the fact.

VI. Governments may employ changes to the tax code for reasons of earning incomes, controlling inflation, exciting industry, or for protecting against socialization (taxes can be applied directly to food, shelter, and clothing to counteract excessive dividends).

When tax ceases to be relied on as the only source of government income it can be utilized as a tool to manipulate the economy. Although the volume of currency involved in an economy would remain the same, restricting personal or corporate incomes can serve the same purpose as constricting the money supply. Lowering taxes translates to a more favorable ratio of earned money to usable money. The value of the currency exchanged will grow proportional to the decrease in taxes. Inflation can then be nullified by a region's reduction in taxes. Taxes can be raised to depreciate the purchasing power of an earned dollar to induce inflation. Regions could react to national interest rate changes with changes in their sales, property, and income taxes nullifying them or exacerbating them. Regional governments could act to complement or contradict national government policies. As a whole the national economy would be better served by having a means to make both universal changes and regional accommodations.

There are no instances of modern government being able to increase or decreases taxes in accord with market pressures. Taxes are always viewed as a necessary evil or unavoidable expanse on income. Commercial governments will be the first to be able to manipulate their economies through market evolving tax rates. But adjusting taxes is not the only tool a commercial government has to manage their economies. Public wealth can be managed under a federalist system of control where the rate of contribution (taxes and consumption), proportion of cash reserves (credit markets), the amount of money devoted to public debt (reducing bond liabilities), direct and immediate tax defrayment (increasing government spending), and the composition of permanent funds (supply and demand for securities, targeting specific industries with capitalization) are all manipulated.

Municipalities and counties can be managed by states and states can be managed by the national government. The Federal government can implement a national economic and fiscal policy and the state governments can implement complimentary regional economic policies. These measures of control imitate the function of the Federal Reserve's ability to control the national currency or national interest rate with a system of regional government institutions coordinating policies. More specific controls can be applied to the national and they will defray the disadvantages associated with national currencies, national interest rates, and federalist tax redistribution systems.

In order to maximize the utility of changing tax rates a region or nation may have to switch to quarterly taxes. Most corporations already pay on a quarterly basis. Ordinary residents could make the transition with ease (especially if employee's rights to be paid as incorporations are protected). Most people have mortgages where the monthly payments already incorporate a partial property tax. It would be easy to simply assess that tax on a quarterly basis as well. The very same people generally earn wages paid on a bi-weekly schedule where taxes are taken out every paycheck. Their employers can continue to deduct the same amount but remit them on a quarterly basis. It may take some time to become accustomed to but it would not be an extraordinary inconvenience. Taxes updated on a quarterly basis will enable governments to manipulate their economies more quickly and more efficiently. Policies that change tax rates can be implemented on a quarterly basis rather than being delayed on an annual basis. Regardless of the trend, whether taxes are being decreased, increased, or dividends handed out, higher governments can change policy on a quarterly basis so they can adapt to most changes in economic growth, consumption, or inflation.

Governments can apply taxes in any proportions they wish to discourage completely subsidized lifestyles. This may become necessary when dividends from C-G Corporations combine with municipal, county, state, and national permanent funds. Normally most governments don't tax necessities like food, shelter, and clothing but if dividends make it possible for certain families and individuals to sustain a lifestyle without working then taxes must be applied to ensure residents remain productive. Otherwise successful commercial governments could decimate their labor forces and rampant inflation would be caused by the greater competition for labor. The only other alternative is conscripting labor and that reeks of traditional socialist planned economy strategies. Increases to consumption taxes must be counterbalanced with higher government subsidies for despondent families but eligibility requirements can exclude health individuals that should be contributing to productivity.

VII. Higher governments have the right to establish minimum contribution, and maximum contributions, with the purpose of creating a MCPFS and manipulating economy.

The Permanent Fund system is mandatory for all local and regional governments. This means that all these governments will need to fund their permanent funds with contributions from taxes. Parameters can establish acceptable maximum and minimum contribution rates. Higher governments can increase local tax rates by mandating an increase to the minimum contribution rate. Likewise, a maximum contribution rate can be decreased so taxes are immediately cut. Within the first cycle of the program changing the contribution rates may lead to insignificant changes to the applied taxes but in future cycles these changes will be more dramatic. If a contribution rate remains the same but taxes have already been reduced by 15 or 20% then what would ordinarily be a 2 or 3% change in applied taxes would be more like a 10% change in taxes.

The further along a nation is in its mandatory contribution permanent fund system the more control it will be able to exert on applied taxes. Manipulating contribution rates is still useful for first cycle governments. The rate translates directly into the amount of capital available for investment into the real estate, securities, bond, savings, or currency markets. This will allow for governments to exert a measure of control over demand for these instruments. Inputting more money into these markets will also increase industrial capitalization rates, credit liquidity, security values, and help fund other governments. The money would be diffuse in the economy; one jurisdiction would be forced to make capital investments into another jurisdiction's industries but another jurisdiction would likely reciprocate in a like manner because of their shared inability to influence or compete in their own jurisdictions.

VIII. Higher governments have the right to dictate whether profits from assets must be immediately dispersed through a defrayment method if the intent is to slow the accumulation of public wealth if it looks to overtake concentrations of private wealth.

If the various regional and local governments establish hybrid accounts and not simple savings accounts, then a higher government could regulate the amount of a government must immediately apply to the budget (defrayment) as opposed to rolling it over in their subsidy funds. Increasing the rate of defrayment can have an even greater impact than limiting the contribution rate. When the fund is more mature it will have earn multiples more in interest than the contribution total and applying that amount for economic stimulus will make more of an impact than reducing an already small tax. In a similar manner higher governments can force lower governments to disseminate dividends to their residents rather than apply proceeds to tax defrayment. Both these measures will more immediately stimulate domestic consumption or counteract inflationary trends.

If the government already has an established defrayment policy then higher governments can limit the amount of money they apply to their budgets and cause tax increases. Normally this would be an absurd premise but this can be an important measure to prevent over appreciation of assets like real estate or currencies or it can help combat inflation. If a nation prescribes to a partial subsidy program then every 25 years taxes will drop by a huge proportion. This could adversely affect an economy with gross inflation. Constricting the proportion of useable income by increasing taxes has similar effects of decreasing the amount of money circulating in an economy and cause inflation when needed. Residents and citizens will have to be disabused of their normal prejudices against raising taxes because it may become necessary for survival.

Instead of using the defrayment method to change tax rates a jurisdiction could immediately apply the difference in funds to increase government spending. Government spending contributes directly to economic growth and consumption rates.

Money can be dispersed in corporate subsidies, commodity subsidies, larger department payrolls, and equipment purchases. This will bolster the revenues recorded by private industries. It will increase resident's abilities to buy certain products. Taxes shouldn't be seen exclusively as a drain on commerce because the majority of government spending is recycled within the domestic economy. Commandeering the defrayment method for use in Supply side economics can produce the same effects without increasing government bond liabilities. It is a win-win situations with only a small sacrifice made to the growth of a permanent fund.

IX. Higher governments retain the right to establish maximum risk allotments, proportions of cash reserves (like deposits), proportions of domestic instruments versus foreign instruments, public equity versus private equity, and market share.

The composition of lower government's investment portfolios can be used to manipulate an economy. In order to increase liquidity in the region's credit markets a higher government can mandate temporary increases to the proportion of cash which must be held in the subsidy funds. More money will be deposited into simple savings accounts and CD's of private or competitive government owned banks within the region. The result is more money available for commercial and private loans. If there were ever a need to limit liquidity than the proportion of cash could be decreased. The central bank could utilize these controls to maximize the efficiency of national interest rate changes much in the same way it reduces the interest rate on money loaned from the Federal Reserve to commercial and mortgage banks. States would be able to accommodate the specific needs of their local economies without compromising national economic policy if policy decisions were left to them.

Higher governments can dictate the risk composition of lower government portfolios. Thus governments can be persuaded to invest more in U.S. securities, municipal bonds, or mutual funds as opposed to hedge funds, high yield commercial bonds, or stock from specific companies. They can dictate the rate of growth of the funds by mandating either more conservative low yield investments or allowing high risk high yield investments. They can even determine the proportion made up of private equity versus secondary equity. Although one may think that the returns earned on investments are the most important function of government capitalization but economic development and stimulus play an even larger part. Higher governments can offer incentives to focus government investment into specific sectors and industries within the national economy. They can even dictate which foreign markets become eligible for lower government involvement.

Higher governments always reserve the right to dictate the proportion of foreign investment versus domestic investment within Permanent Funds. This ensures that government ownership does not over saturate the domestic economy. Government ownership and competition will always be relegated to an inferior position in relation to private ownership. When domestic governments own too much stock of domestic companies, too much market share, or are too heavily vested in the local economies then the money can be moved out into foreign markets. Vested nations can rest assured they will not inadvertently collapse into a Competitive State Capitalist market economy. In Competitive Socialist nations changing the proportion of foreign investment can mark a premeditated effort to create integrated blocks with other Competitive State Capitalist countries. Competitive State Capitalist nations can incentivize investment into emerging or friendly markets as part of trade negotiations.

Higher governments will maintain authority to force divestiture of domestic instruments. A national government can force state or municipal governments to liquidate any position causing conflict. State governments can compel all of their subordinate county and city governments to liquidate positions causing conflict. This may be necessary to maintain competitive dispositions in proportions of government ownership in domestic companies. If a government acquires too large of market share within one region or industry then a higher government can force divestiture. If the domestic economy is saturated with too much government investment forced divestiture can cause those funds to be relocated in foreign economies or less saturated industries. Divestiture of foreign instruments can be forced when higher governments re-evaluate trade agreements or impose embargos. Governments have the right to hold assets and earn incomes but the integrity of free markets or national policy must be preserved.

An ancillary function is to foster more or less demand on local securities by manipulating competition for such products. Depressed securities or commodities markets can be stimulated by contrived demand for such instruments. More money flowing into the security markets will inflate the values of the securities. There will be more competition for better stock. The same is true for real estate, bonds, and currency. When local economies slow, contributions can be increased and risk standards relaxed so that capital flows in and produces stimulus. If a bubble is forming in the securities or real estate markets then higher governments can force future contributions to be focused on bonds, held in simple savings accounts, or diverted to foreign theatres. The reduced demand should relieve some pressure and prices will drop at a fairly predictable rate. These may sound like broad strokes but even a managed economy is not micro managed. Most actions will be restrained to quarters and any trend will not be expressed until several terms have passed.

Manipulating the proportion of a portfolio invested in government bonds will make public finance more efficient. Increasing the maximum allotment will fund local municipalities or national governments. If more money is devoted to municipal bonds then the interest earned on those notes will decrease enabling governments to take on more debt. This in turn will help depress local taxes. Even with public debt earning lower returns they will still provide the most stable and most consistent incomes. Smaller less leveraged governments will earn adequate incomes and larger more debt laden governments will pay less out in bond liabilities. Decreasing the maximum allotment will cause governments to invest more in private securities. Mandates can cause funding to be directed to foreign governments or specific regions within the country. This process can be complemented with tax breaks on funding so that the purchase of bonds imitates government aid.

Lower governments can be directed to move money from savings accounts or other liquid investments into currencies of other nations. A national government could establish its own foreign currency reserve. This will help remove money from economy if glut of investment capital or savings capital causes imbalance in domestic economy. Holding reserves of foreign currencies can be insurance against rapid inflation or currency devaluation. The value of the national currency can be based partially on foreign currencies held for durable periods. Foreign Currency reserves result in an appreciated ability to maintain stable currency values or manipulate values based upon other market movements. A foreign currency reserve imitates the advantages of being on a gold standard without being locked into hording a commodity with a single value.

X. Money borrowed from a permanent fund for use by the general fund must be repaid according commercial rates of borrowing.

Excessive borrowing is a threat to any government. Commercial governments could borrow money from their Permanent or Subsidy Funds. Loaning money to itself would insulate it from political or economy pressures from 3rd parties. Borrowing money for use in the General Fund is only legitimate if a competitive rate of interests is applied. These rates would have to be set by a regulatory agency so that no underhanded money shuffling or political money laundering is possible. When governments take loans out from their own Permanent Funds they conserve the interest paid on the loan. Otherwise a third party private firm or competing government would benefit at their expense. As long as the government pays itself back interest and principal then the debt will not become a fixed liability. Precedent has been set for a government loaning itself money in a number of different situations. The Australian government has appropriated money from its own Future Wealth Fund for improvements in infrastructure within the nation. Rather than paying interest to a private lender the money is being repaid to the Future Wealth Fund according to a competitive interest rate.

XI. No government can force excessive liquidation or another government's permanent fund.

In no case will a higher government be able to force complete liquidation of a Permanent Fund. Higher governments can force no more than half the amount of that year's interest earned to be used in federalist measures of control. If there is ever an economic crisis governments should have the authority to cause economic stimulus especially when they have the means. The nation itself will have to decide whether such commands must be applied uniformly amongst the many states or municipalities or whether different fiscal policies can be applied to different regions. This maximum allows higher governments to cause substantial dispersal without compromising the lower government's ability to continue funding or growing their permanent fund. The volume of money eligible to be redistributed grows significantly with the age of the permanent fund. A fund in its second year of operation will have dramatically less money available for use than a fund in its 20th year of operation. All permanent funds in a payout cycle are naturally excluded from use because their interest is already being applied to budget subsidy or dividend production. Generally a second fund has been created and interest from its principal will be available.

XII. No government can liquidate their own permanent fund to advantage current residents at the expense of future residents.

No government will be able to liquidate its own permanent fund to benefit current residents. This would be a deplorable exploitation of future residents and previous resident's contributions. In a democratic political system it would be possible for some elected official to tempt current residents with massive financial rewards after a fund is liquidated. Imagine how much money current residents would receive if a permanent fund that has been operating for 20 or 30 years was suddenly liquidated. Which residents wouldn't be bribed by a payout that earned each voter tens of thousands dollars? This would severely handicap the effectiveness of a MCPFS if every couple of years they were scratched out. The political system itself would be corrupted by flagrant promises of liquidation. Permanent funds are expected to be permanent fixtures in government finance and any adulteration of its principal will destroy the MCPFS's integrity.

XIII. Governments' ability to subsidize their general budgets with permanent funds will be insured by Permanent Fund Guarantee Companies.

If necessary, lower governments can pay premiums out of their permanent fund proceeds to the national or regional governments for insurance that covers them in the event that excessive losses occur while the fund is being used to defray general budget expenses. This will imitate how private and public pensions pay premiums to the PBGC. The PBGC only pays partial benefits during default but that may be just enough time necessary for the MCPFS to right itself. Premiums should be kept minimal considering the fund does not pay any benefits for its first 25 years and that is adequate time for large enough reserves to be amassed. After the permanent fund reaches maturity it should have already contributed enough to fund itself in the case of economic collapse but premiums can continue to be paid during the final pay out phases to add more security. Premiums can even be raised to such a degree that the Permanent Fund Guarantee Company compensates for all of a fund's losses. The administering government will have to mind the fact that when one permanent fund is depressed others in the same jurisdiction or nation are likely to depressed as well.

Inadvertently this would also subsidize an amazingly large sovereign wealth fund managed by the national or regional governments. If these insurance funds only charge small premiums and only cover partial benefits then it would be in the interests of all governments that there are multiple Guarantee Companies. If one were to cover only 40%, as is the case in the PBGC, then another may cover 40% more and retaining 80% of subsidy will enable a government to minimize its future bond liabilities when compensating for the change in government funding. These Guarantee Companies could be vested in private equities or it could simply traffic in treasury securities much like how the U.S. Social Security system is funded. In any case its investments must be much more conservative than the permanent funds because if the PFGC were to succumb to lower revenue streams when permanent funds experience the same loss then all of the governments would face severe crises. Most funds should be adequately diversified in order to survive down markets. Pension funds have weathered economic downturns without compromising benefits and residents should be confident that permanent fund managers will be just as successful.

XIV. If no permanent fund insurance is available it can be translated into an annuity so that the current level of budget subsidy is preserved.

If a permanent fund is current paying into the general fund and the markets become overly depressed affecting the subsidy it can be changed into annuity so that the loss of value in its assets does not compromise its ability to keep taxes lower. Part of the principal can be released along with the interest earned and the combination will be applied to budget subsidy. This will mean that the fund will eventually be exhausted but the rate it pays out could be coordinated with the maturation of a secondary permanent fund. By the time all of the original fund's assets are released, the second fund should mature and the same degree of budget subsidy can be maintained. If necessary governments can gain extra funding by issuing bonds so that the permanent fund annuity lasts long enough to be replaced by a second permanent fund for budget subsidy. This may delay the government's goal for complete budget subsidy but the system will be preserved. Most economic downturns don't last decades so the permanent fund should recover value fairly quickly and be switched back to a standard schedule with permanent principle earning interest. An annuity phase will compromise a fund's effectiveness and taxes may rise slightly over the long term but because one permanent fund cycle is complemented by subsequent cycles there will still be an aggregate reduction in taxes.

XV. Constructive Market Share applies to all C-G and I-A Corporations.

Market share is tallied when a single government owns multiple assets competing in the same market. If one government owns several concrete making companies in a single jurisdiction than it is their combined market share that determines monopoly. Constructive market share also adds the market share owned by higher government assets with the market share from lower government assets. If a city owns one company that commands 20% of market share in another jurisdiction, and it's State government owns another company that commands 30% market share in the same industry then their total market share is considered 50% for determining anti-trust violations. Depending on federal regulations the state permanent fund may be forced to divest their ownership of the company until it owned less than 49% of the total outstanding stock (or equity) or assets were sold off shrinking its market share.

Constructive market share is more a relation of higher government ownership than lower government and if any action is to be taken then the higher government's assets are subject to forced divestiture first. Lower governments have greater rights to property than higher governments since there are dramatically less conflicts inherent in their ownership. This is also a mechanism to offset the fact the higher government having greater legal authority so that public wealth does not only accumulate in the most powerful tiers of government. State governments can represent themselves in the national congress much more effectively than a city so it is safer to protect the cities interest than the states. Constructive market share diffuses the problem of foreign governments owning large proportions of market share within their national, regional, and local tiers of government. If this way not applied then the collective foreign government could own 100% market share and the domestic government could not prevent collusion within the owning jurisdictions with its regulatory agencies and courts.

Although averting situations where profit seeking companies accumulate monopoly market shares is necessary it is equally important to eliminate situations where I-A Corporations assume to much market share. Government cooperatives can't be allowed to hedge out income producing business and a constructive schedule is applied to their market share as well. This way the focus is maintained on municipal governments as the main suppliers of government benefits and amenities based on residency. Whenever market share is calculated in regards to anti-trust limits higher governments combine their market share with lower government's market share. If Newark City owned an I-A.C. with 25% of market share in the state of NJ and the state permanent fund of New Jersey owned another I-A.C. with 40% market share in the same industry (same benefit) then anti-trust regulators would consider NJ to own 65% market share. In order to shrink market share the state would have to sell assets from its I-A Corporation so that the combined market share agrees with federal statutes.

XVI. Competitive Accounting laws apply to all C-G and I-A Corporations.

C-G Corporations only receive one contribution from a permanent fund when it is bought or created. From that point on it must rely on conventional modes of capitalization. If a C-G Corporation is losing money it will either exhaust its capital store and become bankrupt, or it will apply for commercial loans, sell bonds, sell preferred stock, or divest part of its ownership stake by selling common stock. Further contributions from the owning government's permanent fund or general fund are illegal. Under no circumstances can a government bailout a flailing C-G or I-A Corporation. This should eliminate most concerns over unfair business practices such as dumping because without subsidy from funds it would ordinarily become insolvent fairly quickly. Collusion between governments for an exchange of low cost services or products is also much less likely. This statute should produce enough pressure on C-G Corporations to keep their operations honest and productive.

C-G Corporation accounting must remain separate from each other in terms of profitability even when owned to the same authority or permanent fund. This means that profits can't be combined and applied indiscriminately to different operations unless one is incorporated into the fold of another company adhering to the accounting standards. If two companies owned by the same permanent fund merge they must first be appraised by a private auditor and a virtual exchange must occur. The assuming company must make payment to the permanent fund so that its accounting record remains accurate. Otherwise a owning government could simply reshuffle its assets to float unsuccessful ventures. This is just as true for nonprofit I-A Corporations and every time they expand or reorganize it must be based on accurate exchanges or private capitalization (commercial loans).

If a multi-national or multi-regional company is purchased, the division of the company that operates within the jurisdiction of the owning government must be separated and sold. This includes manufacturing sites and the retail locations but only applies when the government intends to earn profits from its acquisition. Neo-Populist systems can convert previously profit seeking divisions into government benefits. Most governments will steer clear of companies that earn significant revenues from their jurisdictions because there is always a possibility of loss when spinning off the parts in conflict. Higher governments will dictate how quickly this function must be performed and they will determine what occurs during transition periods. They will also determine the sanctions involved when owning jurisdictions fail to comply with the forced divestiture.

I-A accounting laws require profit seeking and nonprofit operations to fund themselves independently even when the same service is provided to different jurisdictions. Well funded governments can appropriate large multinational or multiregional corporations and use their services and products as government benefits. For example the city of Chicago could purchase H&R Block and continue to earn profits with all operations outside of city boundaries while providing low cost subsidized tax services to residents. Operations within the city would be required to fund itself through services charges while operations outside of the city could continue earning profits. Obviously this is intended to protect the integrity of a local economy as much as it protects the integrity of the permanent fund. Never are governments allowed to fund their C-G or I-A Corporations with general fund money. The idea is that they remain self sufficient so they maintain profitability or do not become an overwhelming burden on the tax base.

XVII. News media must remain privately owned.

No government can own any percentage of stock in a company that manages any TV, Radio, Internet, or print news. The potential for egregious abuses is just too high. They can't be involved in political commentary, political advertisements, and civilian oversight. The relationship news has with government is too complicated to introduce government providers and vendors. It would be too dangerous if as a network owner they discriminated against certain opinions or candidates. It would be too dangerous if they advocated certain positions. There is a word that perfectly captures government sponsored media. It is propaganda and propaganda leads to coercion and compromise. Civilian oversight would be neutralized and political abuses would propagate through all tiers of government function. This is especially true in the Competitive Socialist and Populist nations whose economies are heavily saturated by C-G Corporations. In those instances the press would remain Free and continue to be completely privately owned.

XVIII. Auditing firms must remain privately owned.

Whenever companies are merged within a permanent fund an independent third party auditor must first evaluate the complete value of the assets being reorganized or assimilated. They are also needed when companies are dissected into profit seeking and nonprofit units within the same company. In every instance the auditors chosen must be from an unconcerned jurisdiction. The individual or firm may not have residency in the buying jurisdiction nor the selling jurisdiction. This excludes employees of C-G Corporations as well. In the same respects media remains free so must there be free auditors. Both reporters and accountants will keep governments and their business honest. Most governments will require auditors to verify or authenticate sales or transactions they commit to and an estate of free auditors complements an economy rife with politically charged C-G Corporations.

XIX. No government may own or manage a Union. Nor can they discriminate against any union unless a critical service is involved.

No government will be able to form or manage unions in competitor jurisdictions that service private or government owned companies and industries. That would be directly interfering with another government's profits or political power. Governments will not be able to discriminate against unions organizing labor and employees from their C-G Corporations. They will be treated as any other ordinary commercial interest and be forced to negotiate fairly with the unions. Nor will governments be able to discriminate against unionized employees in their own jurisdiction. They can't reciprocate overtones made by a competitor jurisdiction to limit union efficacy in one jurisdiction with unfair limitation on unions within another jurisdiction. These standards do not apply to government employees with critical functions regardless of whether they are working for their own resident government or for a competitor jurisdiction through a C-G Corporations (Private Finance Initiative).

XX. No government may discriminate against businesses owned by other domestic governments with any tax policy, legislation, administrative regulation, or ordnance.

It is imperative to protect the commercial interests of all governments equally within a single nation. If a certain government has entitlements to own C-G Corporations then no other government within the same nation can impose sanctions or restrictions on its ability to procure revenues. Every legislation or administrative regulation created must affect all companies in the same industry in the same way. Neither can a government unfairly discriminate against private industry to advantage C-G Corporations. There should be no significant difference between a government owned commercial interest and a privately owned commercial interest. Many tiers of government can have varied entitlements in different regional or municipal jurisdictions but the integrity or validity of C-G Corporations can never be in question if authorized by a higher government.

XXI. No government can accept a bid from a company it holds investment in.

Not only are no bid contracts a source of conspiracy or corruption and will be summarily outlawed on the regional and local level but any company that is invested in is prohibited from earning contract to work for any government involved with investment. This problem will be adverted by a states inability to invest in companies doing a substantial portion of their business in the state but national contractors are still of concern. If the company solicits a bid for the work and wins the bid, the vested government must immediately sell all its shares of stock in the company. The sale of stock will precede any announcement of who has won the contract thus preventing the government from profiting from the arrangement. In order to decrease the frequency of governments inadvertently being in violation of this statute no company that has been contacted by that government for work in the past three years is eligible as an investment for that government. History is the best predictor of future events and most uncomfortable situations can be averted by limiting contact with firms that are more likely to interact with the jurisdiction again.

XXII. Municipal and county and state governments will be compelled to liquidate their positions in companies that win binds for grants and other mechanisms of economic stimulus.

The same basic principles that government work contracts also cover grants, tax rebates, or any other aspect of economic stimulus or commercial government benefit. Sale or transfer of ownership of the instrument must occur before public announcement of the aid is made. Generally must companies vested in by the government will operate primarily in competitor jurisdictions so must opportunities for graft or self-enfranchisement will be avoided but when in doubt forced divestiture is always the answer. If a government generally hands out grants to companies within the same jurisdiction they can reasonably predict which stock to avoid when making investments. Generalized tax breaks don't exclude any companies but any consumer or industry specific tax incentives will make instruments peculiar to those companies ineligible. Most towns, counties, and cities don't offer too many specific tax breaks so they will generally be unaffected but States often offer stimulus for economic development and they will have to be careful not to transgress any lawful boundaries when investing. National governments will typically be restricted to foreign investments but they disperse the most incentives and development capital so there may be times when they too must divest their positions.

XXIII. No government can conspire with another government for uncompetitive exchanges.

No government can collude with another government for the exchange of subsidized products or services. One government could not offer cheap services if the other government reciprocated with cheap services so that both entered into a mutually beneficial contract based on lower than commercial rates. No government can conspire with another government to offer similar depressed cost services to residents in both jurisdictions. This includes operating nonprofits, charities, and cooperatives. In order to manage nonprofits, cooperatives, or charities they must prescribe to one of the Populist models and they only pertain to the owning government jurisdiction. In order for I-A Corporations to coordinate services between jurisdictions they must be included within the structure of a higher government I-A Corporation responsible for both jurisdictions. Contributions to private charities can't be used to circumvent these limitations. Unfortunately all C-G Corporation managers and all permanent fund managers are forbidden from donating to charities located within their administrative jurisdictions, within competitor jurisdictions, and within foreign theatres.

XXIV. No government official can coerce another official into unintended or unwanted uses of public wealth.

No higher government official can dictate to a lower government official how permanent fund moneys or used or how their C-G Corporations operate unless legislation has been enacted to regulate the activity. Every town, city, and state must be independent in terms of managing their assets if the overall economy is to remain competitive. Coercing cooperation or demanding action contrary to the jurisdictions interests is a form of corruption and that must be stamped out. Governments can coordinate with each other which assets are to be acquired but only to avoid infractions of constructive market share statutes. Higher governments due have the authority to dictate whether or not social and political agendas are applied with lower government assets but they can't micromanage which positions are forwarded and which are neglected. Each government must be thought of as an independent entity and when there is conflict the judgment should always be bent in favor of the town, county, or city with respects to state government prerogatives.

XXV. C-G Corporations can be given no exclusive incentive or advantage separate from private industry.

All C-G Corporations, including those facilitated by collective ownership are treated no better than ordinary commercial interests. This means that anti-trust (monopoly) laws and fair business practices (no price fixing, dumping, steering, etc) apply. Every law that applies to ordinary businesses also applies to C-G Corporations. This complements the fact that no domestic government can discriminate against another domestic jurisdiction's C-G Corporation, section XIX, and works hand in hand with the anti-collusion laws forwarded in section XXII and the anti-coercion laws forwarded in section XXIII. All profit seeking businesses enjoy equal rights and have are subject to the same responsibilities. It is the free market that determines winners and losers and not interloping governments. Even in the Competitive Socialist systems parity between C-G and privately owned corporations much be achieved in respect to government regulation and tax policy. To do otherwise would unravel the entire relationship between governments and consumers, and governments with competitors.

XXVI. All C-G Corporations are securitized in Competitive Socialist and Neo-Populist modes of commercial government, and those instruments must produce dividends for investors.

All Competitive Socialist C-G Corporations are required to translate their assets into public stock companies. Not every company must offer stock but they must be organized into larger holding companies, or authorities, which must be joint stock companies. Inevitably it is the permanent fund which owns the controlling share in the authorities but all types of government and individual investors may own partial shares. None of the permanent funds may be joint stock companies and this is to protect the integrity of the jurisdictions' resident's financial interests. Each stock must in turn produce dividends for its owners. This mechanism is in place so dividends produced by C-G Corporations complement those dividends produced by permanent funds. Securitizing CS C-G Corporations also allows a government to easily return ownership back to the private sector if a nation so chooses to abandon a Competitive Socialist agenda which can remove some of the stigma attached with socialism.

XXVII. All Competitive Socialist and Neo-Populist governments must share profits with residents and citizens by returning a predetermined proportion of common stock back to individual and company investors.

Competitive State Capitalist and Neo-Populist C-G Corporations must also return part of their common stock back to residents or other corporations. Solocorporatic C-G Corporations can hold a maximum of 75% of a company's total outstanding stock (or equity). The rest must be publicly sold to other C-G Corporations or citizens. In certain circumstances the owning jurisdictions can relinquish shares to their own residents through warrants similar to how public companies compensate employees and executives. Monocorporatic C-G Corporations can hold a maximum of 65% of equity and Commucorporatocracies only 55%. By now most, but not all companies will be government owned rather than privately owned. Profit sharing ensures that governments remain honest. Citizen share owners will be represented on their corporate boards and be privy to proprietary information. This is also a check against the proliferation of I-A Corporations because it will impact the public's ability to earn incomes directly.

Permanent Fund managers can target residents for receipt of C-G.C stock by issuing them warrants in a similar fashion conventional companies offer stock options to their executives and employees. Higher governments can dictate what proportion of the total required to be returned to the private sector can be issued in warrants. No C-G Corporation can issue warrants for another jurisdictions residents unless they are employees of the company. If too many warrants are issued it could cause ownership of some particular industry to be too concentrated in one jurisdiction or region. This could be detrimental to the distribution of wealth within a country so it should be guarded closely. Warrants generally provide common stock at lower than current market values so it will still be in the interests of permanent fund and authority managers to sell stock on the public securities exchanges. Not only will the companies be able to capitalize more effectively but it will diffuse the fear of wealth accumulating in too few jurisdictions.

XXVIII. Any company at least partially owned (secondary or primary security instruments) by government may not make contributions to political candidate's campaign or PAC funds.

We are accustomed to the intermingling of corporate and government interests. This is unfortunate because it corrupts the intent of government. Public welfare is subjugated to profits. It is more than reasonable to assert that there must be limitations when government begins to traffic in commerce. There are protections now against comingling of interests and profit. It is already illegal for a company which does business with the government to then contribute to an official's campaign for election. This is naturally extended to include all incidences of investment and business activity. Reinforcing the separation of State and Industry through restrictions on lobbying and campaign contributions is the greatest secondary benefit of government investment. It is a necessary step in reforming current democratic political processes during transition from traditional capitalist democracies to fully vested commercial governments.

Government investment is increased a great deal more than previous levels of investment when only state or county employee pensions were managed, and as a result more companies will be excluded from making contributions to political campaigns. Conservative commercial governments should see a dramatic decrease in frequency and efficacy of private and corporate lobbying. It is inexcusable to allow profit seeking to undermine public welfare. Too often is legislation favorable to a specific industry passed simply because of contributions made during the campaign season. Political systems relying on private campaign financing is exploitative because business owners get to contribute once from their person and then again from their company. Companies are also allowed to make much larger contributions than ordinary citizens can. This makes the political and court systems overwhelmingly partial to businesses and their owners and the expense of the working class voters. The sheer volume of government investment when combined with that of public employee pension management will insulate the government from the coercive effects of industry on local and national politicians.

XXIX. Any company with recorded business transactions with a jurisdiction or its C-G Corporation may not make campaign contributions to candidate's campaigns and PAC funds.

XXX. If a government has authority to manage majority positions in competitive companies then all of the exclusions apply to the assets owned by that company and any business transactions it enters into.

Liberal models of commercial government are the least likely to be influenced by corporations or individuals seeking favor mainly due to the increased investments and business transactions of the government and its incorporations. The interactions of government owned companies and private (or public) companies combined with increased investment into business will exclude a majority of companies from making contributions. Even one C-G C. will have several vendors and clients each of whom will be excluded under this rule. If the C-G Corporation happens to be an incorporated hedge fund then you can bet that several large banks will find themselves on an exclusion list. It will need an office supply vendor, an accounting firm, maybe an employment firm, and probably a legal consulting firm. All of these companies will also find themselves on an exclusion list for political campaigns in the jurisdiction that owns the C-G hedge fund. Its assets are also used for exclusionary purposes. Those companies invested in by the hedge fund are likewise excluded from political interference. Huge swathes of private companies can be excluded by a company's assets and business transactions.

XXXI. Individual owners (more than 10%) of companies invest in by the government or doing business with the jurisdiction may not make campaign or PAC fund contributions).

Even the owners of companies invested in will be excluded and be barred from making campaign or PAC contributions. This is not meant to exclude everybody invested in the company only those that would overwhelmingly benefit from business transactions with the C-G C. or from favorable legislation or regulation. Companies are obviously run for the benefit of stock holders and owners so their interests must be concerned. It would be useless to exclude companies if their owners were not also excluded. It should be expected that mature commercial governments will have extensive lists of persons and companies excluded from making contributions to town council members, representatives, judges, mayors, senators, and governors. These exclusions are based upon specific jurisdictions so if a company and its owner are excluded from interfering with a city's elections they can still contribute to state officials campaigns. Being excluded from state politics does not necessary exclude the company seeking representation from national politics. All in all companies and owners will be prohibited from forwarding their interests when in the process the voters and residents would be exploited.

XXXII. No employee or government owners of a C-G Corporation may attempt to influence another domestic government. They may never lobby government officers and politicians, nor can they contribute to candidate's campaign or PAC funds.

Commercial governments absolutely forbid one government from influencing another with political or economic favor. With the proliferation of C-G Corporations a larger segment of commercial interests will inherently be prohibited from political influence. This combines government investment in private and public companies to exclude the majority of commercial interests from making contributions to political campaigns and PAC funds. One of the most poignant criticisms of modern democracy is the inordinate influence corporations and wealthy have within the political arena. It is certainly a concern for the U. States because it has the most lax lobby and contribution rules of all the modern democracies. Corporations are better organized than the citizenry and have access to vastly more money for political lobby. They are able to forward their agendas in our legislations at the expense of citizen's concerns. Government investment will remedy this. As a result political parties will have to rely on a greater volume of smaller contributions paid directly from their constituencies. Influence will shift from advantaging corporations and the wealthy to favoring ordinary citizens. Corporate influence will occupy a position inferior to that of ordinary citizens as was intended by the framers of the constitution and public welfare will once again become a priority for government officers and elected officials. Democracy can once again be a government for the people, by the people.

XXXIII. No government owning land in another government's jurisdiction shall have the right to vote or interfere in that government's elections, nor will it have any right to claim taxes from those properties.

In order to prevent future confrontations, governments must forfeit any current claim or future claim to any rights of voting or tax collection from that property. No laws current support such rights but the laws and regulations governing over ownership must never be changed or abridged to compromise this natural exclusion. The main purpose of this tenant is to exclude territorial expansion as a reason for the government's purchase of property. Otherwise some governments would react negatively to investment by another government. Hostile takeovers are more a part of colonialism than commercial government and every measure needed to protect the sovereignty of governments must be forwarded prior to any investment being made. If territory exchanges are to be made they will certainly be consensual. Commercial governments are already excluded from lobbying or coercing governments from within the same nation, this naturally includes voting in non commercial elections or referendums.

XXXIV. Prohibition on government employees from personally profiting during their term of (or appointment to) office.

Clearly the personal finances of elected and appointed officials must be watched over especially if they have some locus of control over the jurisdiction's C-G Corporations. It is suggested that they all declare their IRA's, 401 plans, and personal accounts so that some discrete government agency can provide oversight. If necessary these agencies can employ forced divestiture to the personal wealth of public employees. In a world of C-G Corporations and fully vested permanent funds the opportunity for corruption is much more likely and much more disagreeable. It is almost inconceivable that such oversight isn't applied now on a more concerted or organized level. Public employment entails a higher degree of responsibility and every candidate should feel comfortable with others reviewing their assets when they are in the position to enforce regulations, create regulations, determine tax policy, or distribute tax dollars. Those uncomfortable with such scrutiny obviously shouldn't be running for office or seeking appointment because they aren't self confident in their ability to avoid improprieties.

XXXV. Prohibition of elected officials (State and Federal Government only) from working in private sector for five years after abandonment or removal from office.

XXXVI. Appointed officials who are enabled to make decisions directly regarding investment or business transaction will be limited for a duration of three years after the office is vacated.

If there is to be a properly erected separation between Industry and State then our public officials can't earn lucrative paying jobs in the private of quasi-government sector after their tenure has ended. That contributes to the environment of corruption that cripples democracies. How can an observer validate a national congressman who votes affirmative on favorable legislation for drug companies throughout their career and then ends up employed as a consultant getting paid hundreds of thousands of dollars. How does one expect the regulatory apparatus to work when the secretaries in charge of these important institutions are generally retired executives from the very companies they are expected to shepherd? Creating a buffer zone between the elected or appointed official and the private sector is the best way the integrity of our government can be protected. Most nations would be best served in government employees remain in the government sector and private employees remained in the private sector but this is highly unlikely ever to occur.

Instead of a permanent exclusion, former government sector employees and representatives can be forbid from profiting from their service for a period of 3 or 5 years depending on their responsibilities. During this time they will continue to receive the pay and health benefits they are accustomed to. Hopefully those industries seeking influence and those officials peddling their influence will be discouraged by this wait period. Let them work for nonprofits and non government organizations that contribute in a meaningful way to society. Let them reflect on their tenures and write memoires. Let them retire and enjoy family or recreation. But don't let them continue exploiting their privileges and abusing public welfare. Commercial Government Theory is just as much about making public finance much more efficient as it is forwarding public welfare on equal footing with commercial interests.

XXXVII. Having residency in the owning state makes the person ineligible for hire by the government incorporation for three years after relocation.

Residents generally can't be hired by C-G Corporations owned by their principle governments simply because those companies won't have operations within their administrative jurisdictions. In order to eliminate any potential improprieties or unlawful influence peddling they will continue to be ineligible for employment until the end of the third year after relocation. Government officials could otherwise transfer residents that contributed to their campaigns into management positions with their C-G Corporations. This should be considered a bribe and justly criminalized. C-G Corporations are also intended to be staffed by persons from competitor jurisdictions so that its employees have interests in protecting the integrity of the consuming jurisdiction (i.e. their administrative jurisdictions). Employees must first identify with their political jurisdiction, and only then identify with the C-G Corporation. If residents from the owning jurisdiction could be transferred into a competitor jurisdiction for work they would forward the interests of only the owning jurisdiction and this may compromise the consuming jurisdiction political integrity.

XXXVIII. Government officials of the owning government are prohibited from employment by the government incorporation for a period of 10 years after relocation.

No employee from the government sector, be they appointed or elected, is eligible for employment by a C-G Corporation owned by the jurisdiction they formerly worked for. Cronyism would run rampant and disrupt the operation of the C-G Corporation if it was allowed. Residents can gain eligibility in a matter of three years but public officials will have to wait 10 years. If they are picked up by a rival jurisdiction's C-G Corporation review of their work as the regulator or legislator should be made to see if any trends suggest impropriety or coercion was present. There will always be some degree of compromise but adequate protections should be in place to discourage most bad actors. This should not dissuade people from public sector careers. There will always be ample private sector or quasi-government sector jobs to choose from after the appointment ends. This is only meant to discourage flagrant abuses that would be very accessible if formerly public officials could be reassigned, transferred or appointed to positions within the owning jurisdictions C-G Corporations.

XXXIX. Campaign and PAC contributions will be made public.

Due to the drastically increased opportunity for economic compromise campaign finance rules will have to be updated. Every company that is invested in or does business with a jurisdiction is naturally excluded but those companies remaining eligible will have to publically declare their contributions. A list will be compiled of all corporate contributors and this list should be made public for the length of an official's tenure at that position. It will not take much effort to create a city or state government website with the list of contributors for each official. Making contribution lists public would discourage most elected officials from compromising their votes or regulatory charges. Impropriety can be tracked by almost any individual concerned. Journalists, watchdog groups, competing politicians, or competing companies can voice concern over any potential compromise. Private contributors would be tracked as well but those records will remain undisclosed and available for view by concerned government agency employees. If necessary even the spouse's employment record can be publically listed.

A progressive structure in the entitlements section allows a government to slowly expand their powers when they have the regulatory apparatuses necessary to make governments accountable. At any point a government wishes to rescind previous entitlements they can simply amend their administrative laws and sell those assets. Every time they want to expand entitlements they can simply amend their constitutions and use future contributions to begin amassing those interests or instruments. If more specificity is needed then it can be manufactured through more intense scrutiny. If less is needed the superfluous parts can be dropped with little or no concern. Commercial government theory is definitely highly structure and organized but it is not scientific. Science requires empiric testing and evaluations and that won't occur until there is a working model of a completely vested and integrated network of municipal, county, state, and national governments.

There is no way every regulation needed to make commercial governments safe and fair can be included in this book. No significant theory or political unit has ever been posited inclusive with all the rules and laws necessary to perpetuate its existence. The U.S Constitution and Bill of Rights forwarded a limited number of themes and points from which a larger system was extracted. It is still a work in progress as it continues to be adapted to new circumstances and situations. Some tenants are re-interpreted, some are omitted, some are changed, and many more will be added. The Communist Manifesto sufficed into pointing out only a handful of primary characteristics yet it transformed whole nations. In each case the working bodies of law come from direct interaction. They come from scrutiny, experience, and conflict. This book means to be comprehensive enough to portray a commercial government system as a possible path for interested nations but it is not complete in the sense that it is a finished product. All of its sample systems and sample rules and regulations can be reduced to merely themes and examples of a yet unrealized idea.

Annex

The Mutable Boundaries System

Commercial governments are intended to be complemented by a system of mutable boundaries for municipal, city, county, regional, and national governments. An exchange would be created between legitimate governments so that they could sell political territories to one another. Territorial boundaries are not fixed at the moment but there is no institutionalized exchange enabling frequent and structured deals. This is so because most governments don't have disposable incomes to promote expansion or they don't face pressure great enough to warrant their contraction. Commercial governments will have sufficient cause to trade territory for capital and they will have extra income they can spend on acquisitions.

The purpose of a Mutable Boundaries system is to foster contraction and expansion of municipal and regional government's political boundaries to parallel those government's successes or failures at investment. Only governments will be able to participate in the exchange and the primary asset sold or bought are tax liabilities of residents and resident businesses in the territories relocated. Most often towns in the same state will make barter, but exchanges can cross county or state lines. It is even conceivable that two nations participating in an Economic Union may decide to barter territory for extra capital.

Employing a Mutable Boundaries system is contingent on maintaining a democratic process of political governance (even if the larger regional or national political system is not democratic). Every transaction must be first accepted by the residents and land owners who are affected by the transfer of property. A 2/3rds majority will authorize the sale. The swap must then be voted on by government officials in the assuming and relinquishing jurisdictions. These can be based on simple majorities when voting. Profit sharing will discourage all but the most equitable exchanges and ensure no residents are dislocated without adequate compensation.

Probably the most important aspect of any mutable boundaries system would be the contractual obligation for continued government services after initiating an exchange. Each transaction must include secure police, fire, ambulance, and public works for the length of time it takes the receiving government to adjust the size or quality of their services to accommodate the new properties and residents. Once a liquid mode of transporting government services is created a system for reorganizing political districts must be implemented so that residents don't suffer from the lack of dutiful representation. Issuing contracts for services should coincide with the first elections for the new residents and the lasts applicable budget. The transaction should only be considered complete when the transferred residents participate in the next election for the executive officer and at least 1/3 of the municipal, county, regional, and national seats for representation.

The private finance initiative complements a system of Mutable Boundaries. If government services have already been translated into fee based programs with defined contracts then when towns needed to reorganize which towns will continue to provide services and which towns will assume new services there will be a system that can adapt to the changes without affecting the quality of services. The more complicated sample systems were designed to accommodate the public finance initiate because a larger proportion of businesses will be government owned. C-G Corporations are more accountable than private business and can be relied on to facilitate contractual emergency services during territory exchanges.

There would have to be rules concerning sharing of the proceeds from such government sales. Those residents being relocated would need to be compensated with a small proportion of the money exchanged. It would also be prudent to restrict governments from concentrating too much wealth into too few residents through excessive sales of territories. Paying relocated residents compensates them for the contributions they have made into the permanent fund they will no longer benefit from. Residents always have the opportunity to vote the measure down and can do so until they feel their compensation is adequate enough. This may drive prices up for territories but the new jurisdiction is gaining permanent access to a larger tax base so the costs may still be justified.

The largest cities, counties, or states would be forbid from further expansion. Likewise the smallest cities, counties, and states would be restricted from further contraction. In each instance the most extreme sets a minimum or maximum for the others. Jurisdictions are compared in terms of population so a government can add significant territory as long as only a sparse population is assimilated. In a similar respect it could sell a large portion of its territory as long as very few people lived on the lands. No exchange should account for a change in more than half of the original population or acreage and governments could be restricted to a predetermined maximum number of transactions for every year (or decade). Pegging completed territory transfers to representative elections will constrict the season in which certain towns are eligible to participate in the Exchange thus slowing down the rate of change and enabling governments to assume greater oversight.

The most obvious reason for a government to sell parts of its territory and tax base is the gamble that it can earn more from investments than it can by taxing residents. Tax liabilities are guaranteed and permanent but much smaller than interest earned from successful business operation. For residents still belonging to the territory this can mean much lower taxes in the future. The jurisdiction will have to weigh whether having smaller but guaranteed revenue is better or worse than having larger and riskier revenue. Selling jurisdictions have to be careful because they are permanently eliminating income to their general fund. They can't jeopardize the public safety of their remaining residents and would not have to raise taxes in tax revenues drop unexpectedly.

Another reason a particular government may be willing to part with some of its residents is that the population base is unwieldy. Government resources are limited and sometimes awkward areas or specific populations are more expensive to administer services to. Smaller governments have many redundancies that larger governments do not have. Each town needs to have a police chief, a school superintendent, a fire chief, and DPW. In order to save money smaller governments could consolidate services so that less money is spent on administration, organization, or implementation of services. A single large DPW could serve a larger jurisdiction more efficiently than several smaller DPW's serve many less populated districts. If a particular district had more needs and could be served by a larger better equipped government then that section could be sold.

The most immediate reason a commercial government would need to sell some of its territory is to deal with a fiscal crisis. Crisis can result from mismanagement of public resources but it can also come about from failed investments. For the most part capitalized governments won't be subject to excessive losses in subsidy revenue because most permanent fund systems will be accompanied by a permanent fund guarantee system (insurance). Still guarantee systems don't replace all of the lost income produced by permanent funds and a government may be forced to sell some its tax base. A Mutable boundary system allows for an orderly redistribution of property and equity. The government suffering in a financial crisis has a means to salvage its general budget without enacting draconian tax hikes.

Dissolutions may have to be considered due to the increased risks certain governments will bear from investment and competition. Before a government could disband a majority of its residents must second the motion and government boards of the assuming jurisdictions must agree to its dissolution. Dissolving into surrounding jurisdictions may prove to be economical considering the efficiency gained from consolidating social services. In a similar motion, certain jurisdictions could succeed from one county or state and join another. Although less likely, a group of municipal or county government could succeed and form a newly independent state in the union. Popular votes and government boards will always have to adhere to the restrictions and regulations put forth by higher governments or national constitutions.

Although increasing a tax base requires greater expenditures for government services a portion of that tax revenue can be applied for investment and a larger base will eventually allow for much greater investment in the future. Tax liabilities are certain and permanent. A government with a larger tax base has immediate access to much larger contributions. It can displace the tax burden of managing a permanent fund among more people and maintain the same low tax rate to support a larger contribution rate. If commercial governments are more prone to financial crises, then those governments should try to expand their tax bases as much as possible because capital can be raised much more easily from more people.

Governments will no longer be constrained to definite boundaries. A government can immediately purchase land or property to expand its commercial zones, its industrial zones, or residential zones. This can accelerate economic growth within the territory. An expanding industrial zone can be complemented by a larger residential zone, both then creating need for a larger commercial zone. In this respect a government could also acquire natural resources like reservoirs or recreation areas. Cities need water and the easiest way to couple their expansion with resources is by assuming them from other jurisdictions.

Lower governments will not see the mutable boundaries system as a means to spread their influence. For the most part there already is uniformity between state and town laws. However this is not true when it is two neighboring nations. They can have dramatically different laws and it will definitely be to the benefit of one to assume the land of the other. Nations can begin exporting their political process, their social mores, the economic policies. This can lead to spreading democracy, capitalism, or conservatism. This process could be pivotal in peace negotiations because it set precedent for equitable trade. Territories can be returned to countries as long as the residents are comfortable with repatriating and when the owning government is adequately compensated.

Most transactions should occur between neighboring governments but the system does not have to be constrained by proximity. It could be updated to include noncontiguous and distant parts. One government could purchase areas within another jurisdiction despite no immediate connection. In these instances there should be an established minimum size so that one area does not become peppered with too frequent changes in jurisdiction. There should be a degree of uniformity in law and even if a certain zone contributes taxes to another state or nation, and owes it allegiance (bestows citizenship), the owning jurisdiction could make the noncontiguous jurisdiction's laws compatible with the laws of the selling jurisdiction surrounding it.

In this respect a resort town previously in Florida could be transferred to New York. The town would become part of a NY county system and contribute taxes to the county and state. It would continue to elect its own municipal representatives but participate in NY state wide elections. Residents would be guaranteed that emergency services would continue because the assuming NY county would contract with the selling jurisdiction and state of Florida. This municipality could elect to assume New York state laws or it could continue abiding by Florida state laws. When New York's holdings in Florida become larger and larger New York could export its state laws including a fully independent court system. Such changes in governance would be more pronounced if the exchange occurred between two nations but as long as all of the participants agreed to the relocation there shouldn't be any third party objections.

If political boundaries could be adjusted to include non-contiguous and distant parts then Mutable boundaries makes the evolution to a single world government possible through economic maneuvers alone. Nations would coalesce to form competing economic blocks and those blocks could assume more and more of competitor properties. Of course this would require all of a world's government to accept the mutable boundaries process but expendable equity can go a long way in motivating previously reluctant governments to make transfers of property and responsibility. Much more likely is that the internal districts of a nation would shift and change to accommodate their local economies.

Master List of commercial government traits:

I. Account Attributes;
   A. Tier of government owning fund
      1. Federal (Central)
      2. Regional (State)
      3. Local (county, city, village, or town)
   B. Operation (management of fund)
      1. Government must manage own money
         a. Social Agenda
         b. Profit seeking only
      2. Private company (3rd party) must manage government money
      3. Government can choose to outsource management
         a. May apply social agenda when self managing
         b. Profit seeking only when self managing
   C. Purpose (use)
      1. Subsidy of budget (reduce tax liabilities)
      2. Production of dividend checks for residents
      3. Improving government benefits (increase government spending)
      4. Combination of uses
         a. Subsidy/dividend production
         b. Dividend/improve benefits
         c. Subsidy/improve benefits
         d. Unstructured
   D. Method:
      1. Rollover contributions and interest (Savings)
         a. 15 year cycle
         b. 25 year cycle
         c. 40 year cycle
      2. Immediately apply interest earned (Defrayment)
      3. Hybrid:
         a. savings with 15 year cycle/defrayment
         b. savings with 25 year cycle/defrayment
         c. savings with 25 year cycle/defrayment
   E. Domain:
      1. Centralized
         a. One permanent fund for all taxes
            x. separates off budget from on budget expenses

b. Multiple subsidy funds, one for each tax
2. Departmentalized (divided into department, agency, or program)

II. Entitlements:
A. Secondary market Instruments- (modified by degree and jurisdiction):
1. The government may not invest in secondary market instruments
2. The government can invest in broad spectrum instruments only (mutual, hedge, index, REIT, derivatives)
3. The government can invest in any investment instrument (stocks, options, derivatives, and commodities)
B. Debt markers (modified by jurisdiction):
1. The government is prohibited from investing in any debt markers
2. The government can invest in government's debt markers
3. The government can invest in corporate debt markers (bank products, junk bonds, rated corporate bonds)
4. The government can invest in citizen debt (mortgages, credit, past due amounts)
C. Real estate (modified by jurisdiction):
1. The government is prohibited from any investment in any real estate
2. The government can invest in real estate
a. commercial
b. residential
D. Currency (unmodified):
1. The government is prohibited from trading any currencies
2. The government can invest in currency excluding the national currency
3. The government can invest in currency including their national currency
E. Venture Capital (primary markets, modified by jurisdiction and degree):
1. The government is forbidden from initiating a new business
2. The government may initiate and manage new businesses

3. The government may purchase portions of private companies

Jurisdiction (modifies instrument and degree):

x. The government can invest in foreign jurisdictions

xx. The government can invest in domestic territories but not operating within the same jurisdiction.

(c). jurisdiction is defines as same regional government

(cc). the jurisdiction is defined in terms of opposing municipal governments.

xxx. The government can invest in domestic instruments operating in the same jurisdiction (administrative jurisdiction).

Degree (Modifies instrument and jurisdiction):

i. The government is relegated to a marginal share

ii. The government can invest in minority shares.

iii. The government can invest in majority shares.

III. Market Accumulation (<48% rules):

A. Intra-company

1. <48% of collective government ownership
2. >48% of collective government ownership

B. Inter-company

1. <48% of market share
2. >48% of market share

Master List of Sample Systems

Neo-Capitalist;

Capitalocracy, minor:

Code:
I; A.1, B.3.a, C.1, D.1.b, E.1.a.x, II; A.3.x.ii, B.2.3.x, C.2.a.b.x, D.1, E.3.x.ii, III.A.2.x, B.2.x

I; A.2.3, B.3.a, C.1, D.1.b, E.1.a.x, II; A.3.xxx.iv, A.3.x.xx(c).ii, B.2.3.x.xx(c).xxx, C.2.a.b.x.xx(c), D.3, E.3.xxx.iv, E.3.x.xx(c).ii, III; A.2.x, A.1. xx.xxx, B.2.x

Capitalocracy, major:

Code:
I; A.1, B.3.a, C.1, D.1.b, E.1.a.x, II; A.3.x.iii, B.2.3.4.x, C.2.a.b.x, D.1, E.2.3.x.iii, III; A.2.x, B.2.x

I; A.2.3, B.3.a, C.1, D.1.b, E.1.a.x, II; A.3.xxx.i, A.3.xx(c).ii, A.3.x.iii, B.2.3.xx(c).xxx, B.2.3.4.x, C.2.a.b.x.xx(c), D.3, E.3.xxx.i, E.3.xx(c).ii, E.2.3.x.iii, III; A.2.x,A.1.xx.xxx, B.2.x

Capitalocracy, general:

Code:
I; A.1, B.3.a, C.1, D.1.b, E.1.a.x, II; A.3.x.iii, B.2.3.4.x, C.2.a.b.x, D.1, E.2.3.x.iii, III; A.2.x, B.2.x

I; A.2.3, B.3.a, C.1, D.1.b, E.1.a.x, II; A.3.xxx.i, A.3.xx(c).ii, A.3.x.iii, B.2.3.xx(c).xxx, B.2.3.4.x, C.2.a.b.x.xx(c), D.3, E.3.xxx.i, E.3.xx(c).ii, E.2.3.x.iii, III; A.2.x.xx.xxx, B.1.xx.xxx, B.2.x

Corporatocracy, minor:

Code;
I; A.1, B.3.a, C.1, D.1.b, E.1.a.x, II; A.3.x.iii, B.2.3.4.x, C.2.a.b.x, D.1, E.2.3.x.iii; III.A.2.x, B.2.x

I; A.2, B.3.a, C.1, D.1.b, E.1.a.x, II; A.3.xxx.i, A.3.xx(c).ii, A.3.x.iii, B.2.3.xx(c).xxx, B.2.3.4.x, C.2.a.b.x.xx(c), D.3, E.3.xxx.i, E.3.xx(c).ii, E.2.3.x.iii, III; A.2.x.xx(c).xxx, B.1.xx(c).xxx, B.2.x

I; A.3, B.3.a, C.1.D.1.b, E.1.a.x, II; A.3.xxx.i, A.3.x.xx(c).iii, B.2.3.xxx, B.2.3.4.x.xx(c),C.2.a.b.x.xx(c), D.3, E.3.xxx.i, E.2.3.x.xx(c).iii, III; A.2.x.xx(c).xxx, B.1.xx (c).xxx, B.2.x

Corporatocracy, major:

Code;
I; A.1, B.3.a, C.1, D.1.b, E.1.a.x, II; A.3.x.iii, B.2.3.4.x, C.2.a.b.x, D.1, E.2.3.x.iii, III; A.2.x, B.2.x

I; A.2.3, B.3.a, C.1, D.1.b, E.1.a.x, II; A.3.xxx.i, A.3.x.xx(c).iii, B.2.3.xxx, B.2.3.4.x.xx(c), C.2.a.b.x.xx(c), D.3, E.3.xxx.i, E.2.3.x.xx(c).iii, III; A.2.x.xx(c).xxx, B.1.xx (c).xxx, B.2.x

Competitive State Capitalist;

Solocorporatocracy, minor:

Code:
I; A.1, B.3.a, C.1, D.1.b, E.1.a.x, II; A.3.xxx.i, A.3.x.iii, B.2.3.xxx, B.2.3.4.x, C.2.a.b.x, D.1, E.2.3.x.iii, E.3.xxx.i, III; A.2.x.xxx, B.2.x.xxx

I; A.2.3, B.3.a, C.1, D.1.b, E.1.a.x, II; A.3.xxx.i, A.3.xx(c).ii, A.3.x.iii, B.2.3.xx.xxx(c), B.2.3.4.x, C.2.a.b.x.xx(c), D.3, E.3.xxx.i, E.3.xx(c).ii, E.2.3.x.iii, III; A.2.x.xx.xxx, B.2.x.xx.xxx

Solocorporatocracy, major:

Code;
I; A.1, B.3.a, C.1, D.1.b, E.1.a.x, II; A.3.xxx.i, A.3.x.iii, B.2.3.4.x, B.2.3.xxxx, C.2.a.b.x, D.1, E.2.3.x.iii, E.3.xxx.i; III.A.2.x.xxx,

B.2.x.xxx

I; A.2.3, B.3.a, C.1, D.1.b, E.1.a.x, II; A.3.xxx.i, A.3.x.xx(c).iii, B.2.3.4.x.xx(c), C.2.a.b.x.xx(c), D.3, E.2.3.x.xx(c).iii, E.3.xxx.i, III;A.2.x.xx(c).xxx, B.2.x.xx (c).xxx

Solocorporatocracy, general:

Code;
I; A.1, B.1.a, C.4.d, D.2, E.1.a.x, II; A.3.x.iii, A.3.xxx.ii, B.2.3.xxx,B.2.3.4.x, C.2.a.b.x, D.1, E.2.3.x.iii, E.3.xxx.ii, III; A.2.x.xxx, B.2.x.xxx

I; A.2.3, B.1.a, C.4.d, D.2, E.1.a.x, II; A.3.x.xx(cc).iii, A.3.xxx.ii, B.2.3.4.x.xx(cc), B.2.3.xxx, C.2.a.b.x.xx(cc), D.3, E.2.3.x.xx(cc).iii,E.3.xxx.ii, III; A.2.x.xx(cc).xxx, B.2.x.xx(cc).xxx

Neo-Populist;

Monocorporatic, minor:

Code;
I; A.1, B.1.a, C.4.d, D.2, E.1.a.x, II;A.3.x.iii, A.3.xxx.ii, B.2.3.xxx, B.2.3.4.x, C.2.a.b.x, D.1, E.2.3.x.iii, E.3.xxx.ii, III; A.2.x.xxx, B.2.x.xxx

I; A.2, B.1.a, C.4.d, D.2, E.1.a.x, II; A.3.x.xx(cc).iii, A.3.xxx.ii, B.2.3.xxx, B.2.3.4.x.xx(cc), C.2.a.b.x.xx(cc), D.3, E.2.3.x.xx(cc).iii,E.3.xxx.ii, III;A.2.x.xx(cc).xxx, B.2.x.xx(cc).xxx

I; A.3, B.1.a, C.4.d, D.2, E.1.a.x, II; A.3.x.xx(cc).xxx.iii, B.2.3.4.x.xx(cc).xxx,C.2.a.b.x.xx(cc).xxx,D.3, E.2.3.x.xx(cc).xxx.iii, III; A.2.x.xx(cc).xxx, B.2.x.xx(cc).xxx

Monocorporatic, major:

Code;
I; A.1, B.1.a, C.4.d, D.2, E.1.a.x, II; A.3.x.iii, A.3.xxx.ii, B.2.3.4.x, C.2.a.b.x, D.1, E.2.3.x.iii, E.3.xxx.ii, III; A.2.x.xxx, B.2.x.xxx

I; A.2.3, B.1.a, C.4.d, D.2, E.1.a.x, II; A.3.x.xx(cc)..xxx.iii, B.2.3.4.x.xx(cc).xxx,C.2.a.b.x.xx(cc).xxx,D.3, E.2.3.x.xx(cc).xxx.iii, III; A.2.x.xx(cc).xxx, B.2.x.xx(cc).xxx

Commucorporatocracy:

Code;
I; A.1.2.3, B.1.a, C.4.d, D.3, II; A.3.x.xx(cc).xxx.iii, B.2.3.4.x.xx(cc).xxx,C.2.a.b.x.xx(cc).xxx, D.3, E.2.3.x.xx(cc).xxx.iii, III; A.2.x.xx(cc).xxx, B.2.x.xx(cc).xxx

Traditional Variations:

Traditional Solocorporatocracy, major:

Code;
I; A.1, B.2 C.1, D.1.b, E.1.a.x, II; A.3.xxx.i, A.3.x.iii, B.2.3.4.x, B.2.3.xxxx, C.2.a.b.x, D.1, E.2.3.x.iii, E.3.xxx.i, III; A.2.x.xxx, B.2.x.xxx

I; A.2.3, B.2, C.1, D.1.b, E.1.a.x, II; A.3.xxx.i, A.3.x.xx(c).iii, B.2.3.4.x.xx(c), C.2.a.b.x.xx(c), D.3, E.2.3.x.xx(c).iii, E.3.xxx.i, III; A.2.x.xx(c).xxx, B.2.x.xx (c).xxx

Broad-Capitalocratic:

Code:
I; A.1.2.3, B.3.a, C.1, D.1.b, E.1.a.x, II;A.2.x.xx(c).xxx, B.2.3.x.xx(c).xxx, C.2.a.b.x.xx(c), D.3 (national permanent fund is naturally excluded), E.1.x.xx(c).xxx.iv,

III; A.1.x.xx.xxx, B.1.x.xx.xxx

Public Finance Engine:

Code;
I; A.1.2.3, B.3.a, C.1.b, D.1, E.1.a.x, II; A.1, B.2.x.xx.(cc).xxx, C.1, D.1, E.1, III; A.2.x.xx.xxx, B.2.x.xx.xxx

Departmentalized Capitalization;

Fractal Capitalocracy-general:

Code:
I;A.1, B.3.a, C.1, D.1.b, E.2, II; A.3.x.iii, B.2.3.4.x, C.2.a.b.x, D.1, E.2.3.x.iii, III; A.2.x, B.2.x

I;A.2.3, B.3.a, C.1, D.1.b, E.2, II; A.3.xxx.i, A.3.xx(c).ii, A.3.x.iii, B.2.3.xx(c).xxx, B.2.3.4.x, C.2.a.b.x.xx(c), D.3, E.3.xxx.i, E.3.xx(c).ii, E.2.3.x.iii, III;A.2.x.xx.xxx, B.1.xx.xxx, B.2.x

Fractal Corporatocracy, greater (Supplemental):

Code;
I; A.1, B.3.a, C.3, D.2, E.2, II; A.3.x.iii, B.2.3.4.x, C.2.a.b.x, D.1, E.2.3.x.iii, III; A.2.x, B.2.x

I; A.2.3, B.3.a, C.3, D.2, E.2, II; A.3.xxx.i, A.3.x.xx(c).iii, B.2.3.xxx, B.2.3.4.x.xx(c), C.2.a.b.x.xx(c), D.3, E.3.xxx.i, E.2.3.x.xx(c).iii, III; A.2.x.xx(c).xxx, B.1.xx (c).xxx, B.2.x

Competitive State Capitalist variations;

Production Solocorporatocracy, general:

Code;
I; A.1, B.1.a, C.2, D.2, E.1.a.x, II; A.3.x.iii, A.3.xxx.ii, B.2.3.xxx, B.2.3.4.x, C.2.a.b.x, D.1, E.2.3.x.iii, E.3.xxx.ii, III; A.2.x.xxx, B.2.x.xxx

I; A.2.3, B.1.a, C.2, D.2, E.1.a.x, II; A.3.x.xx(cc).iii, A.3.xxx.ii, B.2.3.4.x.xx(cc), B.2.3.xxx, C.2.a.b.x.xx(cc), D.3, E.2.3.x.xx(cc).iii, E.3.xxx.ii, III; A.2.x.xx(cc).xxx, B.2.x.xx(cc).xxx

Commutary

Code;
I; A.1.2.3, B.1.a, C.4, D.2, E.2, II; A.3.x.xx(cc).xxx.iii, B.2.3.4.x.xx(cc).xxx,C.2.a.b.x.xx(cc).xxx,D.3, E.2.3.x.xx(cc).xxx.iii, III; A.2.x.xx(cc).xxx, B.2.x.xx(cc).xxx

Mixed Theme:

Poliplutocracy

Code;
I; A.1.2.3, B.1.a, C.1.b, D.1, E.1.a.x, II; A.1, B.2.x.xx.(cc).xxx, C.1,D.1, E.1, III, A.2.x.xx.xxx, B.2.x.xx.xxx

I; A.1, B.3.a, C.4, D.2, E.2; II.A.3.xxx.i, A.3.x.iii, B.2.3.xxx, B.2.3.4.x, C.2.a.b.x, D.1, E.2.3.x.iii, E.3.xxx.i, III; A.2.x.xxx, B.2.x.xxx

I; A.2.3, B.1.a, C.4, D.2, E.2, II; A.3.xxx.i, A.3.xx(c).ii, A.3.x.iii, B.2.3.xx.xxx(c), B.2.3.4.x, C.2.a.b.x.xx(c), D.3, E.3.xxx.i, E.3.xx(c).ii, E.2.3.x.iii. III; A.2.x.xx.xxx, B.2.x.xx.xxx

Master List of Rules and Regulations;

I. Every government has the inalienable right to own financial instruments, equity positions, real estate, and currencies for the purpose of earning profits but a higher government may limit such instruments and vehicles based on origin, operation, function, and degree of ownership (marginal, minority, and majority), and other mitigating factors.

II. Forced divestiture is applied in a cascading order of eligibility

III. Permanent fund managers have a fiduciary duty to earn the greatest returns possible with the least exposure to risk.

IV. Permanent Funds are incorporated in the owning jurisdiction but its authorities and C-G Corporations must be incorporated within a different state.

V. The vested government has sole right to decide whether income from investment is used for budget subsidy, dividends, or government benefits.

VI. Governments may employ changes to the tax code for reasons of earning incomes, controlling inflation, exciting industry, or for protecting against socialization (taxes can be applied directly to food, shelter, and clothing to counteract excessive dividends).

VII. Higher governments have the right to establish minimum contribution, and maximum contributions, with the purpose of creating a MCPFS and manipulating economy.

VIII. Higher governments have the right to dictate whether profits from assets must be immediately dispersed through a defrayment method if the intent is to slow the accumulation of public wealth if it looks to overtake concentrations of private wealth.

IX. Higher governments retain the right to establish maximum risk allotments, proportions of cash reserves (like deposits), proportions of domestic instruments versus foreign instruments, public equity versus private equity, and market share.

X. Money borrowed from a permanent fund for use by the general fund must be repaid according commercial rates of borrowing.

XI. No government can force excessive liquidation or another government's permanent fund.

XII. No government can liquidate their own permanent fund to advantage current residents at the expense of future residents.

XIII. Governments' ability to subsidize their general budgets with permanent funds will be insured by Permanent Fund Guarantee Companies.

XIV. If no permanent fund insurance is available it can be translated into an annuity so that the current level of budget subsidy is preserved.

XV. Constructive Market Share applies to all C-G and I-A Corporations.

XVI. Competitive Accounting laws apply for all C-G and I-A Corporations.

XVII. News media must remain privately owned.

XVIII. Auditing firms must remain privately owned.

XIX. No government may own or manage a Union. Nor can they discriminate against any union unless a critical service is involved.

XX. No government may discriminate against businesses owned by other domestic governments with any tax policy, legislation, administrative regulation, or ordnance.

XXI. No government can accept a bid from a company it holds investment in.

XXII. Municipal and county and state governments will be compelled to liquidate their positions in companies that win binds for grants and other mechanisms of economic stimulus.

XXIII. No government can conspire with another government for uncompetitive exchanges.

XXIV. No government official can coerce another official into unintended or unwanted uses of public wealth.

XXV. C-G Corporations can be given no exclusive incentive or advantage separate from private industry.

XXVI. All C-G Corporations are securitized in Competitive Socialist and Neo-Populist modes of commercial government, and those instruments must produce dividends for investors.

XXVII. All Competitive Socialist and Neo-Populist governments must share profits with residents and citizens by returning a predetermined proportion of common stock back to individual and company investors.

XXVIII. Any company at least partially owned (secondary or primary security instruments) by government may not make contributions to political candidate's campaign or PAC funds.

XXIX. Any company with recorded business transactions with a jurisdiction or its C-G Corporation may not make campaign contributions to candidate's campaigns and PAC funds.

XXX. If a government has authority to manage majority positions in competitive companies then all of the exclusions apply to the assets owned by that company and any business transactions it enters into.

XXXI. Individual owners (more than 10%) of companies invest in by the government or doing business with the jurisdiction may not make campaign or PAC fund contributions.

XXXII. No employee or government owners of a C-G Corporation may attempt to influence another domestic government. They may never lobby government officers and politicians, nor can they contribute to candidate's campaign or PAC funds.

XXXIII. No government owning land in another government's jurisdiction shall have the right to vote or interfere in that government's elections, nor will it have any right to claim taxes from those properties.

XXXIV. Prohibition on government employees from personally profiting during their term of (or appointment to) office.

XXXV. Prohibition of elected officials (State and Federal Government only) from working in private sector for five years after abandonment or removal from office.

XXXVI. Appointed officials who are enabled to make decisions directly regarding investment or business transaction will be limited for a duration of three years after the office is vacated.

XXXVII. Having residency in the owning state makes the person ineligible for hire by the government incorporation for three years after relocation.

XXXVIII. Government officials of the owning government are prohibited from employment by the government incorporation for a period of 10 years after relocation.

XXXIX. Campaign and PAC contributions will be made public.

Bibliography

Anderson, Ronald A., et al. Business Law and The Legal Environment. Cincinnati: West Educational Publishing Company, 1999.

CalPERS. 2009. State of California Public Employee Retirement System. 18 April, 2009. http://www.calpers.ca.gov

CalSTRS. 2009. California State Teachers Retirement System. 18 April, 2009. http://www.calstrs.com/

2007 Fiscal Budget. 2007. The State of New Jersey, Department of Treasury. 18 April, 2009. http://www.state.nj.us/treasury/omb/publications/07bib/pdf/bib.pdf

2006 Fiscal Budget. 2006. The State of New Jersey, Department of Treasury. 18 April, 2009. http://www.state.nj.us/treasury/omb/publications/06bib/pdf/bib.pdf

Fund, Archon, et al. Working Capital, The Power of Labor's Pensions. Ithaca: Cornell University, 2001.

Hawken, Paul. The Ecology of Commerce. New York: HarperCollins, 1993.

Kuttner, Robert. The Squandering of America. New York: Knopf, 2007.

Marx, Karl. The Communist Manifesto. New York: Penguin Group (USA), 1998.

Perkins, John. Confessions of An Economic Hit Man. New York: Penguin Group(USA), 2005.

SWF Institute. 2008. Sovereign Wealth Fund Institute, Inc. 18 April 2009. http://www.swfinstitute.org

Worldwide-Tax. 18 April, 2009. http://www.worldwide-tax.com/Zinn, Howard. A People's History of The United States. New York: HarperCollins, 2005.

Made in the USA
Monee, IL
08 November 2026

67971948R00129